HIGH STANDARDS, HARD CHOICES

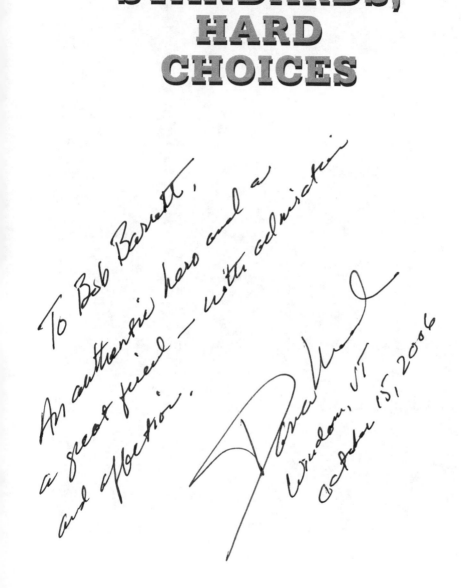

To Bob Bennett,
An authentic hero and a
great friend — with admiration
and affection.

Windsor, VT
October 15, 2006

Dana Mead and Mike Walsh, 1992.

HIGH STANDARDS, HARD CHOICES

A CEO's Journey of Courage, Risk, and Change

DANA G. MEAD

with

Thomas C. Hayes

John Wiley & Sons, Inc.

New York • Chichester • Weinheim • Brisbane • Singapore • Toronto

To our partners, respectively, on The Journey,
Nancy Mead and Nancy Hayes

This book is printed on acid-free paper. ∞

Copyright © 2000 by Dana G. Mead. All rights reserved.
Published by John Wiley & Sons, Inc.

Published simultaneously in Canada.

This publication is designed to provide accurate and authoritative information
in regard to the subject matter covered. It is sold with the understanding that
the publisher is not engaged in rendering legal, accounting, or other
professional services. If legal advice or other expert assistance is required, the
services of a competent professional person should be sought.

Library of Congress Cataloging-in-Publication Data:

Mead, Dana G., 1936–
    High standards, hard choices : a CEO's journey of courage, risk,
and change / Dana G. Mead with Thomas C. Hayes.
      p.   cm.
    Includes index.
    ISBN 0-471-29613-9 (cloth : alk. paper)
    1. Executives. 2. Chief executive officers. 3. Leadership.
4. Competition, International.   I. Hayes, Thomas C.   II. Title.
HD38.2.M42   2000
658.4'092—dc21   99-33866

Printed in the United States of America.

10 9 8 7 6 5 4 3 2 1

CONTENTS

WHEN I RETIRED AS AN ARMY COLONEL AND PROFESSOR OF SOCIAL sciences at West Point in 1978 to start a career in corporate management, there was little hint that I soon would be caught up in a turbulent revolution in the theory and practices of modern business. This revolution took most of the 1980s to gather momentum, but by the mid-1990s it had lifted the economy of the United States back to world primacy.

This success came from tough-minded leadership and the hard, often-contentious work of organizational refocus and renewal throughout thousands of large, complex businesses. Small business has always played a key role in defining new markets, crafting new concepts, and creating exciting new technologies. But it has been the scale and accomplishment of organizational renewal in large corporations both "new economy" and "old" that has been most extraordinary, and has had the most impact on the U.S. and global economies.

Large corporations have led the competitive resurgence of U.S.-based industry. Indeed, many of them now *are* truly global companies, with employees collectively speaking dozens of languages and working in the rhythms of hundreds of different cultures.

I know. My job through the 1980s and 1990s was reinventing big businesses that in some instances operate in more than 100 countries. I also worked closely with hundreds of business and government leaders around the world on trade matters, mainly in the modern industrial economies. We made much progress in our goal to better coordinate and define common rules for a world trading system. As a result, this evolving system has set the stage for huge gains in quality, efficiency, and volume among thousands of global production networks. This, in turn, offers the promise of rising living standards for much of the global population throughout the twenty-first century.

The six businesses I headed for much of the 1990s began the decade as a confederation of industrial producers loosely linked in a financially troubled conglomerate, Tenneco. Conceived as an industrial powerhouse, assembled through acquisitions bankrolled in the 1960s from fast-rising profits in oil and natural gas, Tenneco never achieved that original vision. In one sense, my role as chairman and chief executive from 1994 until my retirement (set for late 1999) became to dismantle it. The seventh and final major step in separating the distinct businesses that constituted Tenneco when I was hired as its president and second-in-command in 1992 was on schedule to be completed late in 1999.

Yet even as the conglomerate gradually was taken apart, its operations were renewed. Now or soon to be structured as seven businesses, four as individual companies and three merged into or acquired by others, the Tenneco operations of the early 1990s included many of the world's largest corporations among their best customers. These operations continue to compete as leaders in many product categories in dozens of countries.

Productivity Gains: Fundamental, Far Reaching

To achieve this, and avoid falling into mediocrity or worse, they had to achieve and sustain a surge in productivity. It was apparent early in the decade, at least to business leaders if not government policy makers, that a momentous new force was rippling through hundreds of large U.S.-based corporations. Costs were declining, quality was rising, innovation was accelerating, and price increases were virtually impossible. We knew this because many of the biggest corporations were our direct competitors, or partners in a variety of ventures. We had daily pressures to match or exceed their passion and their actions to improve. And, from what we were learning from the business news media and from executives we knew personally, most big companies were accelerating the pace, too. The word was getting around.

Productivity gains provided the signature accomplishment for many U.S.-based corporations in the 1990s. We set new world-class standards. We designed and established systems and processes to create innovative products, exploit new technologies, pare costs, buy and sell operations, and assess and pursue opportunities in formerly socialist economies in central and eastern Europe and Asia. And we had to do this faster than ever, under rising pressure from customers, competitors, government agencies, and investors.

Many economists and policymakers were skeptical about enduring productivity gains by big companies posted through the decade, which I and other executives described often in speeches and news media interviews. But as corporate earnings strengthened anew in the first quarter of 1999, *The Wall Street Journal* reported that even the conservative president of the St. Louis Federal Reserve Bank, William Poole, could say, "My best judgment is that the productivity slowdown of the 1970s and 1980s is over."

Average Annual Gains of 5 Percent at Tenneco

For the Tenneco businesses of 1992, revenue per employee jumped 35 percent between 1992 and 1998, from $165,000 in 1992 to $222,000 in 1998. Combined revenues of these businesses rose to more than $20 billion in 1998, from $13 billion in 1992. In the same period, the number of employees in these companies increased to roughly 90,000, from 79,000 in 1992. This amounted to average productivity gains of 5 percent through each of these six years.

Multiplied thousands of times across the organizations and networks of big business, these fundamental improvements brought huge benefits to the economy in the United States, and beyond. In the same period, the manufacturing sector increased productivity by a yearly average of 4 percent, while all businesses improved at a yearly rate of 1.3 percent.

In turn, big businesses generated new levels of efficiency, value, and wealth for customers and owners. These businesses contributed greatly to the rising output, profits and wages, and low rates of inflation and unemployment that now characterize the U.S. economy in its record ninth year of peacetime expansion and within a few months of establishing a new mark of longevity for any U.S. expansion.

To achieve this, many corporate giants had to learn to embrace the hallmarks of small businesses—creativity, customer focus, speed, and innovation—and blend them with the giants' traditional strength in finance, sales and marketing, research, production, and management. For much of the 1990s, big corporations have reaped growing earnings from investments in new technology and innovative products, more extensive global trade, greater productivity, and new organizational structures and processes.

A Chief Executive's Journal, with Analysis

This book examines several issues that confront all senior executives in globally competitive industries. Particular situations and facts are wide-ranging, but all the stories are about leadership and change, strategy, and communications. They also are about crisis and courage and risk.

These are essential elements in any prescription for managing change in large-scale organizations, the constant challenge today for business leaders. These talents and techniques have been outlined and analyzed regularly in an abundance of worthy books, case studies, and journals in recent years.

Being a former college professor, I value serious academic research and scholarship. I appreciate well-documented case studies. Yet this is not a technical business book. My goal is to reward your time and interest with realistic portraits and related conclusions drawn from inside the 1990s' revolution in corporate management. I devoted considerable time, passion, and energy to each situation in the book. My hope is that you will judge the reconstructions here to be credible, authoritative, and instructive. Many lessons should be evident—some unexpected, some familiar, some controversial.

The chapters are organized and written as a chief executive's journal, with a blend of additional analysis and reporting. They emphasize the challenges of dealing with crisis, managing international investments, and influencing public policy in Washington. I want these events and ideas to be accessible and interesting to a general reader as well as to business managers and government policy makers, and professors and students of corporate and public policy, economics, and international business.

Part I describes many personal, leadership, and communications issues and business problems surrounding the tragic brain cancer and aggressive medical treatments that ultimately claimed the life of Mike Walsh. Walsh was my predecessor as chairman and chief executive officer at Tenneco. An outsider with a reputation as a talented turnaround specialist, he rallied the company late in 1991 to avert a looming default and potential bankruptcy, then was the original architect of the transformation plans that I soon took on as general contractor.

During Walsh's battle with cancer, we had to contend with a major business crisis, the troubled farm and construction equipment manufacturer, J.I. Case. The subsequent sale of a strengthened Case generated more than $4 billion in cash and other benefits for Tenneco. This in turn created resources for us to enter the risky but rewarding poker game of mergers, acquisitions, joint ventures, and other investments that dramatically reshaped many of the Tenneco businesses.

Part II describes the risks and obstacles in international investment, illustrated by the challenges of establishing modern production in a poor economy whose leaders are wary and uncertain how to support transition toward Western manufacturing methods. The subjects are developing strategies and policies to establish a potentially high-profit new business on the remote high plains of the Carpathian Mountains in western Romania, and the rough-and-tumble journey starting in 1995 to build and manage Europe's largest wood products manufacturing plant and sawmill.

In Part III, the focus is on the strategies and tactics of pursuing business policy matters in Washington, beginning with our campaign to win support from a divided Congress and Clinton administration for the single largest item in the federal budget—a new aircraft carrier, at $4 billion. The section also examines a closely related effort in which I took a personal role in our lobbying tactics. The goal this time was to reverse Navy policy and a vote in Congress that denied construction contracts for nuclear-powered submarines to Newport News Shipbuilding and Dry Dock Company.

Newport News Shipbuilding, the nation's most technologically advanced and largest shipyard, was a Tenneco company during this period. Like J.I. Case, its future was clouded by major problems. It faced the possibility in 1993 of sharp cutbacks in contracts from its dominant customer, the U.S. Navy, and projected having to slash its workforce to as low as 7,000, from a peak of 31,000 in the mid-1980s, if the Navy's plans and priorities did not change.

The final chapter describes the lobbying effort and broad public relations program to nudge the Federal Reserve Board and especially its chairman, Alan Greenspan, toward monetary policies that would promote a faster-growing economy. I was in the vanguard in 1996 as chairman of the National Association of Manufacturers, the nation's largest industrial lobbying organization with 14,000 companies as its members.

Our drumbeating on productivity was one of many factors supporting the Federal Reserve's eventual gamble on continuing low inflation that began to emerge late that year. If large corporations had not become so efficient, and Alan Greenspan in particular had not become convinced of it, I doubt that the U.S. economy now would be advancing toward breaking a record in 2000 for the longest period of continuous growth in U.S. history.

The research for this book was collected from events that occurred mostly between 1992 and 1997. The manuscript was compiled in 1998 and 1999 in consultation with my Tenneco colleague, friend, and collaborator, Tom Hayes.

Sound Public Policy Decisions

Many sound public policy judgments by government officials in Washington contributed key elements to the 1990s story of improving business productivity and economic growth. Greenspan's Federal

Reserve, the Bush and Clinton administrations, and Congress came into alignment at least often enough this decade to get some important economic fundamentals right. Congress and the Administration achieved the first federal budget surplus in 29 years in 1998. International trade policies that opened the gates to higher living standards around the world continue to be embraced and advanced. This fusion of increasingly competitive industries with sound fiscal and monetary policies has produced the most buoyant economic era in the history of the United States.

This abundance has been accompanied by widespread adjustment costs within our organizations and society in general. Effective leaders in business and government must continue to recognize and manage the ongoing impact of these costs, such as job insecurity, layoffs, rising immigration, and inadequate child care for working parents.

The reasons for these costs are many, and they are certain to remain part of the dynamic, growing economy we have created: downsizing; restructuring; job relocations; global expansion; intense pressures to reduce costs; aggressive improvements in quality, technology and innovation speed; businesses sold or merged with former competitors; businesses acquired; businesses reconfigured into "pure plays" as independent companies.

Each of these factors is a piece of contemporary evidence for what Joseph A. Schumpeter, the brilliant Harvard economist, identified more than a half-century ago as the forces of "creative destruction" in a capitalist economy. Schumpeter predicted dolefully that large bureaucratic corporations would extinguish, or at least minimize, the entrepreneurial drive that creates wealth in capitalist economies. That prediction at times seemed on the mark in the 1980s as fortunes of giant companies like General Motors, Westinghouse, ITT, and Tenneco stagnated, then faded, under bruising competition in an increasingly global, fast-paced economy. But the reinvention of our complex industrial system through the 1990s (with Tenneco a leading candidate for Exhibit A) has proved Schumpeter wrong. He underestimated the ability of huge business organizations to turn up the wick on creativity, customer focus, speed, and innovation. Many corporations have become continuously improving laboratories of creative destruction.

Changes across a Vast
Network of Businesses

My work for the past seven years, first as president then as chairman and chief executive of what was one of the largest U.S.-based conglomerates, required addressing all the issues of corporate transformation. Our corporate decisions directly affected more than 100,000 employees working for part or all of this period in my company.

This large, multinational network of enterprises under the Tenneco umbrella made products in 35 countries and sold them in more than 100. Also, at any given time, we had essential partners in more than 200,000 shareowners, and thousands of customers and suppliers. All these partners relied on us, first, to stabilize our businesses, and then reinvent them for long-term growth.

The nation's 30th largest industrial company when I arrived in 1992, Tenneco had to find a coherent strategy, and operate more efficiently. The corporation had fallen behind the times then in applying several significant management trends and ideas. A partial list of these new management fundamentals included quality measures, cost reduction, rapid innovation processes, shared services, capital effectiveness, working capital management, safety training, equity-based compensation, and environmental performance.

I was recruited in the midst of $2 billion in losses Tenneco accumulated in 1991 and 1992 from past operating problems and charges related to our new restructuring programs. The company was in a serious financial tailspin. To the few who closely examined its balance sheet and operating accounts late in 1991, its survival was in doubt. Tenneco was one of those wobbly American industrial giants that thoroughly lost its way in the 1980s.

A Conglomerate Far Off Course

From its origins in natural gas transmission during World War II, Tenneco had expanded profitably into oil exploration, refining, and marketing in the 1950s. Flush with cash, it acquired manufacturing businesses through the 1960s, as well as insurance, agriculture, and real estate. It was a classic conglomerate, succeeding for a while in the 1970s, but stalling out by the end of the 1980s from financial crises brought on by inefficiencies and a flawed strategic vision.

Getting these businesses into shape demanded change in leaders throughout the organization. As we at the top identified the goals, the objectives and, most important, the leadership talent, we depended on these leaders to set high standards, to make the hard choices to achieve them, and to be accountable for results.

You must have leaders at every level in any organization to create and sustain success, whether in business, government, or the military. At my alma mater, West Point, for example, the central mission of the United States Military Academy for nearly 200 years has been this: *to train and educate leaders*. These are the people who respond to the huge challenges and daily roadblocks in their assignments with initiative, intensity, and persistence. They have the courage, intellect, and good judgment to take risks necessary to achieve tough goals. Most of all, they are people with rock-solid character, entrusted to make the right call for their troops in the heat of battle regardless of the personal cost. Finding these leaders and putting them in place was our first priority at Tenneco.

We had no choice in 1992 but to attack basic performance issues quickly within Tenneco to erase the losses and get the businesses on solid footings. And we made progress on many fronts. We won several important competitive and organizational battles. We adjusted to rapid shifts in global competition, trade, and economics in part by selling or divesting huge pieces of the company and acquiring more than 35 businesses since 1994. I also committed a significant part of my time to getting our businesses more active in markets outside the United States. I participated in several national and international panels and councils concerned with conditions and trends in economics, trade, business, and public policy. These gatherings opened many doors with international trade officials as well as potential business partners and suppliers. Programs to advance the global trade system also were the top priority of the Business Roundtable, the group of 200 top business leaders in the United States, during my 1998–1999 tenure as its chairman.

Playing the Hand We Were Dealt

Pulling away from its brush with bankruptcy late in 1991, Tenneco had few realistic strategic choices available to rapidly alter its weakened condition. Breaking the company apart into six or more separate companies then was not an option. Wall Street already had bid Tenneco's stock market value to nearly $6 billion in anticipation of a successful turnaround. This was positive, a vote of confidence in our leadership. By comparison, our own investment bankers indicated that a breakup and auction of the Tenneco businesses in 1992 would have netted as little as half of that $6 billion stock value for the company's shareowners. Market conditions for each of the businesses, with the exception of our big natural-gas pipeline unit, Tenneco Gas, were eroding, or already poor.

Weak pricing, falling demand, and excess capacity plagued all the manufacturing operations. Breaking up Tenneco then would have been a dereliction of duty. We had to play the hand we were dealt. This meant improving the fundamentals of each operation to the point where we would have the choice of selling at more attractive prices the ones that could not meet our goals for long-term growth and profitability.

So we mapped a difficult, yet potentially achievable course to raise the company's performance across the board. This seemed to many inside and close to Tenneco an improbable vision. Tenneco had been scorned since the mid-1980s by management theorists and Wall Street money managers for its inability to generate real economic value. There were many skeptics. Tenneco had the reputation of an unworkable conglomerate with a poor record in acquiring and operating businesses, criticisms that were close to the mark.

From One Conglomerate, into Seven Separate Companies

I arrived early in 1992, six months after Mike Walsh had been recruited for the posts of chairman and chief executive by company directors after carrying out an impressive revival of the Union Pacific Railroad. The Tenneco businesses then had a combined

78,000 employees and annual revenues of $14 billion, ranging from $4 billion to $900 million in these industries:

- Agricultural and construction equipment (J.I. Case).
- Natural-gas transportation and related energy development projects (Tenneco Gas).
- Military ship construction, design and repair (Newport News Shipbuilding).
- Automotive exhaust systems and ride-control parts (Tenneco Automotive).
- Paperboard and specialty packaging (Packaging Corporation of America).
- Chemicals (Albright & Wilson).

J.I. Case, now Case Corporation, easily was Tenneco's biggest problem in 1991, with huge losses over the prior 10 years that had broken morale and sown bitterness across the corporation. Yet other businesses also held significant threats for Tenneco shareowners, such as more than $1 billion in litigation claims, another $1 billion in looming gas supply contract settlements, major environmental liabilities, the prospective loss of huge defense contracts, and high operating costs. Each business, despite many competitive strengths, had serious flaws or looming troubles that were draining profits and smothering opportunities.

From that start, we guided our businesses to identify and pursue products, markets, and technologies that could deliver the ambitious earnings growth we needed. We identified and embraced our major customers in new ways and, at times, even confronted them in highly public disputes.

Each of those businesses in total is a more stable competitor in its given industry now, but organized and operated generally in very different ways. (See Appendix A and B.) Case and Albright & Wilson became independent, publicly traded companies in 1994 and 1995, respectively, then were on course to be acquired late in 1999 by Europe-based competitors. Tenneco Gas, renamed Tenneco Energy in

1995 after expanding from its core business as the nation's third-largest natural-gas pipeline operation, was merged into El Paso Energy Corporation in 1996. Newport News Shipbuilding remains independent after a 1996 spin-off, despite two takeover bids in 1999 that were thwarted by the Pentagon.

A majority stake in the box-and-containerboard business, once the largest part of Tenneco Packaging, was acquired by private investors in the spring of 1999. The portion Tenneco retained is set to be sold in an initial public offering within weeks of the scheduled publication of this book. That business has reclaimed the name that until 1995 identified all of Tenneco's packaging businesses, Packaging Corporation of America™. With 67 box plants and four mills manufacturing paper for boxes, it has nearly $2 billion in revenues and 8,400 employees. A few weeks after that private sale was completed in April 1999, we announced an agreement to sell Tenneco's folding-carton business, with more than $100 million in revenue, to a former joint venture partner, Caraustar Industries.

Our surgery on the remaining corporate structure was set to send Tenneco Automotive and Tenneco Packaging, now a $3 billion maker of specialty and protective packaging, on their separate ways as independent companies by the end of November 1999.

The sweeping overhaul and, ultimately, dismantling of the Tenneco organization this decade reflect two related pressures and preferences of Wall Street that have gained currency since the mid-1980s. One is for diversified conglomerates—many of which like Tenneco were created in the 1960s—to focus on a few core businesses in which they are market leaders. The breakup and refocusing of Westinghouse Corporation into the new CBS Inc. in 1997, and of ITT into a major hotel-and-casino operator acquired the same year by Starwood Hotels and Resorts Inc., are two examples.

The other force has industry leaders acquiring smaller rivals in strategies to assemble vast assets required to lead and compete effectively, and profitably, on a global scale. The huge deals creating DaimlerChrysler in 1998, and the anticipated Exxon-Mobil giant in 1999 as well as ATT Corporation's pending acquisition of the MediaOne Group are three prominent examples.

Mega-Operating Company, Reconsidered

Our intent back in 1992 and 1993 was to reinvent Tenneco as a mega-operating company, a more focused conglomerate with related businesses operated by a common set of management practices and capable of collectively increasing earnings by an average of 15 percent a year through the business cycle.

The plan by necessity would stretch Tenneco's operations beyond past performance. It also would bury the era in which the presidents of each of the six businesses operated with great independence, with little interaction among these operations, limited oversight from Tenneco headquarters, and few common performance standards.

The changes we demanded were hard-nosed, pragmatic, and necessary, and hardly unique. Multi-industry corporations such as Allied-Signal, Emerson Electric, United Technologies, and Textron already were proving that the model of a streamlined but still diverse conglomerate could generate steady earnings increases. Tyco International, little-known then by Wall Street or the business news media, was gathering momentum. Everyone's favorite example, General Electric, continues as a conglomerate nonpareil with both rare success and scope in its 14 operations in finance, manufacturing, and services. You also easily can argue that Microsoft, Walt Disney, Citigroup, and other giants became more like focused conglomerates as they expanded and acquired through the 1990s.

Yet none of these companies had created their current success from as far back in the field as Tenneco stood in 1991. Moreover, each of them had a strong *core* business generating substantial, rising earnings. This advantage helped buy time for top executives to offload mature, less profitable activities and transfer those resources into more promising lines of business.

Tenneco did not have that luxury. Its only true core business, energy, had been split apart four years before I arrived. Tenneco Oil, a large producer, refiner, and marketer that then would have ranked No. 15 among all U.S.-based oil companies, was sold for $7.6 billion in 1988. Five billion dollars from the proceeds were applied to reduce Tenneco's crushing corporate debt load and, mainly, to bolster Case.

Three years later, though, financial crisis returned when Case again hit the rocks (see Chapter 2). Tenneco's debt at one point in 1991 amounted to more than 100 percent of its book capital after all liabilities were tallied. And few Tenneco business operations had commanding positions in growth markets.

A Microcosm of Corporate Restructuring

The recharting of Tenneco, in terms of multiple challenges and the breadth of its reach, was on a scale equal to those carried out during roughly the same period at Westinghouse Corporation and ITT. Even Westinghouse, with broadcasting, and ITT, with hotels and gaming, were reinvented to capitalize on an existing platform that became its core businesses. At Tenneco, we essentially had to create this core business through a series of acquisitions that we built from a small presence of $500 million in revenues in specialty packaging to $3 billion in 1999.

As at Westinghouse and ITT, the reinvention of Tenneco was a response to the competitive forces that brought a more intense focus on customers, lower administrative and operating costs, and the urgency to compete against international rivals in global markets.

Tenneco's story, then, typified the intense restructuring and refocusing that characterized much of American industry in the 1990s. We raised $15 billion in total value from business sales and divestitures in that period, paid down $8 billion of debt, and invested $3 billion in acquisitions and another $1.5 billion in internal business opportunities. We also returned more than $2.5 billion to shareowners indirectly through repurchases of Tenneco common stock and by issuing shares in onetime Tenneco businesses.

The forces that created these dramatic changes are not abating. As the new global economy requires, the Tenneco businesses of 1992 continued to adjust rapidly in 1999—through yet more acquisitions, mergers, joint ventures, layoffs, and expansions. Like all large businesses in the world's new economy, they cannot be content to keep pace with change. To prosper, they must define progress and success in their industry, and then lead it.

Tenneco's former chemicals business, Albright & Wilson, was set to be acquired early in 2000 by Rhodia, the French chemicals group, after a bidding contest with Albemarle, of the United States. Newport News Shipbuilding, preparing to design and build an advanced new aircraft carrier and submarine, received two takeover offers in the first six months of 1999. The first attempt, by the General Dynamics Corporation, was ruled out by the Defense Department as being likely to reduce competition in nuclear-powered Navy ships. The second offer, from Litton Industries, eventually was dropped for the same reason.

Market conditions for Case, which was forced into laying off 3,400 employees in 1998 by a weak U.S. farm economy and fierce recessions in Eastern Europe, Asia, and South America, wavered with the outlook for the global economy. Case announced in May a planned merger with rival New Holland, to create a $12 billion global business controlled by Italy's Fiat SpA and based in Europe. El Paso Energy acquired another diversified energy company, Sonat Inc., creating the nation's largest natural gas pipeline system, and a company with $15 billion in revenues. It also capitalized on operations that Tenneco Gas originated as long ago as 1943, the year the forerunner of Tenneco started as the Tennessee Gas and Transmission Company. The Tennessee Gas Pipeline survives as an El Paso Energy subsidiary.

Broadly speaking, each of the businesses that comprised Tenneco in 1992 has today what the business revolution of the 1990s demanded for market leaders: single-market focus, lower operating costs, new products, more advanced machinery and technology, and more rigorous operating practices and measurements. Amid unrelenting competition, and unpredictable shifts in markets and economic forces, they continue in most cases to make important economic contributions in the hundreds of communities where they make products and hire, train, develop, and pay workers.

Disassembly and Reinvention

By the close of 1998, Tenneco was so different that 80 percent of the assets that were part of the corporation in 1992 had been sold or divested. Two-thirds of the employees on Tenneco's 1992 payrolls were no longer part of the organization. In turn, through 29 acquisitions made since mid-1994 in automotive parts and packaging, 20,000 of our 50,000 employees had been part of the new Tenneco for less than four years. One of every three employees was based outside North America.

As we took apart the old Tenneco organization and pieced together the new one through these acquisitions, earnings from continuing operations increased in 24 of 25 consecutive quarters through the second quarter of 1998. We had assembled leading product brands in the two remaining businesses of the new Tenneco: automotive parts and packaging businesses. The brands included Monroe Sensa-Trac® shock absorbers and struts, Walker Quiet-Flo™ exhaust systems, Monroe Clevite™ vibration control components, Hefty® trash bags, Hefty OneZip® and Baggies® storage bags, E-Z Foil® single-use aluminum cookware, and Hexacomb® and Jiffy® protective packaging, among many others. Yet our growth pace was not fast enough.

Stock prices of many of the largest and fastest-growing corporations more than doubled during this period in a reprise of the Nifty Fifty stock days of the 1970s. Investors were captivated, and their expectations rose. "New Economy" growth stocks, fueled by the Internet mania, led the way. Tenneco was viewed as an "Old Economy" value stock in this period when value stocks generally were déclassé.

We, in turn, could not reach the high rate of earnings growth we pursued to lift Tenneco into an exclusive realm of "Old Economy" growth stocks. We were seeking to increase earnings at a rate of 15 percent a year or better to validate our strategy, but we fell short. Two damaging setbacks in important segments of our operations persisted throughout 1998: very low prices for containerboard and weak orders from retailers of automotive parts. By July 1998, we determined it would be better to separate the automotive and packaging businesses.

As the 1990s came to an end, each of the six businesses that together formed the Tenneco conglomerate in 1992 stood separately, in seven different companies. These companies had annual sales ranging roughly from $1.5 billion to more than $15 billion, and employee counts from 7,500 to 39,000.

Amid all this turbulence, many awards came our way as thousands of people in our businesses carried out many difficult missions to the highest standards. Since the mid-1990s, nine of our manufacturing sites were awarded the highest designation for safety performance by the federal government, the most of any U.S.-based company. *Fortune* magazine included Tenneco in articles on the best corporate health management and industrial safety programs. *Industry Week* magazine named separate Tenneco-operated plants among its "Ten Best Plants in America" in 1996 and 1997; a third plant was a finalist in 1998. Tenneco also was one of 64 companies included on the magazine's list of "The World's 100 Best Managed Companies" in each of the past three years: 1996, 1997, and 1998.

Army Officer, Policy Adviser, Professor, Business Leader

For 21 years after graduating from the United States Military Academy at West Point in 1957, I was an Army officer with a diverse portfolio in world military and government affairs. Troop leader and aide-de-camp in cold-war Germany; combatant and strategist in the Vietnam War; policy adviser in the Defense Department and the White House, and teacher of politics, government, economics, and national security as a tenured professor at West Point.

Early in my career as an Army officer, I was honored to be selected to pursue advanced studies in political science and economics at the Massachusetts Institute of Technology. My doctoral dissertation, completed 10 years after leaving West Point as a cadet, examined the strategy and logistics of how the U.S. military planned for the "next" war between two world wars of the twentieth century.

Special assignments soon followed in Washington. I wrote several high-level military reports, including four chapters on the Vietnam ground war in the Pentagon Papers project. Later I advised President Richard Nixon and his cabinet as Deputy Director of the Domestic Council.

Drafting the first federal legislation on revenue sharing for states and local governments and coordinating White House responsibilities for governing the District of Columbia were major projects that came my way. After leaving Washington for a professorship at West Point near the end of the tragic Watergate scandal in 1974, I stumbled into another ethical quagmire. One of the worst cheating scandals of the century at West Point erupted in 1976. More than 100 students broke the honor code by sharing answers on a final examination in electrical engineering. I devoted much of the next year to investigating allegations, and mapping administrative reforms to prevent a recurrence.

These experiences gave me both visceral and intellectual reference points for the many difficult decisions I made in my years at Tenneco. They underscored the imperatives of understanding the realities and trade-offs in any situation: being honest and ethical, keeping a cool head amid a crisis, planning exhaustively, executing relentlessly, and surrounding yourself with smart and talented people who have the highest levels of integrity. Above all they strengthened my conviction that the essence of leadership is setting high standards, and making hard choices.

High standards. Hard choices. These basic concepts framed the decisions and programs that remade large corporations in the 1990s. For the tens of thousands who participated with me in remaking the Tenneco businesses, ours was an extended journey through this Schumpeterian world of creative destruction. There were many heroes. There were days of disappointment and triumph. The road was demanding, and often uncertain. For me, it was a prized assignment on the front lines during the most important revolution in business history.

DANA G. MEAD

Greenwich, Connecticut

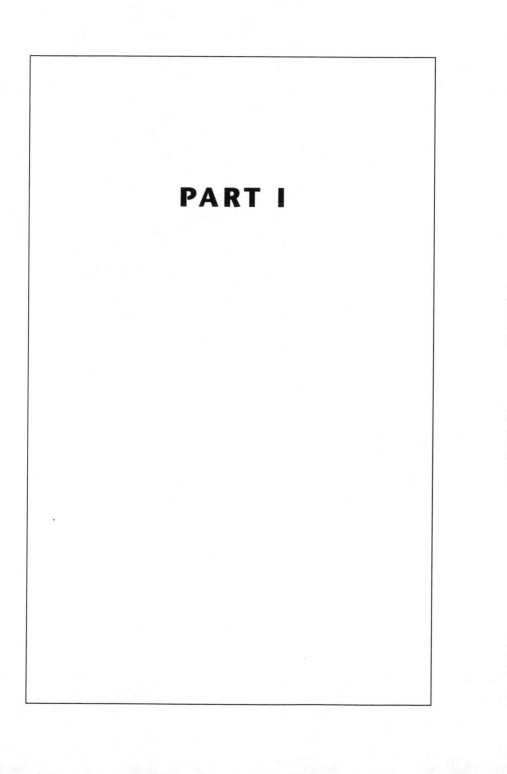

PART I

CHAPTER 1

Two New Leaders, One Lethal Tumor

MY CONVERSATIONS WITH MIKE WALSH ABOUT JOINING HIM TO RUN Tenneco were heating up in February 1992. He had invited me to Houston for some lengthy sessions at the spacious home he and his wife, Joan, had purchased a few months earlier in the Memorial Drive area at the western edge of the city.

We needed to sort through the complicated challenges Mike had taken on, and underestimated, six months earlier when he was recruited into Tenneco's top job from the Union Pacific Railroad. We had to carve out the ones I would take the lead on. We had to consider how to identify and operate the businesses within Tenneco that could get earnings rising at a sustainable, acceptable rate for the future. Then, too, Mike had to prepare to make his case for selecting me to Tenneco's board of directors, and brief me on what I could expect in my "final cut" interviews with three directors who chaired committees. We had to be ready to explain why I was the right candidate to become, as Mike put it, his "copilot" in the corporate command center.

These thoughts left me as I approached Mike's secluded home that morning and saw an emergency medical van parked near the front door. A couple of paramedics were rolling a man strapped to a gurney toward the van. That man was Mike Walsh. Mike greeted me with a shout and a wave. He was on his way to the Texas Medical Center for back surgery to repair a ruptured disc. The surgery had been arranged abruptly to relieve a deepening pain that had bothered him since he had fallen while skiing during a Christmas holiday trip with his family in Steamboat Springs, Colorado. He apologized for the timing, I wished him well, and the van sped off.

This memory of the redoubtable Mike Walsh being rushed away in an emergency medical van still haunts me. It was just a month later that the Tenneco directors approved my appointment as their president and chief operating officer. We then announced that I had resigned from the International Paper Company and would join Tenneco in a few days. I had been an executive for 14 years at I.P., the world's largest manufacturer of paper products, with nearly $14 billion in revenues, or about the same as Tenneco. I'd devoted much of the past six years heading negotiations to buy several large companies and dealing with important trade issues in Europe and Japan. But by this point, the $8/10$ rule had set in; I had accomplished about 80 percent of what I was going to be able to do as an executive vice president with a seat on I.P.'s board of directors. Hard as it was to leave friends and colleagues in the only company in which I'd ever drawn a paycheck, I wanted a broader challenge and new interests. Yet neither Mike nor I could have had any idea at this moment how much his medical problems would frame, publicly as well as privately, our two years as partners in the first stages of recreating Tenneco.

Mike never would be without some pain or discomfort from the brain tumor discovered months later that ultimately took his life, or from the impact of the aggressive medical strategies that could not cure him. Despite these grave obstacles, he stayed in one of the most demanding jobs of any chief executive in corporate America. He would work for periods with great intensity and remarkable effectiveness. But the fatigue from the cancer and from the treatments became overwhelming. He remained in the job almost exactly two years from this day when I saw him off to the hospital.

Competence, Focus to Offset Doubts, Uncertainty

Mike would always voice a flinty determination to beat the cancer. Yet it was natural that his public announcement of this fight, coming in less than 12 months, would generate worries and doubts both inside and outside the organization: about his energy and abilities, about my competence to take over for him, about Tenneco's future. Those doubts, which rarely surfaced directly to either of us, would remain until the disease forced him to leave his post early in 1994. Yet it was our job together, and eventually mine alone, to counter those concerns by staying focused on what was always our mission: strong leadership for the company through a protracted period of difficult, uncertain change.

This disease certainly would be tragic for Mike and his family. For me, it would add more work, faster, than I had anticipated at a critical time. The organization was beginning to feel its way toward a new direction and confidence just as Mike's health faltered. It became our mission not to allow his illness to become a tragedy for Tenneco, some staggering blow that would unravel the successes and new momentum throughout the organization.

It was unclear whether our blurred roles would be temporary, or protracted, or whether it would put me in a position to succeed Mike if the cancer forced him to step down. I would have to rely on my instincts on when and how to assume authority that otherwise would have been Mike's, and to do this as imperceptibly as possible. Achieving this would become one of the most difficult challenges of my business career. It was absolutely vital for Mike. If he ever got to the point when he believed he was too sick to work, it would be a terrible blow to his fighting spirit. It was obvious to those of us around him that preserving his remarkable intensity and mental toughness to battle the cancer was Mike's best shot for a cure.

Piecing together this story of his illness has been emotional at times, despite the more than five years since his death. This account includes details and conversations never discussed publicly during the 15 months from the day he disclosed his brain tumor until we announced his death. It would have been impossible to compile this account without the cooperation and support of Joan Walsh. Joan encouraged the physicians who cared for Mike to discuss his case, including parts that I previously had not known.

Her endorsement for telling the story mirrors the same high standard Mike set through their ordeal. It offered an opportunity to describe how a chief executive demonstrated the courage to confront a fatal disease with a rare outspoken voice and continue to lead. There were special leadership issues, in addition to the anticipated challenges of rebuilding the company, and directing large businesses in different industries selling products in more than 100 countries. Those issues included sophisticated and effective crisis communications with employees, investors, and the news media; the gradual and barely perceptible shift in our two roles as Mike's stamina waned; and management of a vital *sotto voce* link among company directors, the medical team, myself, and Mike. Of all the major changes at Tenneco in the 1990s, none was more difficult and heroic, tragic and inspiring, or as totally unexpected than this period when Mike was staggered by and ultimately defeated by brain cancer.

The story also is a reminder that no matter how thoroughly you prepare and plan for battle, you must have the determination to withstand and outlast the major shocks you are certain to face. Simply put, there are situations when you must make judgments on instinct, with little time for fact-finding or forethought. As the newly arrived second-in-command to Mike in 1992, the notion that his death from an aggressive brain tumor would put me in the position to become chief executive in less than two years was about the farthest thing from my mind.

Ready to Lead

Even so, standing outside Mike's house that morning in 1992, I was confident and optimistic at the age of 55, convinced that I had the bona fide experience and qualifications to run a big company. I had been in serious discussions about different openings for chief executive jobs when I was approached by Tom Neff, president of the executive recruiting firm, Spencer Stuart. Tom was the catalyst who had put Mike on the radar screen of Tenneco's directors. He urged me to hold off on the other positions until I talked with Mike about coming to Tenneco. I agreed.

Mike and I shared much of the same high-level network of contacts in business and government. Both of us had been White House Fellows, working for a year early in our careers at high levels in Washington government—Mike was an assistant to the Secretary of Agriculture in the Johnson administration and I had served in the Nixon administration's Domestic Council. We had never worked together in business, or government for that matter. He was an active, visible Democrat with especially solid credentials in the moderate wing from which Bill Clinton emerged to capture the party's presidential nomination that year. I had a similar resume among moderate Republicans.

Yet I also was familiar with Mike's career trajectory in business. He was far more likely to move on to other challenges than to stay 16 years and retire from Tenneco. He had implied as much in our first conversation about Tenneco over a Sunday morning breakfast at the Waldorf-Astoria Hotel in Manhattan. I think he saw himself going into Tenneco as a turnaround artist, trying to fix it, and then five years later moving on to something else, whether it would be another business or into government. He indicated that morning that if we were successful I was going to be in position to be the CEO in a relatively short period.

Mike then was 49 years old and already a highly regarded executive. His reputation was built on a no-nonsense style in shaking up and slimming down sprawling businesses. *Fortune* magazine had chronicled his successes for six years. In another two, his photo would be on *Fortune*'s cover under huge block letters announcing "Masters of Change," a cover story that also featured John F. Welch Jr. of General Electric, Lawrence Bossidy of Allied-Signal, and William Weiss of Ameritech.

Mike moved to Tenneco in the summer of 1991 from the Union Pacific Railroad, after running the railroad for five years with steadily increasing productivity and profits. Before the railroad, his first corporate job was as a manufacturing executive at Cummins Engine. In that role, he displayed a passion for applying the fundamentals of manufacturing excellence and competing on several

7

levels in global business. He had made several trips to Japan in the 1980s, where he toured many world-class manufacturing plants and leaned on government and business leaders there to open their protected domestic markets. I was working a very similar agenda at the same time at International Paper: improving safety and productivity in our mills and plants, expanding into international markets, and badgering the Japanese to scale back their barriers against paper imports.

It took a close friend from his days at Yale Law School to lure Mike into Cummins and corporate management. Until then, Mike was a fast-rising star in government and law in California. He spent 12 years overall in San Diego as U.S. Attorney, a federal prosecutor, and a public defender. People who knew him from the many high-profile legal issues he tackled or from his role as state co-chairman of the grassroots political network, Common Cause, expected Mike to run for the Senate or the governor's office before the 1980s were out. Many were stunned when he left it to start over in business by the cornfields of southern Indiana, the site of Cummins's headquarters.

Playing with Pain

Mike's back surgery that February day went well. Soon he was active in an exercise program of bicycle riding, walking, and swimming to build his cardiovascular stamina and his overall fitness. Within a few months, though, the back pain flared up again. It was a totally different problem this time, a kidney stone. Mike went into the hospital again to be treated with a sound wave technology that breaks apart the kidney stones. But it was only partially effective, and a special tube was inserted just below the rib cage for cleaning out the kidney. It finished the job but at the price of more aggravation, inconvenience, pain, and discomfort, and further delayed Mike's recovery from his back surgery to late summer.

By this stage in his life, Mike was well used to the idea that reaching for the top often meant playing with pain. An all-state running back during his high school football days in Oregon, Mike received a full athletic scholarship to play the sport at Stanford University. (We shared a passion for competitive team sports. I won all-state honors in football, baseball, and basketball at my high school in Wood River, Illinois, and was a varsity football and baseball player for Army.) One of his ambitions was to play in the National Football League. This was no pipe dream.

He had finished second in the state in total rushing yards during his senior year at his Portland high school, edged out by Mel Renfro for the rushing title. Renfro went on to an All-American career as sprinter and halfback at the University of Oregon and later played 14 years as an All-Pro defensive back and kickoff return specialist for the Dallas Cowboys. Mike did not get the chance to match his prowess against Renfro, or any other NFL players. He dislocated his shoulders so many times in high school and in his freshman season at Stanford that, following three surgeries to mend the separations, he had to give up the sport. He never took the field for the Stanford varsity.

That setback did not shake Mike's conviction about the benefits of regular and vigorous physical conditioning. So he was agitated by summer's end in 1992 when his workouts had not advanced much beyond walks of two or three miles a day along one of Houston's most popular and crowded jogging trails in Memorial Park. It was during these walks that Mike sensed that his left foot dragged. There was no pain, but his gait was a bit awkward. Back patients often have this problem, so it could easily have been related to the surgery. But by late October, it was clear the cause was something more complex. Despite six weeks of therapy, Mike had not regained much strength on his left side.

Working with a physical therapist in his office, Mike repeatedly lost his balance one afternoon trying a simple exercise, extending his right foot backward while bracing himself on his hands and left knee. A previous MRI (magnetic resonance image) had turned up no hint of a recurrence of the skiing injury, of renewed pressure on the spinal nerve or any other reason for continuing troubles with his legs. Three weeks later, Dr. Kenneth D. Wells, a former Army flight surgeon and NASA medical consultant who now was Tenneco's corporate physician, saw no improvement. He feared some disorder of the central nervous system, perhaps in the region of the brain known as the cerebellum. "I recommend we obtain an MRI of your brain," he told Mike.

Bad Timing for Distraction

This suggestion came at a bad time. Mike was in no mood for distractions. It was a few days before one of the most important gatherings for the company: a two-day conference with more than 400 Tenneco senior managers scheduled for mid-November. This would be Mike's second conference of the year, and my first. Mike agreed to see a neurologist that Dr. Wells recommended, a specialist in the nervous system, but he asked if it could wait until after the two-day meeting. "I'd really like to do this conference," he said. "This is a very important week for me and the company." Dr. Wells agreed to delay the MRI for another four days.

Mike and I had prepared a full agenda. We were eager to (1) lay out the evidence that a reversal already was underway in the company's fortunes; (2) make it absolutely clear that continued cost reductions and quality improvements were vital for each business, and (3) motivate as many as we could attending the meeting to adopt our strategies and programs. This was the best gathering for us to display our leadership styles, the breadth and depth of our grasp of Tenneco's problems and potential, and to introduce for the first time to this group several new senior executives Mike and I had recruited.

The meetings went well, but not without friction. On the eve of Mike's keynote speech, presidents of the six operating companies each had presentations ready. Their prepared remarks and slides covered general highlights and news of their operations. As in annual management conferences under previous Tenneco leaders, even the bad times, their tone was upbeat. That isn't what Mike and I wanted. We wanted a hard-nosed assessment of prospects and problems. We especially had to know issues that might blunt sales in coming months or require costly fixes. We knew Tenneco's strained financial condition would make it difficult to withstand any big financial surprise. And we knew our credibility was on the line. It was time to apply and enforce The Doctrine of No Surprises, no holds barred.

I critiqued their presentation rehearsals, leaving the presidents and their staff members to put in a late, late night making the changes we wanted. When they headed home from Houston two days later, few were in a cheerful mood. We had turned up the heat. They knew that their careers at Tenneco would rise or fall with the changing standards they had to meet, and the results they produced. Within the next 15 months, half of the presidents in place when Mike and I arrived would leave their jobs.

Off Balance, but Unfazed

MRI scanners of that day were huge, doughnut-shaped magnets with diameters of five feet or more. Related computing equipment and a motorized table to move a patient into and out of a magnetic field were crowded in with the scanner to fill a large room. It was a harsh, alien setting, doubly so for patients aware that this cold hardware had the potential to deliver the worst medical news of their life.

That is how it happened for Mike. After his scan was complete, Mike moved to a nearby dressing room as Dr. Wells fixed his eyes on an oversized computer monitor in a room adjacent to the hulking scanner. He studied the images of Mike's brain, cross-section by cross-section, as they appeared in sequence on the monitor. There was no round mass, no "golf-ball-size" tumor.

In a way, Dr. Wells was disappointed. Those types of tumor often can be completely removed with realistic prospects for a patient's full recovery. Instead, he saw an unusual brightness on nerve tracts where motor and sensory controls were rooted near the posterior temporal region of Mike's brain. This could have been the inconsequential residue from some brief internal bleeding from long ago. Mike had suffered multiple concussions during his football career, so perhaps this was simply a benign trace from those injuries. Or, as Dr. Wells realized, this might be a spreading cancer. He wasn't sure.

Dr. Wells hung up the phone in Mike's dressing room. He had just received the radiologist's initial interpretation of the MRI scan.

"We don't know exactly what the images represent, or what type of lesion this is," Dr. Wells told him. "But . . . Mike, it looks like you have a brain tumor." No matter how hard Mike might have tried to prepare himself, the spoken words "brain tumor" hit him hard.

This was no surprise to Dr. Wells. It had been more than 14 months since Mike had parachuted into one of the more complex, intense and exhausting jobs in corporate America. The first months especially were brutal, or "back-breaking" as Mike put it. To rescue Tenneco from what could have been one of the nation's biggest corporate bankruptcies, Mike had auctioned businesses generating more than $1 billion in annual revenues, slashed the dividend payment in half, cut $250 million in administrative costs, and eliminated 5,000 jobs. He had put the corporation on notice that any supervisors, managers, and executives not meeting performance targets would be at risk for their jobs. "Results, not best efforts," was the new mantra. "No excuses."

There was more. He had put his reputation on the line, raising $500 million from Wall Street essentially on his vow to resurrect a company that at the time had 80,000 employees, $14 billion in revenues and no earnings. Making these challenges worse, a respected longtime Tenneco executive in his early 60s, Ken Reese, had suffered a heart attack while jogging and died a few hours after a sale had been reached to bring in another $500 million in cash. Reese was among Mike's closest allies in his first months at Tenneco, a trusted adviser he sorely missed. In this same period, Mike had to assemble what was an almost entirely new team of 14 senior managers, most of them like myself coming from outside Tenneco. This blur of constant challenge gave him the sense that his first five months in the job were, for him and everyone else attacking the same problems, more like ten months, as he said once, "counting all the overtime."

He never considered that his health could fail. "I still feel like I'm 18!" he had boasted to a reporter near the end of those first five months. Yet the one part of his life he thought he controlled the most, that he had never taken for granted and that he had conditioned at a level far beyond that of most middle-aged executives, was betraying him at the most demanding time of his business career.

Off Balance, but Unfazed

The medical team accelerated the MRI scans to weekly intervals, creating a more rigorous system to measure changes in the tumor's size and detect any shifts in its growth rate. Meanwhile, Mike's already rigorous routine of physical conditioning became even more intense. It would be another six weeks before many medical questions raised by this initial brain scan could be answered with much clarity. None of that was within his power to influence, so he became determined to master the most of what he could control about his mind and body. His early morning workouts of swimming and weight training took on a more urgent purpose: preserving the physical stamina his daunting work at Tenneco demanded and, potentially, saving his own life.

CHAPTER 2

SINE QUA NON:
RESTRUCTURING CASE

I WOULD NOT HAVE A CLEAR SENSE OF THE GRAVITY OF MIKE'S MEDICAL condition until late October. His absences caused by the back and kidney problems added duties to a naturally heavy agenda during my first months in Tenneco. Yet by the time he learned and relayed news of his MRI tests, I was taking on a more intensive workload to direct the first of our major restructuring programs, this at our farm machinery and construction equipment business, J.I. Case.

This restructuring, which began in force in 1993 and continued into 1997, put the business on solid footing. Now operating as Case Corporation, this machinery manufacturer with a long history in American farming has been an independent company since 1994; its last official ties with Tenneco were severed in 1996. Despite a collapse of Case's markets in Brazil and emerging markets in Asia and Eastern Europe in 1998, the company remained profitable in the capable hands of senior managers we promoted or recruited, a testament to one of the most successful industrial restructurings in the decade. In 6 of the 10 years before we were able to sell Case stock to the public, the business was a money-loser. And if the restructuring of Case had failed, our plans for rebuilding Tenneco would have stalled.

Mike and I had no doubts about that in the summer of 1992, yet at the time the business crisis at Case was one of many urgent matters on my docket. My corporate experience until then had been exclusively in the paper business, and paper was a relatively small part of Tenneco. I had to dig in quickly to learn the fundamentals of all six businesses, and assess the leadership talents in each of them. This was a tall order. Chemicals that create the fizz in Coca-Cola™, make the bubbles in shampoo, and improve cleaning agents in detergent. Nuclear-powered aircraft carriers and submarines. Natural gas transportation and marketing, exploration, and development. Automotive exhaust systems, shock absorbers, struts, and brakes. Boxes, cartons, paper mills, plastic clam shell packages, and aluminum baking pans. Big farm tractors and combines, and small loader/backhoes for construction projects. All of these products and activities were underway every day in the name of Tenneco.

On occasion, it seemed as if I had vaulted into historical reclamation projects for endangered industries. Four of the six businesses had origins in the nineteenth century. Farm equipment (Case) dated to 1842; chemicals (Albright & Wilson) to the English application of phosphorus for matches in 1851; shipbuilding (Newport News Shipbuilding) to 1886; and, automotive (Tenneco Automotive) to an inventor of carriage springs in 1888. Even Tenneco's box-making business (part of Packaging Corporation of America) almost touched the nineteenth century; a forerunner was organized in Ohio in 1903. Oddly, the founding business of Tenneco, natural-gas pipelines, had the shortest lineage of the entire group. The year I arrived, Tenneco Gas was laying plans for its fiftieth anniversary celebration in 1993.

No Priorities among Essentials

A favorite adage from my West Point days as both cadet and professor is that there are no priorities among essentials. In other words, what has to get done must be done. Many things always have to get done. Learning the Tenneco businesses was essential for me, but there were other essentials, too. We had to build cohesion in the new group of senior managers, and meld them with leaders in operations. We had to assess leadership talents in corporate administration and the operations, and make adjustments quickly. I had to be accessible and persuasive to Tenneco's major investors, to our principal outside consultants and creditors, to Wall Street in general, and to the eight nonmanagement directors who represented Tenneco stockowners.

Within our organization, we had to initiate rapidly a program in process reengineering, quality improvement, and cost reduction. Known by the phrase "cost of quality," it was coached throughout Tenneco under the assistance and staff of quality consultants Mike had used effectively at Union Pacific, Armand (Val) Feigenbaum and his brother, Don, of General Systems Company. I had to be on top of this, with good reason. The Feigenbaums gauged the level of inefficiency and waste in Tenneco businesses at 22 percent of revenues, a staggering total compared with world-class ratios of 5 percent, and superior U.S. ratings of 10 percent. In stark terms, it meant that Tenneco customers collectively were paying about $3 billion extra for waste and inefficiency in our systems.

Mike considered the Cost of Quality system the best method for shaking up the organization and getting management and employees focused on cutting costs. The system, widely used by Japanese manufacturers that had hired Val Feigenbaum to teach them, is a disciplined statistical process for quantifying internal and external failures in administration and production. One result is improving product quality, which, in turn reduces warranty payments to customers if equipment fails. And so on.

Companies that joined the quality revolution early gained a large competitive advantage. I saw this during the 1980s at International Paper, where quality improvements regularly contributed to profits. Today, though, quality is the price of admission to the global marketplace, where the world-class companies boast failure costs as low as 5 percent of total revenues.

General Systems' teams worked closely in all our Tenneco businesses from 1992 through 1995, coaching managers on a common language for methodology and measurements. Each Tenneco business previously had its own quality programs before we changed direction. In most cases these programs were unrelated. More important, they obviously were not getting results.

We were committed to these simple ideas about managing work: (1) you can't manage what you don't measure; and (2) what gets measured, gets done. We wanted a more fundamental focus on measuring and reducing failure costs. These are the costs of not doing something right the first time, the costs of not having absolute quality. This emphasis also gave us more clarity in setting measurable goals and objectives with senior executives in each business, and for them to do the same with their leadership teams extending onto the plant floors.

We tied every senior manager's pay in part to their ability to meet specific targets in reducing failure costs. We just said, "Here's your goal. You've got to get so much failure cost out this year. If you don't do it, you won't make your budget. If you don't make your budget, you won't get your bonus. More important, the company won't have as much money to reinvest in your business next year."

We gave them flexibility on how to meet their targets, but they knew we were going to keep score and hold them accountable. We established quarterly meetings where the top executives in each business reported to Tenneco's top management on specific achievements, and the line managers discussed their progress toward annual targets.

Our scoring system had four parts: prevention, appraisal, internal failure and external failures. Prevention activities include product development, training, and defining performance standards. Appraisal requires evaluations such as quality audits, testing, and customer surveys. Internal failure costs include re-work (doing a task more than once to get desired results), scrap (unused or wasted materials or supplies), and unscheduled machine downtown (equipment failures on the shop floor). External failure costs are those not discovered until your product is in the customer's hands, such as warranty costs, policy adjustments, lost sales and liability costs. The challenge is to develop an operating system that lowers the total costs across all four areas. There are many trade-offs to work out, and the optimum balance varies from business to business. Ultimately, it is the customer who defines quality for each product and each business.

There is no rocket science in quality management. Getting it right the first time, satisfying customers, reducing variations in processes, and continually improving products is just common sense in business. Doing this systematically, with energy and dedication, and recognizing the truly remarkable successes that emerge will take you far down the road to achieving your quality goals.

In 1992, we could not count on rapid sales growth of sluggish economic growth in the United States and abroad to raise revenues in any of Tenneco's businesses. We could not count on any technological silver bullets. Competition and excess industry capacity prevented us from raising prices. But we could control how efficiently we worked; we could reduce our costs. In the next three years, we would reduce the ratio of failure costs to revenues to 13 percent of revenues. By the end of 1996, we had eliminated more than $2 billion in failure costs from our businesses. Through 1998, the processes added nearly $1 billion to Tenneco's operating income, or 20 percent of the total since 1992.

Near Miss on a Loan Default

In the final months of 1991, Mike had steered Tenneco through a strong gale. It was a stormy passage, with drama and urgency. There were tight deadlines, the sudden death of an experienced Tenneco senior executive Mike had befriended and trusted, and a flurry of negotiations resulting in $2 billion of restructuring steps completed by the close of his first 120 days in Houston. Several thousand jobs were eliminated, the common stock dividend payment was sliced in half, and many administrative programs were pared. The final two pieces of this effort—the sale of a preferred stock that could be converted into common shares, and the sale of a chemical plant still

under construction and designed to produce a new gasoline addi-
tive—brought in more than $1 billion in cash. Wired from Tenneco
bank accounts, this money beat the year-end deadline on debt payments by a matter of hours. A default on the loans would have been a
calamity, piercing the momentum and rising credibility Mike needed
to keep leaning hard on the top Tenneco managers.

Only a few people in the company were aware of the close call
on the loans. However, the swift actions to pare expenses and raise
cash in the first 120 days were widely reported. This success in alle-
viating this first crisis instilled a new energy and confidence in an
organization that was lacking both. Indeed, a hard-fought, shared
victory is the best antidote for a group of leaders who have tasted
much defeat. This was true for the hundreds of executives, lawyers,
and other staff specialists who worked six- and seven-day weeks for
four months to meet the tight deadlines Mike had imposed. After
years of disappointment and infighting, this group lacked cohesion.
Avoiding a debt crisis in 1991 brought many of them closer together, but it was only a first step. And the long hours had just
begun. "We're still in clenched-teeth time," Mike told them.

The Value of Emotional Detachment

A leader's credibility is a currency that has to be replenished repeatedly through solid, steady results. Three businesses—Tenneco Gas,
Newport News Shipbuilding, and Tenneco Automotive—were reliable in their own right for most of the 1980s, but overall Tenneco
had not produced solid, steady results for more than a decade. And,
despite the early momentum Mike established, we had serious problems to solve. We also had to be cautious. In the first stages of leading a huge transformation, the temptation is to go too far, too wide,
too fast. You risk becoming a leader of dubious credentials, of being
seen as having a portfolio of authority that is a mile wide, and a
level of substance that is an inch deep. So you cannot focus on too
many issues, say 10 or more. You also cannot focus on a single issue,
such as revenue growth or cost reductions. The organizational systems are too complex.

You need to find the most critical three or four issues that should have the biggest overall impact on achieving your goals, make it clear what the results should be, then drive after them relentlessly. It is a tremendous asset to have an outsider's perspective. You have little or no emotional investment in pivotal decisions that either worked or did not work before you arrived. You can exploit a judicial temperament in pursuing facts. This is by no means a behavior foreclosed to executives who have spent 20 years or more in one company. But you've got to have an outsider's perspective to rise above the parochialism that exists in all the big companies. Tenneco's leadership throughout the 1980s could not escape what by most accounts was a stubborn desire to succeed in two global businesses, farm machinery and construction equipment.

One of the true visionaries and risk takers in the high-tech world, Andrew S. Grove, tells how he came to realize the importance of emotional detachment in his 1996 book, *Only the Paranoid Survive* (New York: Currency/Doubleday). Many executives, he writes, fail to identify fundamental shifts in the patterns of competition in their industries. Or, even when they recognize the shifts, they don't adjust. Grove, now chairman of Intel Corporation, almost was one of them. He had to seriously consider as Intel's president in 1985 whether to abandon computer memory chips, Intel's principal business since it was founded in 1968. Intel was an industry leader in memory chips, and Grove one of its most creative forces, but brutal competition from Japan was clobbering profits. Intel was foundering.

"If we got kicked out and the board brought in a new CEO, what do you think he would do?" Grove asked Gordon Moore, the chairman and CEO. "He would get us out of memories," Moore said, without missing a beat. Grove, feeling "numb," replied, "Why shouldn't you and I walk out the door, come back and do it ourselves?" They did. Intel shifted its focus to microprocessors, the electronic brains of personal computers. It was a brilliant move. Two years later, Intel was profitable again and went on to become the world leader in microprocessors. "If existing management want to keep their jobs when the basics of the business are undergoing profound change, they must adopt an outsider's intellectual objectivity," writes Grove, one of Intel's cofounders. "People who have no emotional stake in a decision can see what needs to be done sooner."

The Outsider's Perspective

This was a clear advantage Mike and I brought to our work. But the outsider's perspective brings no guarantee of serenity. Mike and I were jolted many times by unexpected, grim facts that emerged through the spring and summer. We asked a lot of questions and listened carefully. As an outsider, you have to be unsparingly disciplined about what you need to know and what you don't need to know. Most people you deal with will want to tell you more than you need to know. Frequently, they will try to bury you with information. Sometimes they do this to obscure that they don't realize one or two key issues. Also, some people want to avoid making a clear recommendation on something for which they are being held accountable.

At the same time, you will discover a lot of talent buried in the organization at all levels. You need these insiders. They not only know how to work the valves and switches in the middle of the night, but they probably have a lot of ideas on how to do it better. You have to put your ear to the ground and listen carefully to identify the people who are looked to and respected by their peers. You need them as allies to implement your vision as rapidly as possible. These are people with credibility. They have valuable institutional memory and perspective. If they can understand what you want, agree with it, and can lead it, then you will have a good shot at succeeding.

These are insiders who have an outsider's perspective. They are especially important allies for an outsider coming into top positions in a large, complex organization. They can energize the informal but vital political base you must build quickly to make an impact throughout the organization. At the same time, every company has chronic whiners, people opposed to almost any kind of change, and people who simply are unable to make the change. It is a waste of time trying to convert them. In many cases, managers at a midlevel or higher rank who fit these types either leave on their own or are pushed out by the new culture.

Headquarters versus Operations

One of the serious hidden problems we inherited at Tenneco was a corporate reporting system that only a few people at the top could fathom or review in its entirety. It apparently served the purposes of our predecessors. It prevented the six different businesses from analyzing each other's financial books and operating processes. This stifled most initiatives to share best practices across the businesses, such as in safety, purchasing, environmental protection, or human resource management. Frankly, most of the business leaders preferred it that way. The less they had to deal with anyone from the corporate office, the better they liked it.

This conflict between headquarters and distant outposts of subsidiary operations exists at varying degrees in any corporation. It typically is far worse in multi-industry corporations. Headquarters executives have to resist the impulse to micromanage, to dig too far into subsidiaries' day-to-day operations and dictate tactics to the people heading these operations. Decisions should be made closest to the people and places where they will have the most impact, and where fast-changing market conditions usually are most evident. Corporate leaders set strategy, policy, and performance objectives. They recruit or promote the best people available to meet those standards in the business operations, and they give them the authority, responsibility, and flexibility to do it.

This was not how Tenneco had been run. With one notorious exception to be described shortly, heads of business operations expected to be left alone. They avoided telling executives or their headquarters staff in Houston anything they did not want them to know. As a general rule, the corporate executives and staff did not demand information they needed.

By the summer of 1992, all former top executives who either designed or tolerated this nonsense had left the company. But the legacy of hiding bad news caused us fresh problems for months as we dug more deeply into each of the businesses. Mike and I were working 16-hour days and 100-plus-hour weeks with our staff to catch up with the problems we had identified. Then we would realize that these substantial challenges were growing larger as negative surprises cropped up. We kept finding new obstacles to targets we had set for cost reductions, process improvements, and earnings. After a while, these occasions would inspire gallows humor. "If either of us really understood the magnitude of these problems," one of us would say, "we wouldn't have gotten into this. If we were investment bankers, we would have been fired for lack of due diligence."

Identifying Troubles at Case

The most immediate problem was an old one for Tenneco, its farm machinery and construction equipment business, J.I. Case. Case lost $618 million from operations in 1991. It closed out the year with an entire year's worth of production in tractors and backhoes standing idle in dealer lots and company-owned facilities. Meanwhile, factories still were running flat out even though the sales outlook remained poor. Farmers' income was crimped by recession in the United States, depressed land values, and reduced crop prices. A strong dollar dampened sales in Europe.

Case stood Number 2 behind John Deere Inc. in farm machinery, and trailed Caterpillar Inc. in construction equipment. It had 30,300 employees, 24 manufacturing plants, and 4,300 independent and company-owned dealerships in 50 states and more than 150 other countries. Of its $4.4 billion in revenues, 66 percent were generated in the United States, and another 25 percent in Europe. Worldwide revenues amounted to 37 percent of the Tenneco total, twice the percentage of our next largest businesses, the pipeline network and related energy operations in Tenneco Gas, and Newport News Shipbuilding. Case so dominated Tenneco that more than half of the financial analysts following Tenneco specialized in machinery.

Many management miscalculations created the business crisis at Case. Four aspects to the crisis in particular needed urgent attention: overproduction, pricing policies, fixed costs, and excessive product lines. First, the global market for farm machinery was plagued by too much capacity, a situation that had persisted for more than a decade. Case alone had enough plants and capacity to exceed total world demand for farm equipment. *It had to close plants* and dismiss more than 10,000 employees, with the most urgent cuts concentrated in Europe.

Second, its practice of slashing prices to 30 percent or more below the original price for new equipment near the end of a model year conditioned buyers to delay purchases for these year-end discounts. Case's goal was to take sales and market share away from John Deere. But the discounting scheme was a recurring failure, touching off internecine pricing wars that squeezed revenues and profits at Case and also Deere. Deere, responding with its own discounts, could not allow the gap between its pricing and Case to widen too far. Aside from driving down or eliminating profit margins on new products, the yearly deep discounts devastated the used-tractor market for Case dealers, which for them was their most profitable business. Used tractors might sell for $45,000, and new ones for $60,000 without discounts. But with new tractors frequently marked below $40,000 at year-end sales, prices for used tractors also plummeted. Dealers also lost sales in what otherwise were strong spring and autumn sales seasons because customers would wait for the year-end bonanza. Typically Case hurt itself more than Deere. With its prices 7 percent to 10 percent lower than Deere's before the shooting began, Case's narrower profit margins evaporated more quickly.

Looking back, Case's discounting tactics remain a puzzle. Buyer loyalty is unusually high in farm equipment, with 85 percent of tractors sold to repeat customers. You can get a few buyers to shift brands if a particular feature attracts them, or if they are mad about a lemon they recently owned from a competitor. The only hope to gain market share through aggressive pricing was in a thriving market with new customers coming in, which never materialized. The result was that even though Case and Deere competed as a duopoly with market dominance in farm tractors for many years, neither made much money. *Case had to gauge demand more accurately* and gear production schedules to meet it. And it had to minimize the year-end price discounts.

Next, Case had too much capital tied up in manufacturing parts and equipment. This loaded the business with high fixed costs and exposed it to large losses when revenues fell sharply. High fixed costs are anathema in a cyclical industry. Farm machinery and construction equipment are highly cyclical businesses, with sharp moves between peaks and valleys in sales. Competitors in cyclical industries who rely on outside suppliers for numerous parts and equipment have more options to protect profits. They simply reduce costs when sales slip by cutting orders to their suppliers. They also have more choices to utilize the best component technology without having to make big capital investments to develop the technology. During the first stage of designing Case's restructuring, I asked the top people in operations what product features gave Case a competitive advantage or some other appeal over its rivals at that time. Their answer had three major parts: tractor transmissions; engines, which were manufactured in a joint venture with Cummins Engines; and hydraulic valving for loader/backhoes. With that consensus, I directed the leaders in Case's operation to design a restructuring that would enable Case to buy virtually all other parts and equipment from outside suppliers. *Case had to consolidate production* into fewer plants, outsource more of the component parts it assembled, and manage more efficient assembly operations.

Fourth, Case had too many products, including far too many that consistently did not make a profit. We were losing more than 20 percent on average for every tractor we manufactured. So the faster the plants operated, the more money we lost. Case had 48 tractor models, plus another 68 models in construction equipment. This added enormous costs to engineering and parts inventories, as well as making production systems complex and inefficient. It was as if every time a marketing guy came in and said, "Gee, we need an orchard tractor," the product guys would think it over and say, "That's a heck of a good idea." Maybe they would sell 200 of them. Next, the marketing guy would say, "Now we need one for a vineyard," and they would sell maybe 150 of those. In Europe, Case had probably a dozen models of small tractors. Each cost extra money to build, but they really only had one or two unique features. By 1992, Case had three times more models than it needed, and on most of them the sales volume was simply too low for them to be profitable. Studies indicated that the total number of tractors should drop by 75 percent, to 16, and the number of construction equipment models should be pared by 44 percent, to 38. *Case had to simplify engineering and production* by eliminating low-volume and low-profit models.

An Intolerable Situation

Mike scratched at these issues in his first 120 days, taking a charge against earnings of $461 million to cover expenses for job cuts, plant closings, and shutdowns of the weakest product lines. The additional red ink lifted Case's total losses for 1991 above $1 billion. As we intensified our analysis of Case, the following spring and summer, two things were obvious. The business seemed likely to lose more than $200 million from operations that year, and, remarkably, there was no plan underway to cut those losses, except to wait until farmers began buying more tractors. The situation was intolerable. "You've got to get rid of this tar baby," our top strategy adviser on Wall Street, Felix Rohatyn, warned us. "It doesn't matter what you do. You've got to get rid of it or it's going to take you down."

This was no idle warning. The previous chairman and chief executive, James L. Ketelsen, had been removed from power by Tenneco directors a year earlier after continuing disappointments at Case. Ketelsen, a former Case president who became Tenneco's chief executive officer in 1978, had seized the opportunity to make Case the conglomerate's flagship business in the 1980s. Until then, energy had been the dominant group in what had become an increasingly divided organization. From this point of Ketelsen's ascendancy into the chief executive post, manufacturing increasingly would have the upper hand.

The change sparked bitterness and resentment for many within the energy group, and also other manufacturing businesses. It was a natural response. Resources from all the other businesses were funneled toward Case.

This inevitably narrowed opportunities for managers in other operations to expand and improve their business. Less money was available for capital projects, developing new products, hiring new people, and so on. These managers had limited influence over how the cash generated by their successes would be used.

The farm economy was in a severe depression late in 1984, and so was the farm equipment business. Sales of combines in the U.S. would plunge to 11,400 that year (and continue down to 6,000 in 1988), or less than one third of the market total in 1973. The picture was still worse in big, two-wheel drive tractors, which collapsed to 18,000 in 1984, from 71,000 in 1973. Ketelsen knew the industry had far too much capacity, but Tenneco estimated the costs of shuttering parts of Case and selling the rest in a fire sale at more than $500 million.

Gamble on a Farming Recovery

Instead, he decided to lead a consolidation in the industry. He was optimistic that a recovery was due soon in the farm economy. He intended for Case and Tenneco to profit when an upsurge in the fortunes of machinery producers arrived. The healthy turnaround Tenneco had achieved at Newport News Shipbuilding supported this view. Years of heavy investments and mediocre profits had been all Tenneco had to show from its 1968 acquisition of the venerable shipyard, until the builder of nuclear-powered submarines and aircraft carriers began to register large profits and healthy cash flow during the Reagan military buildup. Cash flow is a common standard for measuring the underlying financial strength in a business. It gauges the amount of money earned before interest payments on debt, tax payments, and expenses for aging assets.

Tenneco thought it saw a chance for a similar success at case. Late in 1984, Tenneco acquired International Harvester's agricultural equipment plants and dealer networks for $430 million and combined them with Case. The deal, which Tenneco had considered in broadly similar terms but rejected nine months earlier, catapulted Case into the Number 2 position in farm machinery behind Deere. It was a merger of two historic agricultural businesses that had revolutionized farm productivity, and thereby the American and world economy, for nearly 150 years.

Jerome Increase Case, the inventor of mechanized threshers to separate straw from grain, had founded his company in Racine, Wisconsin, in 1842. The company added farm tractors to its product lines in 1880. It even manufactured automobiles between 1907 and 1927, and entered the Indianapolis 500 race six times. For his part, Cyrus McCormick sold his first horse-drawn grain harvester in Virginia in 1840, and later moved his business to Chicago. The McCormick harvester increased a typical daily grain harvest fourfold to 10 acres, from the two to three acres that a good man could yield swinging a cradle scythe from dawn to dusk.

The Makings of "a Corporate Vietnam"

But in marrying the industrial descendants of these historical figures, Tenneco's strategy was not uniformly applauded. One unnamed Tenneco executive fretted to *Business Week* that the deal had the makings of "a corporate Vietnam." The Associated Press (February 4, 1985) reported that, at least for some companies, the deal would be "akin to swimming toward the *Titanic* before it hit the iceberg." T. Boone Pickens, the Texas natural-gas tycoon then riding high as an oil-company raider, said Tenneco was "investing in a dry hole." But Ketelsen was confident. "I'm very bullish about the Harvester acquisition," he told *The New York Times* in an April 7, 1985 feature article. A superb financial executive Ketelsen had grown up in the heart of farm country, Davenport, Iowa. He was promoted to president of Case when he was just 35 years old, a few years before Tenneco acquired a majority ownership stake in the Case organization.

This first link between Tenneco and Case was remarkably passive, given the far-reaching historical impact the farm-and-construction equipment business would make at Tenneco. Case at the time was a relatively small component in a broad mix of commerce controlled by the Kern County Land Company. The most prized assets in Kern County Land were a million acres of land in California's central San Joaquin Valley, which contained large oil reserves and abundant water resources. Kern County Land was active in agriculture, and became the nation's biggest producer and processor of almonds, pistachios, and dates. It also owned a manufacturer of automotive exhaust systems (Walker Manufacturing) and more than 50 percent of a farm machinery and construction equipment maker (Case). Both companies were based in Racine. Yet when the handshakes in Houston celebrated the pact that brought the Kern County assets and operations into the fold, there had been little time for Tenneco executives to consider much about the condition and outlook for the farm economy or future sales of Case.

It was the oil reserves that had enticed Armand Hammer's Occidental Petroleum Corporation to attempt a hostile takeover of Kern County Land in 1967. Kern County found cover in Tenneco's founder and chief executive, Gardiner Symonds Jr. In a matter of days, Symonds agreed to top Armand Hammer's bid for Kern County. The transaction was one of those whirlwind white-knight acquisitions that increasingly were shaking up big business, adding to the lore of Wall Street's go-go days during the longest economic expansion in U.S. history to that time, the 107 months between 1961 and 1969.

Missing a Strategic Inflection Point

Several Tenneco senior executives anticipated that Gardiner Symonds eventually would sell Case and continue Tenneco's main focus on energy and related operations in chemicals and minerals. Tenneco increased its ownership in Case to 100 percent in 1970 when Case again encountered financial problems. Symonds suffered a heart attack and died unexpectedly a year later. In 1972, Ketelsen was recruited from the president's post at Case to the Houston headquarters as Tenneco's corporate chief financial officer. He also was given a seat on Tenneco's board of directors, an indication to many Tenneco executives that, at the age of 42, Jim Ketelsen was likely one day to run all of Tenneco. This was the period of Tenneco's strongest financial performance, with profits rising and revenues expanding to $15 billion by 1980, the year Tenneco ranked eighteenth on *Fortune*'s list of the 500 largest industrial companies. The organization spanned nine industries. Weak oil prices, high interest rates, and the depressed farm economy in the early '80s added to an already daunting leadership challenge. Ketelsen believed the Harvester deal would be part of the solution for reviving profits.

He moved in the right direction, closing some Harvester plants and consolidating production, but not far or fast enough. Case hemorrhaged cash continually for another three years after the Harvester acquisition. Tenneco continued pouring hundreds of millions of dollars into Case to cover the losses, still convinced of an approaching recovery in farming income, but this would not develop until the mid-1990s.

A huge percentage of this cash for Case was siphoned from energy operations, especially the gas pipeline operations. Its executives considered this constant wealth transfer into Case misguided. Most energy companies, jolted by a 1986 plunge in oil prices, were selling their nonenergy holdings, not dumping cash into them. Even so, Tenneco's energy operations had new troubles of their own. Weak oil prices had crimped Tenneco Oil profits below projections. The pipeline business faced huge legal liabilities, more than $1 billion, from canceling numerous contracts to purchase gas from producers at prices higher than $7 per thousand cubic feet. As the industry deregulated in the mid-1980s, those gas prices plunged by two-thirds or more. Like dozens of other major pipeline companies, Tenneco Gas could not afford to pay the old, high price.

The Selling of Tenneco Oil

The pressure on Tenneco early in 1988 was mounting. Corporate debt surpassed $8 billion. Its credit ratings were slipping as the corporation borrowed and repaid $4 billion in short-term debt every month. Top executives reasoned they needed $5 billion to chop interest payments and retain the company's ample dividend payment. An executive who ran the Tenneco energy operations proposed to combine most of the oil company and pipeline assets into a new corporation, then spin it off under his leadership. The payoff for Tenneco in the transaction might have been close to $3 billion. The new corporation could have taken on that much debt from new creditors, and made a cash payment of $3 billion to Tenneco. The executive, Joe B. Foster, also calculated that a sale of some nonessential energy assets, plus Newport News Shipbuilding, the Albright & Wilson chemicals business, and a 20-percent interest in Case might generate an additional $2 billion.

The plan was turned down. Foster was told that jettisoning the pipeline business might generate an impossibly high tax bill, perhaps $4 billion. He also was told that the shipyard or the chemicals business could not be sold for much and that few buyers would emerge for a stake in Case. The Tenneco directors were convinced instead to sell Foster's prized jewel, Tenneco Oil—all its exploration, production, refining, and marketing operations. Estimated initially to be worth approximately $6 billion, the auction returned $7.6 billion in cash from 14 different buyers, making it the largest industrial auction ever executed by Wall Street to that time. It also ranked as the second-largest deal in the oil industry, after Chevron's $13.3 billion acquisition of Gulf Oil Corporation in 1984. Tenneco Oil had been renowned in the oil patch for developing superior methods of blending talents of petroleum engineers and financial experts. Its processes and culture had been studied by major oil companies. In a matter of months, this business built over 30 years into the nation's fifteenth largest oil company was disbanded. More crucial for 90,000 employees remaining in the still-vast Tenneco organization, internal political forces now shifted decisively against the energy-industry culture of the conglomerate's first business, natural gas transportation, and its leaders. For the first time, Tenneco's fortunes would be created from manufacturing. Case, Newport News Shipbuilding, Tenneco Automotive, Packaging Corporation of America, and Albright & Wilson—all manufacturers—collectively contributed nearly 80 percent of Tenneco's 1989 revenues of $14 billion. The balance came from Tenneco Gas and Tenneco Minerals, a business sold early in 1992. As we revealed our plans in 1996 to divest Tenneco Gas, renamed Tenneco Energy by then, many questioned why I was severing Tenneco's roots in the energy business. In fact, the real decision to do that was made four years before I came to the company, when Tenneco Oil was sold.

By early 1991, the nearly $8 billion retrieved in the breakup of Tenneco Oil seemed to have vanished from Tenneco's balance sheet. J.I. Case again was in trouble. New equipment was piling up on dealer lots as Case factories kept up production, and Case accountants booked sales as the shipments headed off to dealers. But the economy had been in recession since Iraq's invasion of Kuwait the previous summer. Housing construction had slowed and farm income plummeted. The volume of serious buyers coming into the showrooms of Case dealers slowed to a trickle. This time, Tenneco had no oil company to sell. The acquisition of the Harvester business indeed had turned into Tenneco's corporate Vietnam. Ketelsen was forced a week after the Iraqi invasion in August 1991 to relinquish his power to Mike gradually, beginning in October. But the magnitude of Case's mounting losses was made clear over Labor Day weekend, and from then on Mike was in control.

Needing the Facts

Ketelsen formally stepped down as chief executive at the end of that year, then as chairman two months after I arrived. This was a few months before Mike detected that his left foot dragged during those late-summer walks in Memorial Park. Yet, I already had begun stepping in when he had to miss an event to nurse what we thought were continuing back and kidney problems. I often found myself chairing the Monday morning teleconference meeting of senior executives and top business leaders in the company.

Mike had asked Ketelsen at one of the first meetings I attended to make his thick binder on Case's financial and production data available to me and to give me any other assistance I needed. "I've asked Dana to pay a lot of attention to Case," he said. After three or four weeks, I didn't have the numbers. It struck me as clearly intentional, a symbolic brawling over power. Yet once I made an issue of it privately, the data became available. Other than this one initial resistance, he was always civil, businesslike, and helpful despite his public loss of power.

Case's headquarters in Racine, Wisconsin, are a two-hour drive north from Chicago's central business district, the Loop, and nearly three hours by corporate jet from Houston. I traveled there frequently that summer (it was also headquarters then of Tenneco Automotive's exhaust systems business, Walker Manufacturing), gathering intelligence to prepare for the bargaining that Felix Rohatyn had encouraged. We met with bankers, financiers, and executives at every major machinery company in the world. My offer? To give away Case for one dollar, plus its debt of about $4 billion. There were no takers. The common response was, "Sorry, you guys fix it first, and then we'll talk."

Adding Another Assignment

For awhile, Mike and I thought we could count on two seasoned executives then running Case to lead the many changes we knew were required. But that idea withered during a meeting with these two respected industrialists that Mike, myself, our investment bankers, and other trusted consultants held a few days before the Labor Day weekend in New York.

The agenda was set for a daylong review of their plans for saving Case, but it didn't take long for us to realize that these two men seemed to despise one another. While one presented what struck me as a patently flawed strategy, the other buried his head in *The Wall Street Journal,* bored and disinterested. When the roles reversed, the first speaker seemed even more disinterested, jotting nonstop in a spiral notebook. Later, when it was his turn again, he read from those notes for an hour and a half. He wanted Case to expand, to acquire a large dealer network. Together, the pair presented no plan for cost reductions. No restructuring plan. No product plan. No reduction of personnel. No plan for Europe, which was bleeding nearly $100 million a year alone in small tractors. All of us were stunned. I started quizzing them. It was an interrogation of the first order. They had no answers. I was mad, and I wasn't the only one.

Mike and I stayed in New York that evening. We shared a drink together and just sat there looking at each other thinking: we're in deep crap. This place, Case, is killing us. Our most optimistic projections are that it will lose $700 million in the next five years if nothing is done. We've got two guys clearly capable of running it, but who also have no agreement on how to stop the bleeding. Mike continued looking at me for a moment, but said nothing. In our first conversation that previous December at the Waldorf, he had emphasized how vital it would be to get control of Case, to get the real facts about what was going on. He had been warned by then that senior managers there repeatedly had not been adequately forthcoming on fundamental production and accounting issues.

Now, nine months later, I knew what he had meant. We both knew what we were thinking. As Tenneco's chief operating officer, it was my responsibility to make sure Case got out of the woods. This was no time to go searching for somebody else to run it. "What do you think?" Mike asked. "Well, I know what *you're* thinking," I replied. Mike didn't miss a beat. "And *I* know *you* know that what I'm thinking is right." The president and chief operating officer of Tenneco was also going to be the next chairman and chief executive of Case. "You've got to go to Case," Mike said.

Four days later, after a decent interval provided by the holiday weekend, we informed one of the pair who starred in the New York fiasco, the first speaker during the daylong review, that he was out. As the news release put it, he decided to retire. His employment contract would be honored, and so on. But there was no negotiation. Mike and I preferred retaining his estranged, erstwhile colleague, that momentarily avid *Wall Street Journal* reader. This executive knew the Case business well, having worked there earlier in his career. He had been a top executive in another Tenneco business for several years, before moving back to Case. This gave him an institutional memory that helped him interpret and manipulate the corporate culture, such as it was.

We thought we could get him to work with us, a calculation that generally, but not entirely, was on the mark. This executive was dismayed at first when we told him he would not be promoted, but remain president, reporting to me. He grumbled, but stayed, and went on to play a positive role during the first two years in what was to become one of the most successful and enduring industrial restructurings in recent times. When the restructuring program moved into a new phase, he retired with some reluctance after Mike and I concluded we needed new leaders.

Demanding Changes

I had to state the situation as clearly as I could in my first remarks that week to Case's management group in Racine. "Tenneco shareowners and Tenneco management do not have unlimited patience," I said. "This place has been unsatisfactory for too many years." It was a theme I soon repeated before large meetings of Case dealers and customers in Milwaukee, to large groups of Case employees, as well as in private meetings and public gatherings of major shareowners. I also reviewed what we saw as the four cardinal sins of Case: (1) too much capacity; (2) excessive fixed costs and vertical integration; (3) far too many unprofitable product offerings; and (4) ill-conceived marketing strategies that favored an inefficient distribution system and self-destructive pricing discounts. And I said we had to quickly get together a plan for cutting costs, improving the quality and innovation of our products, and listening more effectively to our customers. My closing message was, "If any of you think you can't support this and execute, then you're going to have to leave."

I found many good, but frustrated, managers at Case. While Ketelsen never relented in anticipating a revival in farm equipment sales, few of the executives, managers, and workers on the front lines were believers. You can't lead troops to a victory if they do not embrace the logic for war, or if they are not prepared to fight it. When you looked beneath the surface, many in the Case organization were willing to fight, but not in the wrong war. Many perceptive answers to the problems in strategy and production had been offered from within Case for years. There was wide agreement that only sharp cutbacks and process reinventions would reverse the losses. One of my first moves was to put together a team to iron this out, so we could take a detailed program to Tenneco's board of directors. Working seven-day weeks for several months, the Case team produced a detailed set of restructuring plans to address the issues. But there was a major obstacle.

The plans were far too expensive. They were going to cost perhaps $1.3 billion, a price Tenneco could not afford. The corporation had lost $1 billion dealing with Case's crisis in 1991, including $618 million from operations. Case was on the way to losing another $270 million from operations in 1992. Meanwhile, the other Tenneco businesses were in no position to cover Case's losses. Four of the five other businesses (excluding Tenneco Gas) also were slumping. They could not anticipate higher prices or rising sales volume for perhaps another year.

Moreover, with Tenneco debt still near 70 percent of total capital and weak earnings anticipated in 1992, the corporation would have a hard time borrowing $1.3 billion to fund a Case restructuring. I told the Case team to reduce the projected costs below $1 billion. Our Wall Street advisers at First Boston Corporation believed we could sell $1 billion of Tenneco stock if we had a convincing story about a Case turnaround. In March, the elements of that story were in place. We had pared the restructuring costs to $920 million, still enough to cover plant shutdowns, severance, and pension payments (which amounted to one-third of the total), inventory and other asset write-downs, major production efficiencies, and other actions that would take four years, into 1997, to complete.

Conviction and Credibility

"We can't sell the place, but we can't live with it as it is," I told the Tenneco board of directors when I presented the plans in March 1993. "We have to fix it, and it is going to cost $920 million." These directors had heard a lot of optimism in the past about Case, and had approved billions of dollars in investments that never produced results. I had to make it clear to them this time that I was staking my reputation and my career on what I said would be a final request to fix Case. "I promise," I said, "that if I ever have to come back and ask you for more money for Case, I will bring my resignation with me."

The program was approved. We had been given the green light to spend nearly $1 billion without having the money we were going to need to pay for it.

We wasted no time, immediately announced the restructuring program. The new $920 million reserve we created increased Tenneco's 1992 loss to $1.3 billion, and pushed red ink attributable to Case operations and restructurings in the past two years to $2.3 billion. Within days, we began a two-week campaign—a sales blitz actually—in which two teams of Tenneco and Case executives split the duties of visiting 25 cities and presenting the Case story at 75 meetings with potential buyers of the new Tenneco stock. It worked, turning up more buyers for the stock than we needed and providing $1.1 billion in new equity. This ranked as one of Wall Street's biggest sales of equity by an industrial company to that time. That money immediately went to plug the hole created in Tenneco's equity to bankroll the restructuring, with more than

$100 million to spare. In the restructuring of Case that began that March, we had opened the gate for sweeping changes that followed in the next six years in the Tenneco businesses.

By the fourth quarter of 1993, Case was profitable. To achieve this, we had to shut down production for 28 weeks that year, a good start at getting inventories under control, but not enough. We had to idle production lines for another 22 weeks in 1994. In the first quarter of 1994, Case earned a promising $81 million, its best results in four years. We were elated. This was a solid number. The Case team was beating the tough performance goals we had set for them. There were at least three reasons for this. First, we had made a very clear link between potential cash bonuses for managers and the specific restructuring targets they had to meet. Second, by and large, the restructuring plans were *their* ideas. They knew the problems and the opportunities. These were their solutions, and they had a strong motivation to execute. Finally, we made it clear that the endgame likely would be Case's independence from Tenneco; they were reinventing a company whose fate they soon could control.

As the quarter came to an end, we recruited a French-born executive with proven credentials in international management, Jean-Pierre Rosso, as Case's new president and chief executive. We handed to him a tested executive team with an average age of 40, excepting the 63-year-old head of product design and development, that we had carefully put in place during the past two years. We also had simplified Rosso's task in other ways, eliminating nearly half of the 43 corporate officers at Case in 1990, cutting the total to 23. In 1995, with Case's profits and revenues climbing, *Business Week* selected him as one of its top 25 managers of the year.

By the end of 1994, Tenneco was able to take Case public, selling 56 percent of our holdings in two stock offerings valued at a total of $750 million. At the time of the first sale in June, every Case employee was given an option to buy 100 shares of Case stock at the original offering price of $19. They had to wait three years before they actually could buy the 100 shares. When that day arrived in 1997, as Case's stock price climbed toward a peak of $72 in 1998, each option was worth about $4,500 above the purchase price.

We sold Tenneco's last holdings in Case in March 1996 at a price of $53.75. This put Tenneco's total proceeds from selling all the Case shares at $2.2 billion. Adding the Case-related debt removed from Tenneco, large tax deductions and other benefits from divesting the company, we realized a total economic value of $4.4 billion from the restructuring. Four years earlier, anyone could have taken Case off our hands for $1 plus the debt.

CHAPTER 3

Personal Crisis, Public Communications

I WAS SPENDING AN AVERAGE OF TWO OR THREE DAYS A WEEK PULLING together the people, process, and plans for the Case restructuring throughout the autumn of 1992 and into the Christmas-New Year holidays. The news from Mike about his health during these months continued to slide from bad to worse. He talked about the symptoms, the tests, and the doctors' assessments privately with me and Ted Tetzlaff, Tenneco's general counsel and a close friend of Mike since their days together in the 1960s at Yale Law School. We had all hoped this was all somehow related to lingering problems from his back surgery. Yet by the time the diagnosis had been narrowed in late November to either multiple sclerosis or brain cancer, it was obvious that difficult personal and professional leadership issues lay ahead for us and for the corporation.

The few of us who worked regularly with Mike in this period sensed that whatever had caused his physical problems since the summer had not withered. He limped more when he walked, and his left arm trembled so at times during staff meetings that he would react by gripping it with his right hand to keep it still. Yet Mike was as focused, intense, and quick to joke or laugh as always, and there was no hint of any mental impairment.

By late December, the doctors determined that a biopsy to retrieve, if possible, tumor tissue for laboratory analysis was warranted. The surgery was scheduled for the second Tuesday in January, on the thirteenth. This raised a governance issue for the top corporate officers and Tenneco's board of directors, as well as private fears for Mike and his family. A failed biopsy could leave Mike in a coma, or worse. Mike, Ted Tetzlaff, Dr. Wells, and I had to determine how to keep Tenneco's directors informed about Mike's health problems without stirring up rumors among our employees or outside the company. The board—the representatives of all Tenneco shareowners—needed to understand the risks before the operation. Circumstance helped provide us with an idea, then a system, that worked extremely well.

A daughter of one of the directors, Dr. Peter Flawn, was head of volunteer services at M.D. Anderson. Another daughter was a practicing surgeon. Dr. Flawn himself had been associated with the University of Texas system for many years. In addition to M.D. Anderson, the University System operated four medical schools. As a result, Dr. Flawn was unusually familiar with a wide range of medical procedures and issues, including the confidentiality privileges between physician and patient.

A Yale-educated, Ph.D. geologist who had been president of the University of Texas at Austin from 1979 to 1985 and a member of the Tenneco board since 1980, he also understood the legal and administrative issues raised by the serious illness of an organizational leader. He knew Tenneco's history, had a key role in hiring Mike a year earlier, and was head of one of the more powerful specialized functions of the board, the audit committee. He had the trust, confidence, and respect of the board and would be in a position to get the answers to any question about Mike's condition, and carefully guard those facts.

Mike's decision, with total agreement by Ted and me, was for Dr. Wells to speak directly with Dr. Flawn regarding any aspect of Mike's medical situation. He would keep Dr. Flawn informed about Mike's condition, the medical opinions, decisions, and procedures. In turn, Dr. Flawn would talk directly also to Mike, Ted, or me—providing him with four different sources of information, and he would make judgments about what information needed to be shared with other directors. And, although we never discussed it, I always assumed he was getting accurate information about Mike through his family contacts at the cancer clinic. In any event, this system was credible and effective. "We were fully informed about the disease, the prognoses, the risks and the medical treatment," Dr. Flawn said in an interview. "We on the board were always looking at, 'what is the worst case?'"

Houston's Christmas week in December 1992, was one of the warmest on record. An unusually dense fog shrouded the Gulf Coast and parts of the city further inland. That fog, the balmy temperatures, the humidity, and the late afternoon darkness are all memories of my first days in a Texas winter. It was a gloomy, surreal period made all the more so by our increasing worries about Mike and the unforeseen challenges ahead for both of us.

A few days after Christmas, my wife Nancy took our two adult sons and their families over for a late afternoon visit with Mike, Joan, and their children at their home. It was just the two families. Very informal. Mike and I were alone in the living room at one point, having a few drinks, talking about the company, our families, sports, and the latest news from the Medical Center. He was pragmatic, but hopeful that some new analysis might bring a reversal of the cancer diagnosis. "I really never thought I'd say I was happy to think I was going to have MS," he said wryly, "but if I had my choice . . . " This was typical Walsh. He was in good humor that day, but he was sitting most of the time, instead of standing. His family was very worried. The energy spent on fighting the physical setbacks and handling all the tests, operations, and mental strain clearly was taking a toll.

Deft Touch and a Long Needle into the Brain

Two weeks later, Mike was admitted as scheduled to Houston's Methodist Hospital. Biopsies of brain cells are always risky, even when executed by the most highly skilled surgeons. A long thin needle is inserted through the skull to the site where brain scans have indicated there is abnormal cell growth. The precise location and angle for the path of the 20-inch-long needle is mapped in advance by computer. But the actual pace and depth of the insertion is controlled by the surgeon's hand. Any torn blood vessels, nerve paths, or other critical tissues along the needle's path can cause internal bleeding, infections, paralysis, or death. The brain has no pain receptors, so although patients normally are mildly sedated and a local anesthetic is injected into the skull, they usually are awake through the entire procedure.

"I have only two chances to find this tumor," Dr. Robert Grossman told Mike before the operation. The head of neurosurgery at the Baylor College of Medicine, Dr. Grossman was a prominent specialist on head and spinal injuries who had operated successfully on Mike's back months earlier. He estimated the tumor in Mike's brain to be about the size of the tip of a pinky finger. "I can't probe you with the needle until I find it," he continued. "I'd do a lot of damage to your brain (raising the odds of a debilitating paralysis). I've got to go in there and hit it—once. That would be great. If on the second try I get it, that's wonderful. But if I don't hit it on those first two times, we're going to stop. We'll treat you going forward as if you had a malignant tumor anyway."

Renowned among neurosurgeons for his deft touch with the biopsy needle, Dr. Grossman successfully retrieved the cancerous tissue on the second try a few days later during a tense 2½-hour procedure. Medical teams from Methodist Hospital, led by Dr. Grossman, and from one of the world's top cancer research and treatment institutes, the M.D. Anderson Cancer Center, confirmed within hours that the lesion was a malignant tumor. But how aggressive? Dr. Grossman and Dr. Victor Levin, a leading expert in brain cancers who headed the M.D. Anderson team, were troubled. Brain cancers called astrocytomas are classified in four grades—the lowest one being small, local, and slow-growing and the highest one being infiltrating (into healthy tissue) and fast-growing. Low-grade cancers are the easiest to isolate and remove, with the best chance for recovery. Location is pivotal as well. For patients with tumors in the covering of the brain, the surgery is relatively simple, like plucking a cherry from a bowl of salt.

These two medical scientists, two of the most brilliant and prominent in international cancer treatment, agreed that Mike was not so fortunate. His cancer was at least a grade-two, possibly a grade-three tumor. They could see that the cells already had become enmeshed with healthy neurons, like grains of pepper sprinkled through a salt bowl. It would be impossible to remove those cells without damaging healthy parts of the brain. The only proven treatments were sequential injections of drugs and doses of radiation. The goal: to kill all the tumor cells without damaging too much of the healthy tissue the cancer has infiltrated.

Life Expectancy: Eight to Ten Years? Five to Six?

Dr. Grossman and Dr. Levin had no illusions. The 10-year survival rate for patients with the more aggressive form of these cancers, known as anaplastic astrocytomas, is 200 or more of every 1,000; but the cure rate is perhaps 3 of every 1,000 patients. Few patients who recover are above 30 years old. Mike was 50. He had been in outstanding physical condition, yes. But he was 50. "We never take away hope," Dr. Grossman recalled in a 1997 interview. "We also tell people the statistics. Mike understood this." If this was a slow-growing, grade-two astrocytoma, they told Mike, his life expectancy would be 8 to 10 years. If it was a fast-growing grade three, make it 5 to 6 years.

The two specialists speculated with Mike and Dr. Wells about answers to the difficult questions this preliminary assessment raised. How much damage had already been done? How much could be reversed? How aggressively might the cancer be spreading? Into what regions of the brain? (Brain cancers never spread outside the nervous system.) What treatments offered the best hope for a cure and the least risk of aggravating the damage? How could Mike best prepare himself to beat this? What were the dangers and uncertainties for Joan and their three college-age children? With how many people, and which ones, should he discuss this at Tenneco? What about the board of directors? How much could he say? What was he required to disclose publicly? How long could he continue the demanding work and travel schedule of chairman and CEO for a multinational corporation? If he could continue, what impact would the treatments have on his ability to lead the company's nascent transformation? How would the eventual disclosure of his condition impact investor perceptions of Tenneco and its stock price? What about the company's 80,000 employees?

Planning the Public Announcement

Some of these topics came up the previous week at the regularly scheduled meeting with Tenneco's board of directors. They were prepared for the distressing news that we were getting ready to announce in the days following the biopsy. The only remaining piece of information we needed was the laboratory analysis of the cancerous tissue, which Mike expected by Monday, January 18. So over that weekend, he, Ted, and I drafted a statement we planned to give the Houston news media and major business and financial publications as soon as the doctors completed their pathology report.

Legally, we were not required to do anything of the sort. The Securities and Exchange Commission directs public companies to announce any news they consider "material" to investors. The question is: When does a health problem of a key executive become "material"? This is a difficult call, and each case has to be assessed on its own facts and circumstances. There is much uncertainty involved when medical science takes the measure of what might or might not be a potential threat to life or, for that matter, of an executive's ability to remain visible and effective in a demanding, high-pressure job. Then, too, it is simply human decency to shield any individual or family from the glare of publicity when they are confronting a medical crisis.

On the other hand, the irritating distraction of rumors and innuendo can seriously undermine a leader's effectiveness, by circulating damaging perceptions that might grossly distort the reality. This persuades some companies to make an announcement. Often they are forced into a public statement by the SEC or by the New York Stock Exchange if the company's common shares are listed in that market. Time Warner Inc., the media and entertainment colossus, apparently came to this conclusion late in 1991. Its businesses and the trade publications that regularly wrote about them were rife with speculation and rumor about a serious medical condition involving Steven J. Ross, Time Warner's chairman and co-chief executive officer. The company announced on November 26 that year that Ross was suffering from prostate cancer, but emphasized that the disease was treatable. Ross died more than a year later. That news hit as Mike was developing his own thoughts for how he might have to go public with his medical problems if they became life threatening or raised doubts about his ability to continue as CEO.

Tell the Truth with Clarity, Conviction, and Practical Limits

Mike and I agreed that communication is a key ingredient of effective leadership, especially in big organizations. The only issue before making some statement was getting the facts we needed for it. We all agreed it would be time to go public, with clarity and conviction, when the doctors were able to describe as best they could the nature of Mike's illness and its medical and professional implications for him.

Then, too, Mike's years as a public defender, federal prosecutor, and cofounder of the Common Cause public advocacy movement as well as senior corporate executive had left him with a high confidence and easy manner in dealing with news reporters. He also had a keen sense of news judgment rare among corporate executives— knowing what reporters and editors considered interesting material. He was comfortable, even shrewd, in riding the news waves he created for his broader executive objectives.

Mike never had any thoughts as far as I knew about devising some scheme to hide the truth about his illness. Leaders must be vulnerable. They have to be willing to stand up and take the heat from their actions as well as the praise. Mike and I were committed to leading with openness, candor, and trust. It was ridiculous to think that Mike would be able to keep a diagnosis of brain cancer secret for long. He was limping. He had tremors in his left arm. He was less of a visible presence at Tenneco headquarters because of his frequent trips to the Medical Center. Once radiation and chemotherapy treatments began, he would be away more frequently over several weeks. It was likely that all or most of his full head of thick, dark hair would fall out. And it did.

Mike laughed off any debate about disclosing his medical problem to the public. It was "about a 20-second decision," he said many times. Any attempt to keep the illness quiet would have risked destroying the "open culture" we had to develop in the company. Disclosure was also consistent with the message to lead with candor, clarity, and credibility that Mike had given managers and employees in occasional "town hall" company meetings in the year since he had come on board.

He later told *Fortune* magazine: "What was I going to do, come back from a biopsy with my head shaved and say the barber fell asleep in mid-haircut? Or when I was missing one day a week for radiation, was I going to tell everybody I was having an affair? Because of the terrible impact of a word like 'tumor,' especially 'brain tumor,' trying to hide this would have involved horrible risks to the company."

To other reporters, he explained, "Not making this announcement would inevitably lead to rumors and speculation that could potentially put investors at risk. Moreover, we run this company in an extraordinarily open and collegial way. Trying to hide (the) diagnosis would not only be wrong and foolish . . . it would be impractical."

Don't Let Secrecy Become the Issue

Another reason for making the illness public was to give Mike more time to lead the Tenneco senior management group, as well as direct more energy into his battle with the cancer. When faced with bad news of this magnitude, leaders need some form of disclosure, some mechanism, where they feel they can get this concern off their chests. You want to go public with enough information but not expose all of the gory details. Yet you want to make sure the right people understand the situation, people with good judgment whom you and the business community respect. Then somebody else can be the filter of whatever information has to follow. But you've made your disclosure without totally jeopardizing your privacy, or your effectiveness as a leader. You've freed yourself to *deal with your problem.*

If you don't make any announcement, you've still got to run the company. You've still got to deal with your personal problem. *And* you've still got to keep the secret—manage any potential exposure of the problem. Normally, this is what people do. The best advice is to get rid of the keep-the-secret part. Then you've only got two things to manage, not three. Keeping the secret can be a more overwhelming task than managing the company or dealing with the adversity. We see the sad evidence of this in the news media almost every day.

The communications plan to disclose Mike's brain tumor was set by the morning of Tuesday, January 19. There was a brief statement and talking points for the telephone conferences with security analysts and with news reporters, a two-page new release for the news media and an internal memo from me to all employees. Mike also was set to do a videotaped monologue—his personal message to employees—that would be sent far and wide to Tenneco locations around the world.

As far as we knew, at the time only five members of senior management, three on the corporate communications and investor relations staff, the Tenneco board of directors, a few advisers outside the company, and the Walsh family were aware that this devastating news was imminent. We had done everything possible to avoid rumors within Tenneco or in the greater Houston area, as well as leaks to the news media.

Stunning Coincidence, and a Different Decision

But when we read the newspapers on Tuesday, we were stunned. Another respected corporate leader had brain cancer, and apparently was near death. TLC Beatrice International Holdings had announced the day before that Reginald Lewis, its 50-year-old chairman and one of the most prominent African American corporate executives in America, was in a coma with brain cancer. The company added in a brief statement that Lewis (who would die this same day from a cerebral hemorrhage) had arranged a week earlier for his half-brother to run that $1.5 billion company.

This was a starkly different approach on how to handle serious illness as a management issue, and a grave reminder of how tough a challenge Mike faced. For us, the Lewis story was a wild card we had to factor into our plans. The topic of CEO health and corporate disclosure suddenly was one of the biggest stories on the business pages. We knew we were about to become part of it. But we changed nothing.

Mike, Ted, and I actually had edited the news release Mike began drafting that Saturday. On the advice of Gershon Kekst, head of the Wall Street and financial public relations firm, Kekst & Company, we decided to have Mike make the announcement, rather than the company. This would make it appear more as a direct statement from Mike and would lessen speculation that any advisers, senior company executives, or directors had softened or otherwise muted the message. He also eliminated direct quotes from the doctors, instead using the phrase "doctors told Walsh" or words to that effect, to indicate that Mike and Tenneco were in charge of communications about his illness, and that the doctors would not be commenting beyond what was in the release.

Aside from those issues, the draft we had for release on Tuesday morning, pending the final diagnosis from the doctors, was little changed from Mike's first take. Ted had read that original draft to Gershon Kekst over the phone on Saturday night. While he had worked with Mike on some special projects at Tenneco before I arrived, Gershon's firm was not on a retainer. Ted figured, though, why not check this out with Gershon? After Ted read the statement, which took a few minutes, Kekst was impressed. "Now I know why you guys never hired me," he said. "That's about the best anybody could do."

It was Mike's energetic nature to apply to every task his prosecutorial pursuit and command of relevant facts and logic, and his pragmatic, relentless optimism. This was true even, as his reputation as a corporate leader was reaching new heights, when he had to announce his own life-threatening brain cancer. That step was now unavoidable. We knew—certainly Mike most of all—that the news would open to public scrutiny a private personal struggle with outcomes none of us knew for certain or would be able to control, whether it be heroic, triumphant, or tragic.

A Carefully Constructed Statement

After an introductory sentence noting his name, title, and the next day's date, Wednesday, January 20, 1993, Mike began the draft of the news release this way:

> Having undergone extensive tests in the last few weeks for what I thought was a recurring back problem, my doctors informed me late yesterday that they have diagnosed what is, in their words, a "slow-growth, low-grade" brain tumor, which has been identified at an early stage and is treatable with radiation and chemotherapy.

He noted the results of the biopsy, the role of the Baylor and M.D. Anderson medical teams, and his discussions with Tenneco's directors about the diagnosis, and the need to disclose the news. He went on:

> Dr. Victor A. Levin, M.D., . . . who heads my medical team, informs me that based on extensive past experience, the median survival rate for patients with this condition detected this early, and undergoing the therapy proposed, is approximately 8 to 10 years, with half doing better than that, and some much better. Importantly, Dr. Levin and others around the country are working on research leading to new therapies which may produce more promising results.

Mike had defined the problem, outlined a normal prognosis indicating that he was in no immediate danger, and raised the prospect that he indeed might do much better than the typical patient with this type of tumor. Better yet, medical scientists were pushing hard for better, faster cures. Well and good, but what about his capacity to continue in the demanding job of leading one of the nation's 40 largest companies? He tackled that issue head-on.

> It is the judgment of my doctors, including that of Tenneco's corporate physician, Kenneth D. Wells, M.D., that my medical condition will not in any way affect my ability to carry out the full range of my responsibilities at Tenneco. In terms of carrying out my work, I am symptomless. My mental processes and judgments are unaffected. I feel fine. Treatment will begin Monday.

He described how Tenneco's directors would continue to monitor his performance and his medical condition. He noted the communication link established between Dr. Wells and Dr. Flawn, and his decision to waive the standard right of physician-patient confidentiality. He referred to a seven-paragraph letter from Dr. Wells to Dr. Flawn that would be attached to the announcement. In that letter, Dr. Wells outlined what was known about Mike's medical condition, Mike's otherwise "extraordinarily strong and vigorous" physical condition, and his ability to continue in the job "now, during treatment, and for the foreseeable future."

Mike finished his statement by declaring his continuing commitment to the job, and his defiant determination to beat the disease.

> This unwelcome diagnosis in no way affects my commitment to Tenneco. I remain absolutely committed to continuing the critical work which our excellent team and I began 18 months ago.
>
> My family and I were as surprised by this news as we know others will be. But anyone who has ever known me knows my appetite for challenge. While never in my wildest dreams would I have thought I'd face a challenge like this, our shareholders, our employees, and our many friends can be assured I intend to face it with the same commitment to meet it and beat it that I have brought to every other challenge in my life.

"I've Had Some Bad News"

By late afternoon, I was sitting in the conference room next to Mike's office. It was getting dark outside and the downtown streets were filled with rush-hour traffic. Art House, our vice president of corporate affairs, was with me. Art, like Mike and me, had been a White House Fellow and we had known each other for more than 20 years. He remained in Washington through the 1970s, working for many years as chief of staff for Sen. Abraham Ribicoff, the influential Democrat from Connecticut. Art later held jobs in government, communications, and public affairs for some big Connecticut-based insurance companies before coming to Tenneco a few months after me.

Art and I reviewed details of the communication plans: the timing of the news release; the telephone conference call Mike would lead Wednesday morning with securities analysts who covered Tenneco; another call with news reporters; how we would alert these groups ahead of time to the calls; getting this delicate, complex message to our employees, and other matters.

Ted Tetzlaff was on the teleconference phone from Washington, combing through these issues with us. A close adviser to Mayor Richard M. Daley in Chicago, Ted had just arrived in Washington to see the inauguration ceremonies on Wednesday and to attend a welter of inaugural parties with key figures in and around the new Clinton administration. Mike had intended to go with him.

At Ted's urging, Mike had been one of the first chief executives, and also one of the few outside Silicon Valley, to publicly endorse Clinton over the Republican President, George Bush. That was a controversial move for Mike. He was the newly arrived CEO of what was then the largest company based in Bush's adopted hometown, Houston. Even worse for some traditionalists around Tenneco, Mike had swept away the long-standing Tenneco political dogma of only supporting Republicans financially, and never backing Democrats.

After the November election, Thomas F. (Mack) McLarty III, the senior Clinton adviser from Arkansas and former pipeline company executive, had written Mike's name onto the short lists of candidates for Defense Secretary and Commerce Secretary, with the eager approval of the President-elect. In the usual ways of Washington, a trial balloon soon was sighted. Mike got a few questions from reporters. But he never had any serious discussions about a Cabinet-level appointment. He told the White House from the start that he was committed to Tenneco.

Mike and Joan Walsh had eagerly anticipated joining the inaugural celebrations for the new Democratic administration. It was a spectacle that would include dozens of longtime friends and professional colleagues. Instead, they spent that week in Houston, not Washington, coping with the most devastating medical news of their 25-year marriage. The pathology report about the cancerous tissue removed a week earlier could hardly have been worse. Patched in from the car taking the Walshes home from the Medical Center, Mike's voice was coming through to us on a speaker phone. "I've had some bad news," he said. "You've got to cross out 'slow-growing' from the press release. You've got to change the life expectancy, too, to 'five or six' years, not 'eight to 10.'"

The medical odds against him were soaring. "Mike," I said. "I'm sorry to hear this. We're going to make these changes. We're going to get this final. Tell me what else you want to say."

A long, silent moment passed. There wasn't much else he could say. Neither could we. We focused again on the urgent task before us. Aside from changing those few grim facts Mike had noted, the release still covered the key points as he knew them and as he originally had written them. We quickly reviewed with Mike the timing and mechanics of how we were going to get the word out. It was well past 5 o'clock. Art and his staff began to execute their steps in the plan. I made calls to inform the six presidents of Tenneco's operating divisions. On my drive home that night, I braced myself for the uncertain, additional demands that Mike's illness was bound to place on my shoulders in the months ahead.

Communicating to Shareowners and Security Analysts

The next morning, January 20, Mike opened his remarks to the analysts with the key points from the statement. Then, with as much conviction he could generate, he vowed to remain in the job and went on to describe many of the changes, and performance improvements, that were happening at the company. The point, never explicitly stated, was that if any analysts on the line now were considering advising their clients to run for cover and get off the Tenneco train, they would soon regret it. He bragged that there was no corporation in the United States that was reinventing itself in such a positive, sustainable way as Tenneco: sharp improvement in operating earnings despite "lousy" markets; aggressive reduction of a stiflingly high debt burden, and a restructuring of remaining debt on more favorable terms including lower interest rates; assets sold in the billions; hundreds of millions of equity raised.

When Mike finished, one analyst had a question. Given the fairly harsh statistical odds that Mike might not reach the median life expectancy of five to six years, wasn't it likely to assume that he was considering leaving Tenneco? And, if that happened, wouldn't that bring changes to the strategies, policies, and processes we were still putting into place?

"Hell no," he barked. "I am 50 years old—I didn't even get into this management game until I was 37. What are the statistical probabilities of someone that started out as a public defender, and then was a federal prosecutor and didn't even go into major management until he was 37, becoming chairman of the country's 25th largest company 13 years later? I mean, you'd say they're nuts! It wouldn't happen! So that tells you a bit about what I think about statistical probabilities. Very little is going to change. Dana and I have run this company in what I call a copilot basis. That is the way we have run this company from day one, and it's the way we will continue to run the company. Not because something is going to happen to me and my responsibilities are going to change. That is just the way I run things."

The news release had been out since 7 o'clock. When the financial markets opened at 9:30 eastern time, traders at some of the big institutional brokerage firms lined up to sell Tenneco shares. I was not surprised. Mike had a huge reputation on Wall Street. His success in particular in carving out useless bureaucracy, bolstering communications and generally focusing Tenneco's businesses on delivering what customers wanted had brought a big improvement in earnings in a short time. On the two days after Tenneco announced his hiring in August 1991, the company's shares jumped 14 percent, or $5.25, to $41.875. That confidence was warranted, as the company's results in the previous 15 months had demonstrated.

Moreover, we were preparing to announce in another week that Tenneco's operations in 1992—our first year together in running the company—had improved by a remarkable $5 per share.

The Wall Street Response

The initial rush to sell our stock created an order imbalance, so officials at the New York Stock Exchange delayed trading for several minutes. Within an hour of the opening bell, Tenneco shares were down $1.25 to $40.75. Eli Lustgarten, a respected machinery analyst then at the Paine Webber investment firm, had put out an advisory before the market opened, reducing his rating on Tenneco shares to "neutral" from "attractive."

Lustgarten's decision was the one major negative, hard-nosed business response that day among the group of 12 or so securities analysts who followed the company. That was all it took to weaken the price even though the Paine Webber analyst remained enthusiastic about our strategies and long-term prospects. He thought news of Mike's brain tumor would keep investors away for some uncertain period so he was advising his clients to take some money off the table, but also to keep their hand in the game. In his report to Paine Webber clients, he wrote: "The sad uncertainty caused by the health of the clear leader of Tenneco's cultural and financial turnaround will likely limit the near-term upside potential of Tenneco's stock." Our shares remained under selling pressure, and finished the day off $2. Nearly 1.4 million shares were traded, more than three times the average daily volume.

Most analysts stayed in our camp. Mike, myself and others in the corporate management group that day spoke with several analysts at mutual fund companies, insurance companies, bank trust departments, and other major holders of Tenneco shares. At each turn, we emphasized that Mike and I had put together a strong team, we were executing an ambitious, credible plan and, aside from Mike's treatment program of chemotherapy and radiation, nothing was going to change.

These comments quickly were relayed through the tightly connected financial network on Wall Street. One part of that network, John McGinty of the First Boston Corporation, another top analyst of machinery manufacturers, was among many who agreed with us. He made a few comments I particularly appreciated in an interview with one reporter.

"Will this put a cloud over Tenneco? No," McGinty said. "One of the marks of a successful chief executive is to have players behind him that are very good players. Mike Walsh has done a lot of very positive things at Tenneco. Of first rank in importance was to bring in Dana Mead as president." McGinty asserted that I was "perfectly cast" in the role to straighten things out at Case, a "no nonsense, no excuses type of guy." "He is the perfect complement to Mike Walsh," McGinty went on. "Walsh has laid out the parameters, and Dana Mead is going to execute the game plan."

Communicating to the News Media

By 9 o'clock, we again were in Mike's conference room to discuss the news in an audio conference with about 15 reporters. Most had been contacted the night before and alerted to an urgent news conference. They knew nothing more until some had read the news release that had been faxed to their homes and offices after 7 o'clock that morning. They called in from cities and towns around the country where Tenneco had its largest centers of employment—Newport News, Virginia; Racine, Wisconsin; Burlington, Iowa; Chicago; and Houston. Regional correspondents in the Southwest for *The Wall Street Journal* and *The New York Times* were there, too.

Mike began again, reading every word of the news release and added that he would repeat much of what he had said on the call with the security analysts. "From the beginning," he said, "I have told you there is only one story around here . . . not one for the press and a different one for the analysts."

"Why am I making this announcement at this time?" he said. "The answer is a lot simpler than you may think. Let's start at the top with the single most important point. I am not making it because I think anyone's investment is in any kind of jeopardy or because there are any kind of new management risks at Tenneco. This simply isn't the case.

"As indicated in Dr. Wells' letter, I am totally symptomless," he said, his voice rising. "Let me repeat that. All of my mental processes and judgments are unaffected . . . I intend to stay doing exactly what I am doing. The board is 100 percent behind that. I am fully committed to that task and, as you know, the task continues to go very well."

As he did with the securities analysts, Mike shifted the focus quickly away from the medical news to describe many Tenneco accomplishments of the past 15 months. He was able to do this in virtually the same breath as he presented the medical facts of his illness. For those of us in the room, it was a dramatic moment.

A reporter asked, "I see the (Tenneco) stock has been downgraded. Do you think Wall Street is spooked after what happened yesterday to Reginald Lewis?" The issue was relevant and the topic not unexpected in this forum, but the reporter's crude delivery was insulting. We exchanged quick glances around the room, silently venting our anger. Mike didn't pull any punches.

"Hey, look! I learned of this yesterday afternoon at 3 o'clock. I've got to tell you something. At a point in time like this, you don't pay attention to anyone else's set of circumstance. You don't have a plan. You do what in your gut you feel is the correct thing to do. I don't know a thing in the world about Mr. Lewis's situation. It has absolutely nothing to do with this. I took this initiative frankly without much reflection. It is the right thing to do. The only risk would be not disclosing."

Moments before in this 45-minute conference, Mike had acknowledged that he harbored some doubt that he could lose the fight he was about to take on. It was only the slightest backing away from his declaration earlier in the news conference. At that point, he had said he had agreed to notify the Tenneco board "at the earliest moment," then added that there were no plans for me to step into the chief executive post, even temporarily. "We have no contemplation of that occurring," Mike said.

Yet he clearly was aware that a time might come when he no longer could keep his job running Tenneco. "The board [of directors] will decide to disclose any additional medical information if it is relevant to the [medical] judgments communicated today," he said. "In other words, if those judgments change, and there is something in the situation that requires action, the board will take it. But let me tell you something, given what I hope you will find is in keeping with the extraordinary openness we are demonstrating here today: *I hope events will never require that."*

A few weeks later, after his radiation and chemotherapy treatments were underway, Mike gave a more blunt assessment of his crisis. "Look, I know this is bad," he told John Huey, then chief of *Fortune*'s Atlanta bureau and now the magazine's managing editor. "In fact, this is tragic. But it's up to me to keep it from being tragic. To a point, you have to concede to medical realism and admit there are elements you cannot control. But there's a personal dimension, too. It includes the will to live, support systems, and hope. These are things under your control, and nothing says you can't be a 9.999 on that scale. Where those two grids meet determines how it all comes out. But I'm not one of these people who believes that just by scoring a 9.999 I necessarily win" (*Fortune*, February 22, 1993, p. 76).

Within 24 hours of receiving the medical conclusions from the M.D. Anderson Center, Mike and I had contacted each key group of investors, news media, and employees with essentially the same messages. We felt we had made an effective start, but it was only a start. We had to support this initial effort with dozens of one-on-one telephone conversations with key players in each of these groups to continue to avert a crisis of confidence through the next two days.

The Story Is Out—Far, Fast, Accurate

The news of Mike's brain tumor was reported that evening on CNN's national business news program, *Moneyline with Lou Dobbs*. Mike was a White House Fellow classmate of CNN president Tom Johnson and had been Dobbs's guest on *Moneyline* a few times. In the next day's major national, regional, and financial newspapers, on Thursday, January 21, Mike's announcement was one of the top business stories. "Tenneco Chairman Has Brain Cancer But Says He'll Stay on Job Indefinitely," was the headline on one of two *Wall Street Journal* stories. "Tenneco Chief Discloses Brain Cancer."

said *The New York Times*. "Tenneco Chief Reveals Illness," in the *Financial Times*.

The *Journal* included my answer, correctly, about how I viewed the implications for me. "It may mean I'll work 85 hours a week instead of 80," I said. In New York City, listeners to radio business reports on the Bloomberg News station heard a vote of confidence in Tenneco, and in me, from David Fleischer, an analyst then affiliated with Prudential Securities. "This is no one-man show," Fleischer said. "Dana Mead is the chief operating officer and president. This extremely top-quality, high-quality individual was brought in by Mr. Walsh from International Paper. I like the division heads across the board. They've got many good people in this company."

Regional newspapers whose circulation covered areas with large Tenneco operations, typified by the *Chicago Tribune,* also gave the story heavy coverage. Donald M. Jacobs, dean of the highly rated J.M. Kellogg Graduate School of Management on the campus at Northwestern University, two blocks from the headquarters of Tenneco's packaging business in suburban Evanston, did not know us personally. But he knew the Tenneco story and Mike's leading role. Our going public with the medical news "will only enhance his reputation," Jacobs told the *Tribune*. "It demonstrates an enormous feeling of security. If I were a board member, I would like this kind of openness so I could make decisions with a full deck of cards" (January 21, 1993).

In Omaha, where Mike had made a big impact as a civic leader while leading the Union Pacific railroad for five years, the *World-Herald* published three stories: a long one relaying information from the telephone news conference, another on reaction from Omaha's mayor and business leaders, and a third on the medical diagnosis. Charles M. "Mike" Harper, then chairman and CEO of Conagra, the big Omaha-based food products company, and later chairman and CEO of RJR-Nabisco, echoed sentiments in hundreds of calls and letters we were getting from all over the country. "He's a very capable young man, and I just hate to see that happen," Harper told the *World-Herald*. "It's just a damn shame. But he's strong. He's tough. And I'm sure he will be able to deal with it. But it will be very difficult" (January 21, 1993).

By Friday morning, our concerns about how investors and the financial and general news media would respond to the Wednesday news were easing. The Tenneco stock price had slipped to a low of $39.125 during Thursday trading, rebounded as high as $40.875 and settled that day at $40.375. From the stock traders' view, we had stabilized and were bouncing back from the lows of this episode. Within two months we would top $45. News coverage, despite unavoidably alarmist headlines, included many laudatory comments about how we had gotten the story out. The coverage also relayed accurately, quickly, and broadly the difficult facts of the diagnosis as well as the policies and principles that would govern our handling of Mike's personal crisis in the months ahead.

Communicating to the Employees

My internal memo, along with copies of the news release and Dr. Wells's letter to Peter Flawn, was on the desks of all 3,000 Tenneco employees in the headquarters building before they arrived that morning, as well as on the way through various channels to the other 77,000 company employees. The news release and letter had the details—including Mike's about the illness, life expectancy, Mike's determination to stay at his post, and so on. My task as his second-in-command was to reiterate those points briefly, add background, and the reminder that we all still had jobs to do. "Be a leader," I concluded. "Mike is positive about this and expects you to be as well. Remember: the best way to demonstrate Mike's continuing leadership is to hit or exceed our business targets. Thanks for your help. I know you join me in supporting Mike."

The day of the announcement and in the days and weeks that followed, our employees were among the most anxious and attentive followers of the news coverage of Mike's announcement, especially in the United States, where most of the information was available. Even though we had made our own extensive internal announcements on Wednesday morning, Mike was dissatisfied with the impersonal process of "cascading" the news through multiple levels of managers and supervisors to the shop floor.

So on Friday morning, after two days of responding to a rush of phone calls from deeply concerned friends and business associates all over the world, he focused his gaze toward a single video camera set up in his office. Without a script, and marshaling his polished courtroom skills of presenting and summarizing a tough case before the jury, Mike spoke for 22 minutes. Much of what he said was a reprise of facts, policies, and emotions repeated many times in the previous two days. For the employees, though, he stressed the "incredible" improvements the company had achieved, the business challenges ahead of us, his conviction that nothing in the management policies or processes would change, his confidence in them, and his eagerness to get going with his medical treatments and beat the tumor.

"I'll start Monday," he said. "That process is not going to be, of course it won't be, fun. Many of you have friends and relatives who have had to go through that. You wouldn't wish it on anybody, I'll tell you that. But the tumor is treatable, the response is appropriate. . . . There is a small risk that you become somewhat fatigued. But I'll tell you, working 80 hours a week for the last 18 months, I am somewhat accustomed to fatigue, as I know all of you are. What do you do about fatigue? Do you let it affect you and control you? Or do you just get on with it? The issue that I played out in my life a long time ago, and I am sure you figured out, is that there are things outside your control and there are things inside your control. If you let the ones outside your control drive you nuts, you are going to be driven nuts a lot."

He finished with a call to look beyond his medical troubles and to focus on the hard work of converting Tenneco into a world-class competitor in every critical area of performance. He wanted the organization to send a message not just about Tenneco, but about the rapidly improving performance global manufacturing corporations could achieve.

"I am telling you that you are incredibly important to the continued success of this company," he said. "And the continued success of this company is incredibly important, not just to me, but to this nation. At the end of the day, it really isn't just Tenneco or just one of the operating companies in Tenneco that counts. It is demonstrating what we are doing at Tenneco: Showing that large industrial companies can reform themselves, that they can fundamentally change, and as a result can become competitive on a global basis. That is the ball game."

With a glancing reference to the five or six years of median life expectancy cited by doctors as part of his brain tumor diagnosis, Mike added a dispiriting footnote. He estimated that the organizational changes he envisioned for Tenneco, and a resurgence of the U.S.-based manufacturing economy certainly were going to take longer than those five or six years.

Mike was wrong about that. U.S.-based manufacturing was reinventing itself so aggressively when he spoke those words that in two years, in 1995, the United States would regain the lead as the world's most productive economy. The advance in productivity and profits among manufacturers was playing a big part. As for Tenneco, we were making rapid improvement in cutting costs, raising product quality and safety performance, and building profits in most of our core operations. We had much hard work ahead of us. In today's global competition, the pressures on market leaders never fade. Compaq Computer Corporation's stumble after acquiring Digital Equipment provided fresh evidence of these pressures in 1998 and 1999. So did our own problems in the retail markets for auto replacement parts. But, along with much of the American industrial sector, most of Tenneco's businesses entering 1993 were showing signs that they were measurably on the mend.

A Great
Oak Tree

IN A TYPICAL YEAR, 10,000 PEOPLE IN THE UNITED STATES ARE diagnosed with malignant brain tumors. This is about the same number as those who learn for the first time that they have either Hodgkin's disease or multiple sclerosis; about one in every 25,000 people. Medical scientists have no clear understanding of what causes brain tumors. Unlike lung cancer, and its causal link to toxins from smoking tobacco, environmental influences have never been identified as the cause of a brain tumor. Genetic factors, an individual's biology, are the most likely source.

Most lethal cancers strike first in one area, such as the pancreas, lung, or breast, and then spread to many other parts of the body. Brain cancers are different. They rarely spread outside the nervous system, yet are extremely difficult to cure. These cancerous cells become so intermeshed with the neurons that form thousands of signal paths within the brain that it usually is impossible for doctors to consider surgery.

In Mike's case, surgery to remove his motor and sensory cortex, where his tumor was first identified, at best would have left him paralyzed on his left side—with tumor cells still active in his brain. The best chance for a cure, then, was some combination of radiation and chemotherapy. Dr. Levin, the top specialist at Houston's M.D. Anderson Cancer Center in treatment for brain tumors, put Mike on what was at the time an aggressive, experimental course. Mike was going to get the maximum radiation dosage, the most his body reasonably could tolerate in a lifetime, in one month. The pace was three radiation sessions a day, one every four hours and each treatment lasting five minutes or so (excluding 15 minutes of preparation), for five days. Then, two weeks off.

In addition, Mike received automatically timed, intravenous drug infusions consistently over that period, always in the minutes prior to a radiation treatment. The drugs were delivered by portable pump from a cassette-sized pack strapped to his body. The basic idea behind chemotherapy is easy to grasp. Because cancerous tumors are faster-growing collections of cells, they absorb poisons carried by the drugs more rapidly than healthy cells. If the process goes well, the poisons kill the cancer cells at a much faster pace than healthy cells, then the patient gradually recovers from damage done to healthy cells. This treatment has contributed greatly to extending the lives of millions of cancer victims, but never comes with a guarantee.

The Will to Lead and Take Action

Mike insisted to us before he announced his tumor that he would lead the regularly scheduled, hour-plus meeting on February 2 that we already were preparing for the security analysts and investment officers from Wall Street firms following Tenneco. The agenda was routine: to disclose and review Tenneco's fourth-quarter and full-year operating results. It would require him to fly with the rest of us on our senior management/investor relations team to New York City. This also would be his first public appearance since the tumor announcement. And it would come a week after the start of his radiation and chemotherapy treatments. The gathering now would be anything but routine. We would be under unusually close scrutiny by 120 Wall Street analysts, money managers, and investment bankers.

Mike prepared hard, rewriting his speech on the plane trip and expanding it to more than 20 minutes. He was determined to prove that, as he had declared two weeks earlier, "I am symptomless. My mental processes and judgments are unaffected." In the speech, he put the business and financial facts of Tenneco's results in 1992 into the more theoretical context: the challenges of the emerging global economy. This might have struck some in this unsentimental Wall Street crowd as arrogance. To those of us who knew him, it was something more compelling. It was a discourse on industrial leadership by a successful practitioner. It was also something of a public declaration by a man choosing to continue his pursuit of a goal despite the stark prospects of his life-threatening circumstance. "I have two basic messages," he began. "One is that the main shortcoming or gap in producing results in U.S. businesses is not knowledge, but the will to lead and take action. The second is that Tenneco has responded to that challenge."

He built his theme around a recent editorial in *The Wall Street Journal* (January 28, 1993) with the headline, "A Need for Vision." The piece assessed all the turmoil in American industry, noting massive layoffs and changes in executive command at General Motors, International Business Machines, and Digital Equipment, among others. It asked, "Where do we go from here?"

Mike's response was something that he and I had discussed at length prior to my coming to Tenneco. The years in graduate academic studies and teaching made me comfortable with these more abstract ideas about business and the global economy. My years in training and leading Army troops and industrial managers also had convinced me of the basic fundamentals of successful manufacturing businesses. What we had said often in our management meetings in Tenneco is what Mike now was repeating before this crowded room at the Waldorf Astoria Hotel.

"My view is simple—that the best defense is a great offense," he said. "A well run, focused organization populated with excellent people who work well together is the best answer to inevitable and unending uncertainty. And when you're 'lean and mean' like this you can create markets because you're more agile—you react faster, you're easier to deal with, your people are more highly motivated to go the last mile. Beyond that, when the industrial world recovers, you're posed to take full advantage of it. . . . My real interest is in the competitiveness of the American economy."

An Untimely Concession to Fatigue

Brain cancer patients usually tolerate radiation and chemotherapy treatments far better than other cancer patients. There is less nausea, few headaches, or severe pain and discomfort during the first months of chemotherapy, although this becomes a major discomfort over time. For brain cancer patients, the major physical challenge from the start of treatment is fatigue. Mike was no exception. Within four weeks, as we prepared for what was going to be the exhausting series of meetings across the United States and Europe, it was obvious he was not going to be able to take a major role. He knew that. We had scheduled 72 investment group meetings in 25 days. This was the high-stakes campaign to sell $1 billion of new Tenneco common stock to raise money we needed for the restructuring of Case. Mike's mind was sharp as ever, but he tired on many days by mid-afternoon. His hair had fallen out, an expected reaction to the radiation.

We limited Mike's participation to the two cities with the highest concentration of potential buyers, New York and Boston. He was going to lead meetings in late morning, over lunch, and several in the afternoon. Then, because of his fatigue, we pared his schedule back to three meetings a day, with only one in the early afternoon.

Even at the dramatic hour we were preparing to set the price with our investment bankers, Morgan Stanley, on the stock we would sell—a $1.1 billion transaction—Mike had to bow out. He had flown to New York from Houston the previous day. Six of us on Tenneco's senior management team had huddled in a suite at the Waldorf Towers that morning, reviewing order books the Morgan Stanley bankers had assembled that listed prospective bidders—the customers for this deal. We were excited.

The strength of the orders indicated that we would be able to negotiate a price between $46 and $48 per share. That easily was more than we needed to get our balance sheet in better shape, to fill the equity hole left after creating the $920 million reserve for the restructuring. We were on the brink of a significant victory that would keep our ambitious plans for remaking Tenneco on track.

But as we got set to depart for the short ride to the Morgan Stanley offices, Mike signaled he was not going with us. "You've got the parameters," he told us. "Go ahead and do the pricing without me. If we get out of this range (between $46 and $48), somebody call me." We could see he was deeply disappointed to miss this final round of high-stakes poker. Pricing a $1 billion deal is a great thrill. I've been fortunate to be in that position numerous times during the past 20 years. The big game is on the line. You want to take the winning shot. On this day, none of us, including Mike, was disappointed with the outcome. The price was $46.75.

Experimental Treatments and Huge Doses of Steroids

During the next six weeks, Mike battled the fatigue and increasing occurrences of nausea and other symptoms of the poison that was starting to accumulate in his body from the chemotherapy. The intensive radiation treatments had ended by early March. One day around that time, his eldest daughter, Kim, asked him why he wanted to keep working in the demanding job of running one of the largest corporations in the country. "I only hope I can be an example to others," he said.

He would be a dazzling sprinter in his work on many days, displaying a laserlike brilliance and intensity on business issues, but never again was he the 80-hours-a-week, long-distance runner he had been. He arose most days for early morning workouts that combined swimming and weight training at the fitness complex a few miles from his home. He spent fewer hours at the office, but came in most days for important meetings and otherwise kept in touch by phone and fax machine when working from home.

"Mike was on an experimental, incredibly aggressive treatment program," Dr. Wells recalled. "The radiation and chemo dosages just sapped his strength, but he continued to fight back against that. Psychologically, having a place to go and to focus on his work was important. His work was a major part of his life. He used this goal to sustain him through the difficult physical side effects from this aggressive treatment."

By early May, he was having a harder time moving around because of a flare-up of phlebitis in his left leg. For the annual stockholders' meeting at the Doubletree Hotel a few blocks from the Houston headquarters, we arranged the dais so that Mike, myself and Karl Stewart, our vice president and corporate secretary, could just speak into microphones placed before us instead of walking to a podium. With a blue curtain draped around our table, no one saw that Mike's left leg was propped up on a chair. Not one stockholder asked about Mike's health.

By this time and through the summer of 1993, Mike was putting on a lot of weight, perhaps 40 or 50 pounds. It was a reaction to the steroids that had become an essential part of his chemotherapy. When radiation and chemotherapy treatments are effective, they do kill tumor cells. But radiation also causes swelling of brain tissue in the same region. This mixture of dead cancer tissue and swelling can seriously injure other nearby parts of the brain. The brain is in a closed container so swelling puts pressure on the nervous system and nearby structures of the brain. It was the doctors' puzzled search for the cause of Mike's slight limp a year earlier that led to brain scans that caught the tumor in its early stage. The limp was a symptom of that tumor crowding against his motor and sensory strip.

Physicians prescribe steroids such as cortisone-derived drugs as the best neutralizer for that swelling, which is what Dr. Levin had done for Mike. He also wanted the benefits steroids bring to the signaling functions of normal cells in the neurological network. By any standard, Mike was taking what Dr. Wells considered very large doses. They did reduce the swelling. They also aroused a voracious appetite that put the weight on Mike, they caused his shoulder and hip muscles to weaken, and they made his sleep much more difficult. By Labor Day, he often was noticeably more tired and less focused. He seemed to get a lift in September when the doctors eased back on his chemotherapy. Yet brain scans at M.D. Anderson suggested to a concerned Dr. Levin a rising level of radiation-induced injury to healthy tissue, and he also saw evidence of continued tumor growth.

At approximately the same time, however, brain tumor experts Mike had been seeing for some months at the Brigham and Women's Hospital in Boston were more optimistic. Their brain scans were compiled with new imaging and nuclear scanning technology not available in Houston. Dr. Jay Leffler, the head of Mike's medical team in Boston, felt these tests indicated the tumor growth had slowed significantly. Many of Mike's symptoms, he felt, were due to the buildup of dead tumor tissue along his motor and sensory cortex. The Boston scans indicated no new tumor growth.

Diverging Views from the Two Medical Camps

In Dr. Wells's view, the brain tumor clinics at M.D. Anderson and Brigham and Women's were the world's greatest. Their methodologies and opinions might occasionally clash, and their experience and sophistication with new technologies and treatments varied, yet no brain cancer patient in 1993 could have asked for better, cutting-edge medical support. The decision by Mike and Joan was to consult continually with both camps. By this point in the fall of 1993, the diagnoses and medical strategies from these two camps diverged irreconcilably.

"The scientific diagnosis and treatment of brain tumors continues to evolve," Dr. Wells said. "Unlike many other forms of cancer, no highly reliable and effective course of treatment had been developed for the aggressive, malignant brain tumor that Mike had. And because of the evolution in the science of brain tumors, we expected to find differing opinions. This was true among the specialists in Houston and Boston. Moreover, high profile cases, as this one surely was, have a propensity to heighten even minor differences of opinion among experts. In the end we always made our decisions after analyzing and assessing the best information and opinions available to us."

Late in October, Mike, Joan, and Dr. Wells flew to Boston for another brain scan. When Dr. Wells gave them the laboratory results over the weekend, Mike and Joan were overjoyed. The Boston doctors concluded there were no signs of growth in the tumor, that it probably was now dead tissue, and that there also was a chance that the tissue might break apart and gradually be reabsorbed by the body through natural processes. If not, surgery would be possible to remove the dead tissue.

Mike, Joan, and Dr. Wells celebrated over dinner. The three of them now had been battling Mike's escalating physical problems for 20 months, since the comparatively routine surgery to repair his ruptured disc. Maybe this new diagnosis signaled better days ahead. Maybe these radical, aggressive treatments somehow had found the cure. They eagerly signed the label from a $30 bottle of Far Niente wine that night, a souvenir of their newfound hope.

For several months, our senior management team had prepared for what we called the "Tour de Tenneco," a whirlwind tour of four key operating sites with more than 70 securities analysts as our guests. It would be our first chance over two tightly scheduled days to give the Wall Street crowd a first-hand look at some of the major changes and progress we had made in four of our six operating companies since Mike and I had taken charge. It also was a chance for the analysts to meet informally with us as well as other key corporate and operating officers. We leased a Delta Air Lines commercial jet for this tour, shuttling the group from LaGuardia Airport in New York City initially to Newport News, Virginia, for a look at the shipyard. We followed with visits to a Walker exhaust systems pipe plant in Marshall, Michigan, a specialty packaging plant near Chicago, and a major tractor assembly plant near Case's headquarters in Racine, Wisconsin, before the return flight to New York.

A Buoyant Declaration, and Dismay

Mike joined us the first night for the big reception and dinner for the analysts and about 80 people from Tenneco headquarters and operations. It was just a few days since he received the new diagnosis in Boston. He had been more energetic anyway in the previous few weeks because the doctors had cut back his drug intake for awhile. Now he was buoyant, enthusiastic, joking, and spirited. Some of us cautioned him against making any strong statement at the dinner about a cure, but he ignored that advice. Toward the end of his welcoming remarks, he told the dinner crowd of the diagnosis and that, barring unforeseen circumstances, his doctors now believed he could live a normal life span. The response was prolonged applause, and a standing ovation.

In the news release we put out on his new diagnosis immediately following that tour, Mike said a "full regimen" of chemotherapy treatments would continue through the following spring. These treatments were intended to prevent a recurrence of the tumor. "The program of accelerated radiation combined with aggressive chemotherapy has been tough, but it has worked," Mike said in the release. "That's all that matters."

The Houston medical team was dismayed. They had not seen the news release until after it was on the news wires. The latest brain scans from M.D. Anderson, as from Brigham and Women's Hospital, also suggested the buildup of large amounts of dead tumor tissue. But Dr. Levin believed there also were signs of worrisome radiation damage to healthy tissue, as well as new tumor growth. He told Dr. Wells and Mike that he strongly disagreed with the Boston opinion. Mike continued having brain scans conducted and drug treatments monitored at M.D. Anderson, and he continued meeting regularly with Dr. Levin. But he increasingly would look to Boston for his medical guidance.

His immediate problem by mid-November, whether or not the tumor was dead or still growing in some way, was containing the serious effects of the radiation and chemotherapy inside his brain. The swelling related to healthy and dead cancer tissue was causing pressure on his motor and sensory nervous system, and slowly was choking off the strength and muscle control on his left side. Dr. Wells and Dr. Levin worried that some swelling might have flared up near Mike's emotional control center. It would be normal for anyone with an optimistic, vibrant persona such as Mike to suffer bouts of depression and wide mood swings. I never saw any.

Experimental Treatments and Huge Doses of Steroids

More Steroids, or High-Risk Surgery

The doctors were uncertain. In conversation with Dr. Wells, Mike at times seemed to be less engaged, more distant or disinterested. On occasion, his temper flared. Was it simply the enormous psychological burden he was under? Or was it swelling related to a new tumor, radiation damage, or the side effects of his massive steroid doses? Aside from surgery, there was no way to know. The doctors stayed with the prescription: large doses of a steroid derived from cortisone called dexamethasone, an especially effective antidote for swelling brain tissue.

This created more physical problems. In addition to his increasing weight and fatigue, and weakened muscles, Mike's troubles now extended to his pancreas and liver. His short-term memory was waning. The Boston medical team encouraged Mike to think about a "debulking" surgery. It was the only way to remove the dead tumor tissue and reduce swelling. They knew surgery carried high risks; aside from usual dangers of permanently damaging brain functions, it could stimulate the spread and growth of live cancer cells if any were in that region. The Houston doctors adamantly opposed it for that reason. Dr. Levin repeatedly tried to persuade Mike not to have the surgery.

Mike still was holding onto the hope that at some point the swelling would abate, he could quit or reduce the heavy doses of steroids and recover at least a part of his lost strength and control on the left side of his body. He also knew the steroids were taking a heavy toll. One day he said to me, "I'm fighting this thing. I'm trying to get my energy back. But this stuff took a lot more out of me than I expected. The doctors told me, if we don't keep the swelling down, I'm going to be paralyzed. My left side is going to go. So I've got to stay on the steroids."

This was just days before his last appearance at any major Tenneco event. The event was the 1993 Tenneco Leadership Conference, coming almost exactly one year from when the very first brain scan indicated that Mike might have a brain tumor. Mike was determined to give his opening address, standing, before the 400 members of senior management. Naturally, he wanted to convince this crowd that he was in command, that he was recovering, and that he was going to stay on as leader.

My Silent Mission: A Seamless, Unobtrusive Transition

Those of us aware of his recent struggles were very wary. Mike had led the October board meeting as Tenneco chairman and CEO, but had missed most weekly senior staff meetings for two months and was rarely in the office. As a precaution against a possible slowdown in some key administrative tasks, the board had extended to me the power to approve large capital projects that exclusively had required Mike's signature. For the same reasons, I gradually became more assertive within the senior management group in deciding policy issues, disputes, and disagreements that naturally arise in such a large organization. No one in the group ever confronted me; I think this was because we all knew what had to be done and that it was my job to set things in motion as long as Mike's condition was weakening.

Mike's decision in January to disclose his illness had been the right one, and it made my job easier by not having to keep the secret. Yet it also made my job more difficult in other ways. We had to constantly play Mike's own enthusiasm and optimism and his public statements of being fully in command and control, against a difficult situation where he was becoming more fatigued and more distracted. As it would be for anyone, it simply was hard for him to project command and control as he became less engaged in the administration.

By staying as chairman and CEO, while fighting the brain cancer through the fall, Mike was clinging to a role that helped him keep up his fight. Given the hard-driving person he was, quitting the job would have been an admission that the cancer was beating him. I don't think he ever had in his mind that he simply was going to hang onto the position to maintain the power and the control.

My goal amid this uncertainty was to make the transition that seemed to be developing as seamless and unobtrusive as possible. It was a complex problem that I had to solve carefully and privately over the course of several months. I had to avoid any perception that

I was attempting to elbow Mike out of the picture. This issue was even more sensitive because several members of the senior management group had been recruited by Mike before I arrived, or had a much longer relationship with him than with me before coming to Tenneco. Moreover, the organization was still on "red alert" as we said often, under pressure to improve performance and uncertain how much of it would hold together, or for how long. I couldn't think of worse elements to toss into this volatile brew than gossip and intrigue surrounding divisive maneuvers to grab power at the highest level. If Mike's illness eventually could force him to step down, then I had to take on the responsibility of keeping the rest of his leadership team intact at corporate headquarters. (No one would depart until 1997.)

At the same time, Tenneco could not abide indecisiveness at the top. Human nature being what it is, a perceived weakness in our leadership team could have caused many senior managers throughout the company to stiffen their resistance to the demanding assignments we were giving them. A chorus of "We'll just wait these guys out" would have risen behind our backs.

A Final Performance

In advance of the Leadership Conference, we set up a bedroom for Mike just behind the stage on the third level of the cavernous George R. Brown Convention Center. Mike could sleep or rest as much as possible before walking to the dais. At that point, our security chief, John Bales, would be standing right in back of the curtain behind Mike's podium. If Mike stumbled or collapsed for any reason, John might be able to cushion his fall. It wasn't necessary.

Mike made what overall was an inspiring presentation, rooted in a 50-minute script he had rehearsed repeatedly, and dramatized, of course, by his vulnerable health. He faltered briefly in the final 15 minutes, wandering from the text of the speech scrolling before him on a Tele-Prompter as his energy flagged, but even the ad-libs were coherent and relevant. His doctors later said they were amazed that any patient in such an advanced stage of brain cancer treatment could have attempted the performance.

In his speech, Mike boasted about the "absolutely astounding" progress in the company's results during 1992 and 1993. He criticized inefficient management methods that get in the way of productivity on the factory floor, saying, "We need to take failure cost out of the management process, not just out of the manufacturing process." He cautioned that none of the six Tenneco companies could rest on its laurels, and indicated that the pace of change was going to accelerate for each of them. "Most of the strategic opportunities for each of our businesses will have to be met by re-deploying rather than simply adding resources; we . . . are obligated to put our capital in the highest return, most productive places we can."

And he challenged the group to create and execute the "big, bold strokes" that can catapult and keep the businesses ahead of competitors. "Make no mistake about it. We are going to become a world-class industrial company, and you are going to make it happen." The managers were on their feet, applauding, as he finished. Mike smiled broadly. He took a seat near the front, sat through my talk on world-class performance and a few presentations by our operating group heads, then departed for home.

Wearing the same, bright red v-neck sweater he had chosen for the speech, Mike returned for the closing afternoon session the next day. It was an informal hour where he and I took questions from the floor and also answered others handed in before the conference. I gave many of the responses, but Mike was very animated and forceful when he spoke. He had rested for a day, and he still had the ability to pick himself up for a big event. Once the show started, he could do it:

> Question: How important is culture change in reengineering a division, and can it be accomplished quickly without making extensive management changes?
>
> Mike: In some circumstances, you absolutely have to change the people in order to change the whole approach to the business. In many others, you don't. My presumption has been from the beginning that we can teach and develop our best people to learn different ways, and I think that has been demonstrated here over the past 24 months.

I'll tell you one rule that is absolute: Anybody standing on the air hose has to get knocked off it if they don't get off it voluntarily and in a hurry. Because, as you all know, when someone is in a leadership position, if he or she is not with you, they are against you. They're clogging up the process or they're failing to exercise leadership, which is the key value in the whole thing.

Over the course of the hour, we sparred and joked about salaries and other things that came up. We had a lot of fun. In his two appearances, Mike seemed to have convinced this group that he was the man in charge. Their evaluations of the conference gave him high marks for his speech and, for both of us, that open forum. Except for the few dozen of us whose offices were in the Houston headquarters, hardly anyone in that room would see him again.

"We're Not Going to Accept the Status Quo"

Mike's battle with cancer, along with our strategies and achievements at Tenneco, were the focus of a long *Business Week* cover story, "The Fight of His Life," in September. During one of many August interviews with the correspondent and writer, Wendy Zellner, Mike declared he would be skiing with his family at Christmas. It was typical Walsh bravado, and Zellner used that line in her story. Yet as Mike and his family made final plans for a holiday fortnight at their home in Steamboat Springs, Colorado, hitting the slopes was hardly his biggest worry. Shadowy lesions in his frontal lobes were evident on the most recent brain scans. New tumor growth or radiation damage? The doctors did not know for certain, but a consequence was more swelling. It was near the center that controls emotional response.

Mike knew that surgery could hasten his death if the procedure went badly or more cancer cells were stirred up. Still it appeared to be the only choice that *might* improve his condition. By late January, he decided to take the risk. "This was something he had to do," Dr. Levin said. "It was very hard to change his mind. I didn't know how to approach it." To Mike, the Houston option seemed to offer only more chemotherapy, more steroids, and no solution to the brain swelling that eventually could kill him.

"His view was, 'We're going to think positively about this, we're not going to just accept the status quo,' Ted Tetzlaff recalled. "Whether it was going to the fat farm, getting on a diet, working out, surgery . . . he was going to *do* something. Well, he needed the calories to function. He had this voracious appetite that just undermined any kind of dietary approach. He didn't have the physical ability to work out. The guys at Harvard always said surgery was a long shot . . . it could improve the situation . . . it might hurt the situation. But it was not without hope."

The surgery at Boston's Brigham and Women's Hospital lasted more than three hours on a Saturday, January 29. First signs were encouraging. The doctors were confident they had removed much of the dead tissue. Mike seemed to emerge with no obvious, urgent difficulties. He was quiet, but coherent in talks with Dr. Wells. Ted, Art House and I put together a brief statement we released to the news media Sunday afternoon:

Houston, January 30, 1994—Tenneco today announced that Tenneco chairman and CEO Mike Walsh completed surgery on Saturday at Harvard Medical School-affiliated Brigham and Women's Hospital in Boston to remove dead tumor tissue remaining from a brain tumor discovered a year ago. The surgery was performed following tests and evaluations concluded on Friday. The procedure was made possible by the progress of his treatment program. Mr. Walsh tolerated the procedure well and is resting comfortably."

The operation is a standard one performed to advance the healing process. Pre-operative and available post-operative tests performed at both the University of Texas M.D. Anderson Cancer Center in Houston, Texas, and Brigham and Women's Hospital confirmed earlier diagnoses that Walsh appeared to have no active tumor lesions.

Walsh is resting and recuperating at Brigham and Women's Hospital, where he will remain for several days before returning to Houston.

Cancer Identified in Multiple Locations

The following day, however, laboratory results confirmed the doctors' fears and erased their initial postoperative optimism. Mike's brain still had active cancer cells, which had spread to several areas from the original growth at the front-right motor strip. When I first heard the news, I felt double-crossed by the Boston doctors and their first report after the surgery. Events seemed to be heading toward the bad outcomes Dr. Levin had predicted.

Mike's energy level during that week after surgery was unusually flat, another discouraging sign. Joan and her children, Ted, Dr. Wells, I, and others close to the situation including the Tenneco directors hoped for some indication of a renewed spark. But privately, many of us feared the worst, including Tenneco board members. "It was a shock to us on the board when the cancer was found within 24 hours of the successful surgery to remove the dead tissue," Peter Flawn said. "We all had been very encouraged, then we had the very bad news about the additional lesions."

Mike remained on chemotherapy and steroids. He immediately began rehabilitation exercises. Within a week, he was moved to a rehabilitation center outside Boston, in Woburn, Massachusetts. In mid-February, he suffered there the first of several seizures. His condition began to slip. Ted and Mike agreed that all of Mike's energy now had to be focused on his medical recovery. Ted relayed that message to Tenneco's directors. On February 22, my fifty-eighth birthday, Dr. Wells delivered to the Tenneco board a letter from those doctors confirming that Mike no longer could continue as chief executive. The next day, the company announced that the board had elected me to succeed Mike. Dr. Flawn remembered this about the board's discussion about the leadership succession issue:

> I remember saying that I thought Dana's great strength was in his ability to execute. The board was very pleased about how he had carried out the strategic plan that he and Mike had put together. As Mike's illness had sapped more of his strength, we had concerns that Dana get all of the help he needed. He was carrying a big load, having to do an enormous amount. He led many meetings with

investors and analysts, he had the Case problem to fix, and was heading operations of all six Tenneco businesses.

For that matter, everyone in the senior management had to push harder. But they put their shoulders to the wheel to get the work done. That was a great achievement for the company. The board did raise the question when we met in Houston that day of whether we wanted to look more broadly outside the company for a successor to Mike, or to make Dana the CEO. The board was unanimous. We wanted to go with Dana.

The doctors would keep Mike on chemotherapy, offset swelling with steroids, and do what they could to make him as comfortable as possible, for as long as possible. But they were out of solutions to stop the spreading tumor.

Two weeks later, on March 4, Joan brought Mike back to Houston. He was admitted as a patient to one of the nation's finest rehabilitation centers for head and spinal injuries, The Texas Institute for Rehabilitation and Research, a few blocks away from the M.D. Anderson clinic. The institute is renowned in the Southwest as the wellspring of many inspiring recovery stories. Virtually all patients who enter improve, not die. Staff physicians and therapists initially thought Mike's case would be no different. Although he rarely spoke, they saw signs of improvement in his coordination, his energy level, and his eye contact. The final few times I visited him, his mind was active and alert, but he could not communicate. Ted Tetzlaff has the same lasting image, of a man whose mind retained a large measure of its brilliance until the moment his once-vigorous body finally wore out. Mike died of respiratory failure at 3:15 P.M. on Friday, May 6, 1994 two months before his fifty-second birthday.

Memorial for "An Immensely Gifted Leader"

More than 1,000 people attended a moving memorial service the following week in Houston. Ted read a letter of condolence from President Clinton. Mike's three children recalled poignant stories about their father. John W. Gardner, Mike's most valued mentor, a visionary thinker about leadership in both government and business, and the originator of the White House Fellows program, gave the eulogy. Gardner eloquently summed up what had made Mike's life so remarkable, and so continuously successful:

> He was an immensely gifted leader . . . an immensely gifted leader and manager. He came into the corporate world at a time when U.S. competitiveness had been called into question. Large organized systems, corporate and governmental, we had designed to accomplish our shared purposes simply were not working very well. Mike and I talked quite a lot over the years about those large-scale systems. Mike developed a passionate conviction that they could be made to work well. He believed that to do so was the best service he could render to this country. He gave it everything he had, with extraordinary results.
>
> I have heard it said that Michael was struck down at the peak of his career. But I disagree. I believe that he was just coming into his greatest years . . . I once lived in a house that had a great oak tree out front. And one night, in a terrible storm, a big wind came in and tore that oak tree down. Always after that, when I looked out front, all I could see was a big empty space where that oak tree once stood. That is how I feel now.

It is one of the great frustrations of brain tumor specialists that medical science has developed no better weapons against this killer, especially compared with the great progress against cancers that originate in other parts of the body. Surgeries like the one Mike gambled on, to remove dead tumor masses and relieve swelling, remain an option. When patients can tolerate it, this surgery is followed with radiation treatments that have prolonged many lives. The treatments Mike received throughout 1993 and into 1994 have extended lives of some brain tumor patients 9 or 10 years. Cures still are very unusual, especially for patients 50 years or older. Therapies focused on molecular and genetic sciences are considered medicine's best hope for beating this cancer one day.

"All of This Is Just Chance"

Mike's case turned out to be an exceptionally challenging one, one of the most difficult ever encountered by his medical team. "We can treat 10 patients with the exact same fields, exact same radiation, exact same chemotherapy, and only a couple of them will get the side effects Mike had," Dr. Levin said. Mike was in a group of 20 percent of all brain tumor patients who suffer significant radiation damage to his nervous system. He also was in a group of 10 percent of patients with the same classification of brain tumor, the grade three, anaplastic astrocytoma, whose cancers spread from their original location to other parts of the brain.

"All of this is just chance," Dr. Levin said. "Mike lost more things, faster, than we had expected. We do not understand the genetic abnormalities, but damage to the nervous system as he had is most certainly genetic. We were optimistic in the beginning that he would live for years. He survived, from the first time I saw him, for a year and four months. There is nothing we could have done to reverse his condition, or make it better. There is nothing available today that would have changed things."

PART II

CHAPTER 5

Strategic Choices: Into Romania

THE FAILURES FROM THE HEAVY INVESTMENTS IN J.I. CASE THAT HAD nearly wrecked Tenneco in 1991 also limited our options to rebuild the six businesses. Most were not reporting adequate profits through 1993 in part because their markets were weak or growing only very slowly along with the modest recovery that was underway in the United States. As we considered possible strategies to strengthen earnings, there was not much we could do to raise cash by selling parts of businesses that appeared to have the least attractive prospects. We were pessimistic, figuring that sales at this point would amount to our giving away assets. You want to sell into strengthening markets. Prices typically are stronger when a business's performance is improving and the outlook for that particular industry is good. It is much harder to find a buyer willing to pay a good price in a weak market. For proof, we had our frustration trying to find a buyer for Case in the summer of 1992.

This combination of weak finances and poor business conditions in the early 1990s made Tenneco's road to recovery steep and uncertain. In direct and indirect ways, it caused thousands of employees to lose their jobs as production was trimmed and assets were sold in many of the businesses. But after Case became profitable and we had sold more than half of our ownership in that business for $750 million in cash by the end of 1994, we began to have serious options to make sizable investments and acquisitions.

This included several attractive prospects outside North America. We had important strategic choices to make, each with varying risks and uncertainties. One was whether to build a large sawmill and manufacturing plant in Romania. The plan was to export panels and other products made at the site from timber collected from nearby beech forests that were among the finest in the world. If the project were successful, it would generate good profits for Tenneco and provide a boon to the depressed Romanian economy.

This chapter is about the broad strategy and policy issues we assessed and confronted in committing to go into Romania. The issues were similar to those we faced before expanding into Asia, Latin America, the Middle East, and South Africa. But our experiences in Romania best capture the wide range of challenges that arise in making global investments.

The Logic and Appeal of Global Markets

Like hundreds of other U.S.-based manufacturers plotting their future growth, we were eyeing expansion into both the modern industrialized and emerging markets of the new global economy. And why not? Economic trends were heading our way. Newly industrialized countries were developing a faster-growing segment of middle-class consumers. These consumers wanted more of the Western lifestyle of increasing mobility, safety, comfort, and convenience. This implied rising demand for all kinds of products that Tenneco businesses supplied directly or indirectly: energy (natural gas), automobiles and auto parts, food prepared outside the home (packaging), and basic foods and housing (farm and construction equipment). The window of opportunity to get established in these markets was not going to last long, so we knew we had to move quickly. As one of my favorite Chinese expressions puts it, "A man will sit in a chair with his mouth open for a long time before a roast duck flies in."

More broadly, economic growth in general outside North America was accelerating. That is where the money is, or where it soon would be, for companies willing to pay the price of admission. In 1950, shortly after the industrial strength of Germany and Japan had been eliminated in World War II, the United States generated 59 percent of total global output. By 1994, however, 74 percent of the global economic activity was outside the United States, with Japan and Germany back at the top of the list. Those statistics underscored why international trade was becoming more important to the U.S. economy as well as the global economy.

To be sure, we thought our best opportunities were in the advanced industrial economies of Western Europe and Australia. We moved quickly from 1994 through 1996 on the continent and "down under," where several Tenneco businesses had been active for decades. We strengthened our position as a leading supplier of exhaust systems to prominent European automakers (e.g., Mercedes-Benz, Volkswagen, BMW, Porsche) and, in Australia, as the leading manufacturer of shock absorbers sold through retailers as replacement parts. At the same time, we moved forward on some intriguing opportunities in China, Southeast Asia, and Latin America and in some emerging markets in formerly socialist countries in Central and Eastern Europe. We were seeking new relationships in markets where some Tenneco businesses had little or no presence in the previous 50 years. In Latin America: Mexico, Argentina, Brazil, and Chile. In Asia: China, India, Taiwan, Thailand, Singapore, and, a real long shot, Vietnam. In the Middle East: Abu Dhabi and the United Arab Emirates. Ventures in Israel and Egypt would come in another few years. In Europe: the Czech Republic, Poland, Hungary, and Romania.

To emphasize the urgency for our business leaders to expand outside North America, I linked a portion of their annual bonus to progress we could show in these emerging and newly industrialized markets. This was part of our standard procedure in determining compensation. Business priorities had to be included as much as possible in measurable criteria for calculating bonuses. I had to be realistic, however, in setting expectations for performance targets. Few people who have never tried to establish a business in an emerging market truly appreciate how difficult it can be.

A Weak, Isolated Economy

Of all the countries we entered in this period, Romania was among the most improbable. It was one of the poorest nations in the Balkan region of Eastern Europe, and one of its most isolated. At first glance, Romania offered little appeal for potential investors in the West, Middle East, or Asia. Its profile included an aging and uncompetitive industrial base; a lack of administrative and managerial talent competent in the basic rules of capitalism; a labor force largely unfamiliar with the concept of being paid for performance; high rates of inflation that at times exceeded 50 percent; unpredictable political, economic, judicial and social climate; and a stunningly deficient healthcare system.

As a result, capital inflows were only a trickle into the mid-1990s. This was especially discouraging for many Romanians. Most had become more aware of rising living standards in the new market economies of former Central European satellites of the collapsed Soviet Union. This was the so-called first tier of formerly socialist nations: Poland, the Czech Republic, and, along Romania's western border, Hungary. Yet the Romanians lived in a very poor society that had fallen far behind the modern world during more than 40 years under a Communist government in a centrally planned economy. Annual per capita income was less than $1,000 in 1996. Life expectancy fell consistently during the 1970s and 1980s, to age 69 in 1992, less than every European country except Albania and Slovakia. Infant mortality was 24.3 per 1,000 births in 1993, nearly triple the level of 21 developed nations in the Organization for Economic Cooperation and Development. Population was declining, with birth rate falling and people leaving in search of better jobs and living conditions elsewhere in Europe. Leaders in the first years of the post-Communist era in the early 1990s had failed to halt this decline, but were under growing political pressure to find the answers.

A Wealth of Natural Resources

The best potential for improving Romania's economy and living standards, more so than most of the former Soviet-bloc countries, lies in its natural resources. Romania has large, valuable, and underutilized wealth in its rich soil, forests, energy, and ore reserves. Farmland covers 40 percent of the country, which is roughly the size of Oregon in the United States, or two-thirds as big as reunited Germany. Romania's forests cover 28 percent of its land. Its oil reserves, clustered in the southern lowlands, along the Black Sea coast and beneath the Black Sea coastal waters, were a major energy source a half-century ago for Nazi Germany's war machine. In 1938, Romania was the world's seventh-largest oil producer, and second largest in Europe. Its potential for supplying the industrial economies of Western and Central Europe remains very real. Even in the 1970s, before it pulled further into economic isolation, Romania was the world's fifth largest producer of natural gas. The country also is a large producer of a variety of ore and minerals.

If well managed by modern standards and practices, these resources could provide the most immediate and pragmatic path to increasing trade and steadying, then expanding, Romania's weak economy. In economic terms first noted by David Ricardo, the nineteenth-century British philosopher and economic theorist, Romania's natural resources and its abundant, literate workers represent its main wellspring of comparative advantage for increasing its trade with richer, more economically advanced nations.

By most accounts, Romania's economic profile seemed to offer little that meshed with Tenneco's growth strategies. We intended to build our assets in global markets with a growing middle class; it would be years before Romania could achieve a growing middle class. Our strategy also was to focus on three core businesses for the future: automotive parts, packaging, and unregulated natural gas operations; in Romania, fewer than 2 percent of the households owned an automobile. Much of the food is raised in 1½-acre plots many families own (and only recently were returned to them from state control); an unlikely market for large farm tractors and combines. Few manufacturers can afford Western-style packaging. Finally, the large financing packages that would be required to develop the nation's appealing natural gas reserves were a distant dream.

Yet Tenneco's forest products and packaging business, the Packaging Corporation of America, managed more than a million acres of woodlands in the United States. It also operated four sawmills, a pole mill, and four large paper mills in the United States and supplied much of the pulp, or processed wood chips, for those paper mills from our own woodlands. Our experts in forestry management knew how to cut, grow, and nourish forests profitably and as a sustainable resource.

Romania, in turn, has more than 20 million square miles of forests. This is roughly two-thirds as much as the abundant timberlands of Georgia in the United States, a state in which Tenneco was one of the largest manufacturers of wood products. Romania's forests, which cover more than one-fourth of that country, were managed by a state-owned company, RomSilva. The methods and technology of RomSilva and the thousands of men who cut and haul logs to dozens of small, aging sawmills across the country were decades behind Western practices. They were similar to what was seen in the rural United States during the Depression years prior to World War II.

Vast Forests of Beech Trees

We had become aware through contacts in the European wood products industry that the foothills and mountains of Transylvania in western Romania had some of the world's finest and largest virgin forests of beech trees. For reasons ranging from inaccessible locations to bureaucratic inertia and black market politics, Romania was not on anyone's list as a likely source for future supplies. The reputation of Romanian forest products was that the timber was both superior and abundant. Yet traders and brokers in Europe complained mainly that the country's economy, everything from inadequate roads and rail lines to banking services, was too backward for the forest products sector to develop into a dependable industry.

This represented a terrible waste of resources. Lightly colored beech is highly popular in Western Europe and Asia. It typically is used in paneling, hardwood floors, shelving, and solid and veneer-coated furniture. Because supplies are limited, it is very expensive. What little volume entered the markets from Romania was harvested from the forests by fairly primitive methods. Hand saws, axes, and small chain saws were common tools for cutting down large beech trees that, by law, had to be at least 80 feet tall and nearly two feet in diameter. These usually were between 100 and 150 years old, an extremely rare and valuable wood source. The only comparable hardwood stands were in the wine country of France, where the climate and mineral content in the soil were similar. But the French forests had been harvested for decades, and the annual cut was limited. Much of the Romanian timber, however, was untouched, to a fault. It was wasting away, rotting on the ground.

Rotting Timber and a Legacy of Neglect

Nicolae Ceausescu, the Communist dictator who ruled Romania for more than 20 years, had decreed in the 1960s that forestry management was a peasant pursuit. His Stalinist bias was to cluster jobs and capital in massive factories and other industrial settings, and neglect agriculture and any related activities in land management. The only significant activity in Romanian forests during the Cold War years was conducted by Russians. They often ventured south across Ukraine and Moldova to exploit the forests as well as crops and mining sites in Romania. In the 1980s, Ceausescu was able to reduce most of Romania's ties with the Soviet Union, and the Russian incursions abated. As a result, for nearly 20 years some of the world's most valuable stands of beech wood, as well as sizable forests of spruce and oak timber, had been left to rot on Romania's mountains and hillsides.

It was mostly chance that brought these beech forests to our attention. At my suggestion, Paul Stecko, the new president of our packaging business, had taken a trip in early 1995 to inspect some old sawmills and paper mills that the Romanian government wanted to sell. His job was to assess whether there might be something we could salvage and operate either as owners or through a joint venture. Paul and I had worked closely for 15 years at International Paper, where he had become an expert in mill operations. I had brought him into the top job at our packaging operations late in 1993. The operations he inspected in Romania's south and north left him cold. It seemed to him like a worthless trip, with nothing of any value in Romania likely for Tenneco.

Then, on his flight out, Paul gazed down from the air onto those vast forests of prime beech. In his mind a business proposition began to take shape: If roads could be built into these remote forests, sufficient timber supplies obtained, a modern saw mill and manufacturing plant constructed, and a few thousand workers trained to operate equipment and reliably deliver raw materials, food, and other essentials, Romania could quickly take its place as a significant supplier of high-quality beech products. The business could generate hard currency from wealthy economies in Western Europe and Asia. It could provide attractive pay, benefits and working conditions for a few thousand unskilled and semiskilled workers. Most important for Romania's leaders, it could demonstrate to potential investors that Romania was both willing and capable of taking a bigger role in the global trade network.

We were intrigued. Nothing in that basic formula posed a prima facie problem for us. So we started thinking about how to put a project together. We knew experts who had managed timberlands, built big manufacturing plants and operated mills in Third World countries. My experience at Case helped in gauging the risks and opportunities involved in building roads in distant, isolated places. We reckoned we could maintain adequate controls on each of these factors, even in Romania. A full-blown business analysis soon suggested that there could be an appealing profit margin, the difference between likely costs and likely revenues, over the first 5 to 10 years of operation. But we would have to invest more than $40 million initially over about two years to bring the project to life. We would have a good shot at starting to make money sometime in 1997 or 1998. Then, if most of our financial projections held, we could begin earning substantial profits fairly rapidly.

Ignorance of Basic Methods of Business

Obstacles related to Romania's government, politics, and culture were another matter. We were confident about the basic economics of the business proposition, but we were not naïve. We would be spending millions of dollars in a country where untested democratic leaders had little understanding of the predictable dynamic interplay among supply, demand, and price. These leaders had lived all their adult lives in a socialist economy, where the production of capital goods was dictated with little regard to what volumes actually could be sold.

The freely elected, post-Ceausescu leaders genuinely sought capitalist reforms. They wanted to hitch their Romanian cart to the fortunes of the West. More important, for some, was qualifying Romania for membership in NATO, the North Atlantic Treaty Organization. Modern Romanians hold a deep suspicion of foreigners. They had a long, violent history of invasions from all directions, beginning with the Rome of Emperor Trajan in A.D. 106 and ending with the occupation by Stalin's Russian troops in 1944. Romania had lived under Soviet-style, military communism for nearly 50 years. With a wary eye on the suddenly dormant Russian bear to the north, many Romanians want to join the industrialized Western democracies in a military alliance as quickly as possible.

Politically and economically, all this was going to require a much higher level of sophistication and conviction among Romania's leaders about the ways of the West. If they were hesitant about the norms and rules of capitalism, we wondered, would they block us when we sought to apply those norms and rules in their country? If the national leaders did support us, would the National Parliament and state and local bureaucrats fall in line? In Russia, answers for Western companies that invested shortly after the collapse of the Soviet Union in 1991 too often had been the wrong ones—a resounding Yes! and an emphatic No! It was why we had been keeping Tenneco people and investments out of Russia.

We also realized that few Romanians anticipated the economic difficulties that surely lay ahead of them. To become competitive and attract foreign investment, their economy needed massive changes. Many aging and obsolete factories had to be shut. Ceausescu's economic austerity policies in the 1980s had kept managers from ordering any new equipment, or badly needed spare parts, from outside Romania. The bloated payrolls of most state-run factories and government agencies had to be sharply reduced. This was the familiar dilemma of all post-socialist economies, only worse for Romania. Inefficient, state-run industries had far too many employees, with products of very poor quality. There was an urgency for Romanian industry to create at least some profitable segments. This would require reducing costs—primarily labor costs—and improving the quality of their products. The Romanian economy would have to attract capital the country did not have. To do that, it had to offer investors a return high enough to justify the risk that they could lose all of their money.

The first tier of formerly socialist economies in Central Europe was far ahead of Romania in traveling this politically unpopular course. Inflation soared initially as socialist subsidies were taken away and prices rose to true market levels. As payrolls were cut, unemployment ranks swelled, and crime and other social tensions mounted. Yet economic growth, improvements in living standards for many, and new freedoms for businesses and consumers became evident within a few years. Stores were stocked with more and higher quality goods. Groups of wealthy, educated entrepreneurs and professionals schooled in the law, accounting, banking, and other mechanics of capitalism emerged.

By the mid-1990s it was clear that popular sentiment would continue to support foreign investment and market reforms in those countries. We had been participants in these historic transitions in market reforms, and we had seen them develop month by month. Tenneco businesses were active in each of these countries, with retail sales or wholesale distribution of auto parts in Poland, Hungary, and the Czech Republic; and box manufacturing in Hungary. We felt we knew how to calculate the risks, and we understood the patience, discipline, and vision it took to be successful.

Stumbling toward Capitalism

In Romania, though, the first steps toward creating a market economy in 1990 had been halting ones. Ceausescu had been arrested and executed by army officers at the conclusion of a popular insurrection in December 1989, a month after the fall of the Berlin Wall.

Yet compared with formerly socialist economies in Central Europe, not much would change economically for the average Romanian. Ion Iliescu, the former Communist elected president in 1990, and re-elected in 1992, ran a left-center government with oft-unpredictable stabs at go-slow economic reform. This was not a surprise in the West. Most Romanian experts here figured that the political momentum in that country was too feeble to carry through the economic reforms that in the short run would drive up unemployment and raise inflation.

Two months after Iliescu was elected president in June 1990, correspondent Steven Greenhouse reflected those views in a report for *The New York Times* from Bucharest. "Romania desperately needs Western help to rebuild its industry and retrain its workers and managers," he wrote. "But it will probably receive far less Western aid and investment than most other East European nations." Nearly a year later, Iliescu's changing policies were beginning to demonstrate why the West would be reticent. Bowing to pressure from within his cabinet, Iliescu put the brakes on aggressive market reforms. The dominant view of his ministers was that the masses of poor Romanians could not accommodate the shock therapy solutions taken by Poland and other countries in Central Europe.

In the previous six months, inflation had erased 50 percent of the value of the Romanian currency, the leu. In an interview with *The Times* (April 7, 1991), Iliescu conceded that he was constrained by opposition in Parliament and outside the government. "We bear a very heavy legacy, an atmosphere of general suspiciousness created by the old regime," he said. His cultural minister, the writer Andrei Plesu, echoed the sentiment. "A post totalitarian neurosis with a very bad effect on everything" pervades Romania, he said. "We are all of us infected by a perverse illness. This has created a huge social tension and a toxic intolerance."

Not much changed in the ensuing four years. Iliescu's administration continued to be deeply split over whether the country should, or could, embrace "shock therapy" reforms as Poland, Hungary, and the Czech Republic had done. Economic "shock therapy" requires transferring control of state-operated industries rapidly to investors who, along with their managers, can create a largely privatized, competitive market economy. Yet the National Parliament in Romania, with representation from dozens of political parties, was immobilized by the debate. Progressive steps to liberalize industry ownership and practices regularly were blocked by socialists and other opponents of change.

A First Meeting in London

Despite encouraging rhetoric and efforts occasionally to woo investment from the West, Iliescu's government had generated little interest by the time we first began to see opportunities for Tenneco. My first meeting with Iliescu came late in 1994. I was a panelist in London at a conference of corporate chief executives organized by *Business Week* magazine on global competition. Iliescu, Romania's first democratically elected president, was in the audience. I knew from our contacts in Romania at that time that he was concerned by Romania's poor record in attracting Western investment, management expertise, and technology. With more Romanians aware of improving conditions in Central Europe, Iliescu knew he would have a problem in the 1996 campaign if he could not demonstrate some benefits for Romanian workers from attracting foreign investment.

During a question-answer session, he asked our panel what advice we CEOs had for a country trying to modernize and privatize its economy. Knowing who he was, I said as pointedly as seemed appropriate, "The best advice I can give *to those of you who run the governments* is to get the governments out of the way as fast as you can. Get them out of the ownership of the plants; get government out of making the deals, or controlling the deals. Do the things that facilitate the attraction and retention of foreign capital."

Iliescu approached me a few moments later after the session with his small entourage and asked what specific ideas I had in mind. In a few minutes, we were able to describe our doubts and frustrations about Romania. This somehow engaged Iliescu's interest in Tenneco, and I have to say that this former Communist became one of the most consistent supporters of Tenneco investment plans through the remainder of his presidency, much more than the putatively West-leaning politicians who succeeded him.

I suggested to him that day that Tenneco's capabilities in managing ventures in wood products had many possible applications in Romania. At that point, though, we were discouraged by what to us was an impractical approach that negotiators from the Romanian government had taken on one deal we were exploring. They wanted us to buy full ownership of a big mill producing linerboard, the heavyweight brown paper used to make corrugated boxes. They also insisted that we put in a certain amount of investment to set up more modern equipment and get the mill into better shape. I explained to the president that if we were to take full ownership, *we* would have to decide how to make the mill competitive, not the Romanian government. And our view was that the business prospects for the mill, modest at best, did not justify the high investment sought by his government. I told him this was a good example of why government generally was not capable of making or controlling deals in the private sector.

We also told Iliescu that we were aware of the high quality in Romania's large beech forests. We would be interested in harvesting the wood, building roads into the forests, manufacturing beech products for export, managing the forests, and so forth. Iliescu said he wanted to talk further. He and I then left for other commitments, but Art House, my corporate affairs executive, and one Iliescu's economic advisors continued talking, mainly about Tenneco and our forest products business. Art noticed that the man suddenly seemed very distracted. "Should we meet some other time?" Art asked. "No, no," the Romanian said. "It's just that Henry Kissinger is the next speaker and I've never seen Henry Kissinger."

Art had worked on Kissinger's staff at the National Security Council 20 years earlier and knew the former Secretary of State and head of the National Security Council quite well. Kissinger knew something about Tenneco too. He had been on the board of directors at Union Pacific Corporation when Mike Walsh left his job running the Union Pacific railroad to go to Tenneco. Kissinger now was standing by the entrance to the big meeting room. Sensing an opportunity, Art asked the Romanian, "Would you like to meet him?" "This is not my intention," he said with some embarrassment. Undeterred, House brought the fellow over to where Kissinger was waiting to go up to the dais.

"Hello, Doctor," House said. Kissinger turned around and laughed. "Art House! What the hell are you doing here?" Art mentioned my panel and talk, then said, "I want you to meet Mr. so-and-so from Romania. Tenneco has this great idea for a project in Romania. President Iliescu is interested in it. We're going to have further discussions about it." Kissinger nodded at Art, glanced knowingly at the Romanian official and said, "Very good. Good, good company. Good people to do business with." In a second, Kissinger was on his way to the dais but his spontaneous endorsement had the right effect. Art handed his now starstruck Eastern European his Tenneco business card and said, "We'll be glad to talk to you later about this."

The Plan for Action

Six months after Paul Stecko's airborne vision first took shape early in 1995, Paul and I determined that this unexpected opportunity should be pursued aggressively. This was an opportunity for Tenneco to do well for itself and for others; we could create a profitable wood products operation in Romania, and generate more than a thousand new jobs. There was a chance to outsmart other forest products companies by taking the lead in supplying the potentially large market for beech products, while making an acceptable profit and possibly an even larger return. I thought overall that we had the odds in our favor.

Before we could take action we had to have the approval of Tenneco directors. After months of preparation and armed with an inch-thick document that analyzed the business logic for the deal, Paul and I presented the proposal to the directors for an investment initially projected at more than $20 million:

- We would build Europe's largest sawmill in a remote southwest region of Romania.

- We would build under the same roof an adjacent plant to manufacture wood products for export to many of the world's largest wood products, furniture, and home-furnishing dealers.

- We would construct approximately 500 kilometers, or 300 miles, of roads into otherwise inaccessible hardwood forests.

Every capital project we put before our directors must describe the amount of expected profit and the months or years required for us to deliver it. This is one of the basic functions of the capitalist—determine what makes any one deal more appealing than dozens of other investments, then allocate limited financial resources into the most productive activities. Every major company has some system of adding an increment of required return, or profit, for financial risks and political risks wherever they are mulling investments.

When we made decisions about investments situated in the United States, we looked for projects we estimated could deliver at least $15 of after-tax profit for every $100 invested; a rate of return of 15 percent. In countries where political and other market risks are greater, that bogey must be higher. In Romania, we figured any deal would have to deliver at least 25 percent on paper, making the "risk premium" for that country an additional 10 percent for projected profits. We needed that extra 10 percent of profit to cushion us from problems that could push costs higher or delay the day when the project would start making money. We showed our directors how we figured the costs. Then we explained why this was a rare opportunity: we could supply light colored beech products into Western Europe and Asia at prices that should comfortably exceed that 25 percent goal.

Concerns about Anti-Semitism

Several members of the board had some hard questions about our presentation, and the discussion developed into one of our more vigorous debates on a single capital project. All of the obvious issues were out on the table: politics, crime and corruption, market potential, project execution hazards and risks, historical tensions and rivalries among various ethnic groups in the region, and Romania's own past record in state-sponsored pogroms, notably against Jews and Gypsies. The last point was a particularly sensitive one for one of our directors, W. Michael Blumenthal.

Born in Berlin in the 1920s, Mike and his family escaped from the Nazi persecution of the Jews to Shanghai, China, where he lived much of his later youth. The Blumenthals mounted a second exodus in 1947, this time to the United States and away from Mao Tse-tung's communist revolution. Mike earned a Ph.D. in economics from Princeton University, taught on the Princeton faculty, and then became a successful business executive, heading the Bendix Corporation and the Burroughs Corporation and its successor, Unisys, in the 1970s and 1980s. He also was a top economic policy maker in the U.S. government between 1977 and 1979 when he was Treasury Secretary in the Carter administration.

Mike was also a prominent Jewish leader and became even more involved as his business schedule permitted. He led the development of the new Jewish Museum in Berlin as its president and chief executive. One of his close colleagues in these pursuits has been Elie Wiesel, the Nazi camp survivor, Jewish writer, chronicler of the Holocaust, and Nobel Peace Prize winner. Wiesel is a native-born Romanian. Along with much of his family, he was among hundreds of thousands of Romanian Jews swept off to Nazi labor camps during World War II. An estimated 400,000 of the 750,000 Romanian Jews living at the time perished during the war.

All of this, plus recent reports of incipient, anti-Semitic attacks in Romania, was on Mike's mind during the board deliberations about a Tenneco investment in Romania. "Do we really want to deal with people who have this kind of [anti-Jewish] history?" he asked. "Isn't it possible that we as a company could be tainted in our business relationships elsewhere in the world by choosing to associate now with the Romanian government?" These were serious policy questions, and fair ones.

Inevitably, when a chief executive presents to his directors any proposal for a major investment into uncharted markets, his or her credibility implicitly is on the line. For me, this was one of those moments. My response to Mike was that Iliescu had taken strong public stands against anti-Semitism in 1991, with positive results. My sense was that Iliescu genuinely was as committed to democracy and market reforms as he was to combating ethnic and racial discrimination of all varieties. After weighing all these comments, the board approved our plans. It was time to get going.

Business and Diplomacy in Washington

By the time I shook hands again with Iliescu in Washington in September 1995, the Romanian president was, if not starstruck, certainly enthusiastic about Tenneco. From my view, he had several good reasons. With help from our high-level contacts in Washington, led by Commerce Secretary Ron Brown, we had helped arrange a private meeting for Iliescu with President Clinton, and another with several key members of Congress. President Clinton also hosted a state dinner for him.

Before these events could be scheduled, Brown had to overcome some strong reservations at the State Department. Eastern Europe specialists there perceived Iliescu as a holdover from the Ceausescu regime, and suspected him of being more communist than capitalist. Brown was convinced otherwise. So was I. We both believed Iliescu understood that major investments by American businesses were the best hope for Romania to improve its odds for lasting democracy and economic reform. Brown also knew that Tenneco was in the vanguard of prospective American investors.

A member of Brown's staff for international business, Sally Painter, had joined Tenneco's Washington office for government relations that spring. She had urged Brown's involvement that led to Iliescu's official working visit at the White House, where he met privately with President Clinton for half an hour. The trip was important for Iliescu, who needed the meeting to score some sorely needed political points in Romania. An official working visit included a high level of pomp and circumstance available in Washington to foreign heads of state, a ritual capped by the same formal White House dinner that had been enjoyed by Europe's most important leaders. For Iliescu, it would send a signal to Romanian legislators and voters that he was leading the country into a new status and legitimacy with the West.

Meanwhile, I had arranged a pro-Romania show of force from major American corporations. A group of CEOs from prominent companies, including Procter & Gamble, Martin Marietta, Marriott, and McDonnell Douglas, gathered with me during Iliescu's Washington visit for a formal luncheon at the Romanian ambassador's residence. We talked about our companies, business prospects in Romania, and Iliescu's progress in economic and legislative reforms. The timing was especially good for Tenneco, coming a week after our directors had approved the plans to start the wood products venture in Romania. For Iliescu, after more than five years as Romania's president, our project was one of only a few examples he had to demonstrate his campaign pledge to attract foreign investment from the West and improve general living conditions.

On that day, we at Tenneco still had many details on our venture to nail down with the Romanians. The biggest set involved specific contract terms for location, price, quantity and time span related to the exclusive rights we were seeking to harvest in their beech forests, and the location and number of roads we would agree to build into those forests. After our luncheon, I met privately with Iliescu. He was appreciative, excited by Tenneco's commitment. We reviewed the status of the various contract items. He pledged to have his government place top priority on getting all the key state agencies and leading members of Parliament to give their approvals. When we were about to depart, I handed this former member of the Communist Party's Central Committee in Romania a stylish pen as a gift. "Mr. President," I said, "I hope this is the pen we use to sign the final contract."

Business and Diplomacy in Bucharest

By the following May, still without a signed contract, I accepted Iliescu's invitation to visit Bucharest. The groundbreaking for our wood products plant, held up for months by delays in a variety of required government permits, was nearly ready. In making the trip, I wanted to signal the project's importance, our concern about the political and bureaucratic opposition that had been holding us back, and the project's potential importance for Romania.

A two-hour meeting was set with Iliescu and members of his cabinet on May 28. He would be joined by several members of his cabinet as well as the youthful Romanian ambassador to Washington, Mircea Dan Geoana, and one of most talented, and rakish, international tennis stars of the 1970s, Ilie Nastase. Nastase now had his hand in several investments in Europe, including a nightclub in Bucharest favored by the local nouveaux riches. Nastase also had entered his first political match. With Iliescu's support, he was running for mayor of Bucharest.

It would have been hard at that time to assemble a more potent group of politicians in Bucharest. Yet their clout wasn't enough to prevent some bureaucratic foul-ups that came close to aborting—or sabotaging, it never was clear to us—this trip. The day before I was scheduled to arrive, Paul Stecko and the head of our international packaging group, Paul Griswold, flew into Bucharest on a Tenneco corporate plane. Two of our government relations officers from Washington, Ted Austell and Sally Painter, had arranged for the two men to be met on the tarmac by Romania's foreign minister and chief of protocol, the staff of the American embassy, and reporters from newspapers and television stations.

Always Expect the Unexpected

It was a warm day, close to 100 degrees Fahrenheit. This official reception committee was there a half-hour before the appointed minute, waiting in the hot sun. These officials then waited for more than three hours in vain for the Tenneco jet to come in. Actually, the jet had arrived. A disgruntled air traffic controller had ordered the plane to a remote part of the same Octopeni Airport in Bucharest. Stecko and Griswold, unable to locate the official reception on the tarmac, were greeted instead with machine-gun toting soldiers. The soldiers herded them into long lines in the main terminal, where they waited behind foreign laborers and others queued up for mandatory customs inspections. Once outside the terminal, Stecko and Griswold hailed cabs and rode off without further incident to their hotels. They were furious. They wondered, will Dana Mead, who is committing among the most dollars of any single Western investment into the Romanian economy, get this kind of treatment when he lands tomorrow?

I didn't. My arrival at Octopeni and ride to and from the presidential palace went off without a hitch. In the past 24 hours, Iliescu's office had fired the malcontent in the traffic-control tower and disciplined his supervisors. The entire staff of the airport had been alerted before my arrival. Security was tightened. If loaded rifles were going to be pointed at anyone, our people were assured, they wouldn't be pointed at me. The president greeted Stecko and Griswold, standing at my side, with apologies and embarrassment that afternoon over their rough treatment at gunpoint. Yet, that episode demonstrated the conflicts and miscommunications that make the basic logistics of business more difficult in premodern societies, often leading to bizarre situations. Six years earlier, Iliescu's foreign policy adviser described the problem this way to *The New York Times* (June 18, 1990): "The system in Romania does not function in a logical manner. That is not a reason to forgive, but to always expect the unexpected."

One of the more critical negotiating issues for us had been to secure exclusive rights to harvest and manage specific acreage in certain beech forests. This would give us an assured volume of wood supply, and increase our confidence in Romania's commitment to foreign investment and in the odds that the mill-manufacturing facility could supply a large volume of high-quality wood products. We needed all this to achieve our optimistic financial goals.

The terms we wanted were to cover five years in each location where we would build access roads at our expense. We anticipated it would take that long to construct all of the needed roads. We estimated the total distance at about 500 kilometers, or 300 miles. As roads were completed, we then would have five years of cutting rights in that location. We figured it would take five years to finish all the roads, so the total contract would cover a cumulative 10 years of exclusive cutting rights. Iliescu endorsed those terms. Most but not all of his cabinet members had agreed by this point, but we still needed approval from Parliament. It was clear there would be no final contract signed on this trip.

A Vulnerable Political Ally

Before the news conference, Iliescu assured us that the remaining administrative and political obstacles would soon be overcome. He also confided that he was worried about the approaching national election in November. His go-slow approach on market reforms had done little to revitalize the economy. His opponents were attacking him for not moving more rapidly. He knew he was vulnerable. He considered the Tenneco project, with more than 1,000 potential new jobs for Romanian workers, one of the best illustrations of his efforts at attracting foreign investment and bolstering national economic development. His political prospects could only improve if more Romanians knew of it.

At our news conference that day, we met informally with reporters who covered the president's activities and chatted about the mill project. As we expected, Iliescu was as enthusiastic about the mill project in public as he had been behind the scenes. The news conference went well and generated a smattering of positive publicity for us over the next few days. Stories were published about the significance of Tenneco's size, global activities, and commitment to Romania.

After the news interviews, our small Tenneco group sat down with the president and about 20 other Romanian leaders for a delightful, mostly casual discussion over lunch. Unlike some American corporate CEOs, I consider it insulting to consistently focus conversation on "the deal," whatever that may mean for any two groups at a given moment, when meeting with hosts outside the United States. Europeans and Asians are much more civilized than Americans on this score, preferring first to take measure of the personal interests and the character of a potential partner.

Power Serves and Power Saws

During this hour in Bucharest, we talked tennis a lot. This was relaxing, but also good salesmanship. Politicians are simply customers of a different stripe. Instead of selling a product, you want them to support public policies that can help your business succeed. This at times can require great persuasive skills, and sometimes very little at all. Once you've established some common ground, persuasion becomes easier for both sides. I mentioned to Nastase that I thought tennis had changed since he was competing at the top of the professional circuit in the 1970s. There used to more emphasis on finesse shots and ball placement. Now players like Pete Sampras hit their serves so hard it was nearly impossible to return them with any accuracy. Quickness and agility had given way to raw power. "Exactly right," Nastase said, and then he launched into a long analysis on the strengths and vulnerabilities of some top-seeded players.

I did make a few formal remarks that day about our mill project, which we intended to build on a farming plateau in the western Carpathian Mountains, near the small town of Buchin (pronounced *boo-KEEN*). The theme I stressed to Iliescu and his senior ministers and advisers was that we intended to be a long-term partner. "We are business partners with a responsibility to each other to make our venture not only work, but be profitable for all involved," I said. "Most importantly, we hope that this will enrich the lives of Romanian citizens. We are here not only to listen and learn from you, but also to share our knowledge and expertise. Tenneco does not want to be an American company in Romania, but rather a Romanian company thriving in Romania.

"We intend to be partners with you down the road," I continued. "Our plans and investments for Buchin are only a first step. Working together to solve problems as they come up will be the key to our success. One of our priorities in all of Tenneco is to be easy to do business with. I hope you will find that this is true of us in Romania as well." My parting benediction was to wish them all success in the November elections.

"Market Reformers" and a Long
Step Backward

They did not have that success. Iliescu lost by a popular vote of 54 percent to 46 percent. Nastase lost his race for mayor of Bucharest. Emil Constantinescu, a bearded academic geologist who returned to his home country following a sabbatical at Duke University,

Top: Days before his doctors detected a possible brain tumor, Mike Walsh (*left*) fielded questions with Dana Mead (*right*) at a 1992 conference of 400 Tenneco leaders. (Credit: Michael Hart.)

Bottom: Tenneco committed nearly $1 billion to restructure Case in 1993. Dana Mead told Tenneco's directors he would resign if the maker of farm and construction equipment needed still more rescue money. (Credit: Manuelo Paganelli.)

THE McKINSEY MYSTIQUE I CLINTON'S HEALTH-CARE PLAN

BusinessWeek

SEPTEMBER 20, 1993   A McGRAW-HILL PUBLICATION $2.75

THE FIGHT OF HIS LIFE

Tenneco CEO
Mike Walsh's
Remarkable
Battle With
Cancer

Mike Walsh's cancer battle attracted major international news coverage from the day he announced his illness in January 1993. *Business Week* published a cover story later that year. (Credit: Steven Pumphrey, and *Business Week*.)

Dana Mead at a Houston news conference in May 1994. This was four days after Walsh's death, and two weeks after plans for an initial public offering of Case shares were announced. (Credit: F. Carter Smith, for *The New York Times*.)

Shawn Kelly (*left*) and Paul Griswold at the wood products plant in Romania. Kelly had worked in "pioneer" projects in Costa Rica, Brazil, and Argentina; and Griswold in Russia, Turkey, and Colombia, among others. (Credit: Thomas C. Hayes.)

Top: Two-thirds of Tenneco's Romanian employees are women. Timber quality problems forced an indefinite shutdown of this sorting line in 1999.
Bottom: Iulia Ilianu (*left*), one of the first hires in Buchin, is a workforce specialist. Tina Padure joined Tenneco for higher pay, better safety, and benefits, and soon became a supervisor. (Credit: Thomas C. Hayes.)

Growing tensions between Tenneco and the Navy, Tenneco's largest customer in 1993, were put aside during this christening ceremony for the *John C. Stennis* aircraft carrier. *Front row:* Pat Phillips, president of Newport News Shipbuilding, and Mrs. Margaret Stennis Womble. *Back row:* Navy Secretary John Dalton, Vice President Al Gore, Admiral Bruce DeMars, Senator John Warner, and Dana Mead. (Credit: Judi Baldwin, Newport News Shipbuilding.)

Ron Dellums, chairman of the powerful House Armed Services Committee, at a 1993 news conference. The liberal Democrat opposed adding $4 billion to Pentagon budgets for a new aircraft carrier, but ultimately did not block the legislation that became law in 1994. (Credit: Reuters/ Mike Theiler/Archive Photo.)

Top: A section of the *Ronald Reagan* keel being lowered into drydock in 1998, two years after Newport News Shipbuilding became an independent company. (Credit: Chris Oxley, Newport News Shipbuilding.)

Bottom: Dana Mead (*left*) advocating policies for faster economic growth at a 1996 news conference with Jerry J. Jasinowski, president of the National Association of Manufacturers. (Credit: Ray Dixon, National Association of Manufacturers.)

Business Week's coverage advanced the "growth" debate Mead sought in Washington beginning in 1995. This May 1997 cover would have been as timely in the autumn of 1999. (Credit: *Business Week*.)

Top: Mead with Alan Greenspan at the 1999 annual meeting of the Business Roundtable. (Credit: Ben Zweig.)

Bottom: Greenspan testifying before the House Banking Committee a month later in July 1999. The economic expansion in the United States will enter an unprecedented tenth year in the spring of 2000 if output continues to rise as expected. (Credit: Reuters/Ira Schwartz/ Archive Photo.)

campaigned against Iliescu on the theme of accelerating market reforms and improving the weak economy. Many Romanians celebrated his election as a final break with their Communist past. Sincere, unpretentious, but with no experience in governing, Constantinescu spoke at every turn about his policies to attract more foreign investment, create jobs, and bolster Romanian living standards.

In an interview days after his election, he told *The New York Times* (November 11, 1996), "Economic reform hasn't started in this country except in propaganda." He said he would court foreign investment "especially from the United States." The irony is that his victory ended up costing us many months in additional delays from both unvarnished bureaucratic obstruction and political indecision.

It was frustrating. The steel structure of our new mill was starting to take shape on the high plains of Transylvania. Bureaucratic officials, Constantinescu's political opponents and other less visible forces were holding up our progress. Even many Constantinescu allies mistrusted us. His appointments in key ministries had been longtime Iliescu opponents dating back to the years Iliescu wielded power in the Ceausescu dictatorship. These ministers assumed that most any deal Iliescu had made in his six years as president must be corrupt, stupid, or unnecessary.

The Tenneco project was among the most visible of these deals, so an ample share of the new government's suspicion was focused our way. Hundreds of permits and approvals related to construction, labor, environment, export licenses and other issues were reopened, reexamined, reversed, or put on ice. Still, we had to keep working on the problem—at the plant site in Buchin, in the halls of government in Bucharest, and through diplomatic and U.S. government channels in Washington. Our elusive objective was to get the support we needed within the Constantinescu government to complete our wood-supply contract.

Despite Emil Constantinescu's appealing rhetoric, it was going to take us a lot more time, money, and effort to overcome the administrative setbacks we would suffer after Iliescu lost the election. In the subsequent three years, we asked ourselves a lot of questions. Had we misjudged the difficulties of transferring our expertise in forest products into an emerging economy? Could we have averted the frustrating setbacks dealt by the "reform" government that considered our ties with Iliescu suspect? Were we diverting excessive amounts of management time into framing continual adjustments to keep our Romania project on course?

Six Points of Caution

After we entered Romania, as well as Poland, China, India, Thailand, and elsewhere, we often examined our calculations and assumptions about building a business in developing markets. Here are six points of caution, some of which apply directly to our Romanian project:

1. *No political situation is as stable as it appears.* The situation is more confusing when the government retains a large investment in the privatized company. Who has the final power? If you negotiated a deal with government officials, you might be back at square one with five different interest groups involved in the bargaining—the labor union, the new business leaders, the government leaders, the government investment managers, and government officials from Washington. This happened to us in Poland simultaneously in two different industries. Also much of the industry in formerly socialist economies is state-controlled. Real wealth often is in the hands of politicians and the cronies who want to hoard it. Even progressive government officials are uncertain and wary about market economies. Decisions made by government officials can be reversed when a state-controlled business is transferred into private hands.

2. *Promises will not always be kept.* Government leaders often make promises to lure outside capital into these economies and for infrastructure development. It is not necessarily a ploy, but reality inevitably means these leaders will not have the resources to meet their ambitions.

3. *Too many companies blindly fall in love with international projects.* You have to be just as cold-eyed about an international project as any other. When a business leader proposes some idea with "strategic value" that might offset some obvious high risk, you have to say, "Quantify this 'strategic value' for me." My guidance: if it

doesn't smell like a good business deal on its own merits, it isn't a good deal. Whether it is in Beijing or Bogalusa, the project has to stand on its own merits.

4. *Enter every project agreement with an exit strategy.* Under what circumstances would we consider this project a failure? How would we be able to pull out at the lowest financial, political, and social cost?

5. *Economies with explosive rates of growth cannot continue at double-digit rates forever.* The Southeast Asian economies—South Korea, Taiwan, Thailand, Malaysia, and Indonesia—were upended when massive debts and the currency crises of 1997 created economic shock waves that lasted into 1999.

6. *Competition is going to increase, and much of it will be generated from your own successes.* Competitors are not always going to be fragmented, confused, or underfinanced. They're going to get smarter and tougher. Access to capital does not differentiate U.S. companies. The world is awash with capital; it goes where it is welcomed, and stays where it is well-treated. The competitive strengths of U.S.-based corporations will continue to be technology and managerial know-how. The often-painful education that U.S.-based corporations acquired by reinventing themselves in the past 20 years has become their most tangible competitive edge.

CHAPTER 6

Project Management: A Capitalist Frontier

"ALL PROJECTS ARE ON TIME AND UNDER BUDGET, UNTIL THEY BEGIN."
Nowhere is that axiom more accurate than in developing countries, where living conditions, culture, and politics make new projects all the more challenging. Here you have to double the time estimate and the anticipated degree of difficulty. The story of what it took to assemble and begin operating Europe's largest sawmill and wood products operation in one of that continent's more remote settings features many heroes, surprises, and setbacks.

The managers who raised Tenneco's flag in Romania were tested often in strange or frustrating circumstances. They had to (1) adapt to local culture, laws, and recent industrial practices; (2) analyze the primitive, fragmented timber and sawmill industry; (3) create programs for construction engineering and operations management; (4) design financial plans and treasury management; (5) frame and execute nimble legal strategies and develop political relationships. And so on.

A bigger challenge was dealing regularly with government officials and bureaucrats who seemed still to function as they had under Ceausescu's communism. Our forces had to outwit, defy, steamroll, cajole, occasionally knuckle under, or otherwise improvise in dealings with hundreds of assorted functionaries in Bucharest and in the local region of the small village, Buchin, that became Tenneco's outpost. Construction plans were approved, then disapproved after work had been completed. Wood supply and road construction contracts were signed, then invalidated by authorities or rival politicians at the highest levels. Worst of all was the dispiriting epidemic of delay and indecision, which a senior government official once suggested was exacerbated by our refusals to pay bribes.

To be sure, it is a common bureaucratic affliction to never part from past practice, or to always seek approval from some higher authority before taking some new action. But this virus was severe in Romania. Under Ceausescu, bureaucrats were jailed or executed for making a "bad" decision. Even in the post-1989 era, most officials continued to fear the potential of harsh retaliation if they acted in some "wrong" way. It was safer to do nothing, or do nothing different than in the past because they incurred less risk of being fired or jailed if an opposing party came to power in the future. Romania had 80 political parties in the mid-1990s, so this fear was a real one. But rigid bureaucrats hold back economic change. Until they overcome these attitudes, the bureaucrats will continue to throttle and frustrate those Romanian political leaders and citizens who seek a more open and modern economy.

Two Complementary Leaders

The two men we selected to develop and manage the Romanian project had complementary skills and experience. Our top U.S.-based executive for Tenneco Packaging's international operations, Paul Griswold, had joined us from Pepsico's international bottling business. At Pepsico, he had arranged and managed deals with local bottlers and distributors of the company's beverages in Turkey, Russia, and several other countries. A New Yorker in his mid-40s and towering at 6 feet 9 inches tall, Griswold had been a starting center on Fordham University's varsity basketball team in the early 1970s. His roommate at Fordham was another hard-nosed kid, named P.J. Carlesimo, the future basketball coach at Seton Hall University and of teams in the National Basketball Association.

"Grizzy," as we call him, is a quick study, very analytical and a shrewd competitor. A math major in his undergraduate years at Fordham, he specialized in finance for his master's degree in business administration from Seton Hall. Before signing on with Pepsico, Grizzy had worked for me and Paul Stecko at International Paper on projects that involved a lot of systems work, as well as on a joint venture with W.R. Grace & Company at a paper mill in Colombia. Grizzy had good instincts for structuring and negotiating deals and agreements. These strengths would be put to the test in Romania and elsewhere in other deals he would pursue and be responsible for in China and the Netherlands.

The leader we put on the ground in Romania was Shawn Kelly. Kelly, in his mid-50s, was a colorful industrial soldier of fortune from Canada who had developed sawmills or wood product manufacturing sites in North America as well as Costa Rica, Brazil, and Argentina for other companies. An industrial engineer by trade, Kelly knew what kind and how much milling and manufacturing machinery was required to make a certain volume of product. What mattered most to Paul Stecko, who hired him for the Romanian assignment, was Kelly's talent for getting results in chaotic conditions that were sure to surround a frontier venture like this one.

Kelly was a blunt-spoken master of the art of the impossible—tongue-lashing or pacifying difficult government officials and vendors; lecturing or stroking his managers and employees; being tough, clever, and fair-minded while bargaining with motley, local dealers to arrange reliable purchasing contracts. Kelly had the instincts more often than not to succeed in situations when the rules of engagement often were up for grabs. We all agreed that he would have a loose, yet defined structure in which to operate. After all, he represented Tenneco in Romania and if he ever did anything outside the limits, Tenneco would have to live it down. He couldn't lie, cheat, steal, physically abuse the employees and so on. And, by all accounts relayed to us at headquarters, he never has.

Kelly also had reasonably good instincts for appropriate times to ignore or defy his bosses and their lieutenants back at Tenneco Packaging's headquarters in Lake Forest, Illinois, north of Chicago. One day, for example, he violated purchasing rules by running up a charge of more than $20,000 for tools and other hardware for the Buchin site. He bought all of this at a Sears department store not far from those very Lake Forest headquarters. Packaging's chief financial officer was aghast later when he scanned the American Express bill that Kelly submitted as part of his expenses. A purchase totaling $20,000 needed executive approval, and Kelly had neither sought it, nor obtained it. But Paul Stecko, aware of Kelly's practical problems in trying to buy quality tools in southwest Romania, approved payment.

The site Griswold and Kelly selected for our Romanian mill was in a remote cornfield near the town of Buchin on the high plains of western Transylvania (Figure 6.1). It was about 100 miles from the Hungarian border to the northwest, 50 miles from Serbia to the southwest and 200 miles from Bucharest to the southeast. Rail access was good, with a major line right next to where we planned to be. The site also was on a north-south, two-lane road that had been well maintained by the military when Romania was part of the Soviet Union's response to NATO, the Warsaw Pact. It was just south

Figure 6.1 Map of Romania.

of the state-owned Mocars furniture plant, and distant enough from Bucharest to make it inconvenient for any opponents who might be inclined to stir up trouble. And it was near abundant beech forests.

The preferred practice in a modernizing industrial country where a Tenneco business was getting started was to find an existing business, then create a joint venture with the owner by making an investment large enough to give us operating control. This limits the amount of equity we put at risk while we learn these local markets. Yet this approach is not so effective in a backward economy where by Western standards the quality of existing plants and equipment is poor and the local management inept. Griswold and Kelly convinced us that Tenneco should be the sole owner of its assets in Romania, and that we should build an entirely self-contained new plant and sawmill.

There were two immediate problems in executing this strategy: (1) by law, no foreigner could own this or any other Romanian land; and (2) before we could do anything at the site we had selected, we would have to negotiate through an intermediary with 28 separate land owners. Mostly these were peasants who had been given control of these parcels after the 1989 revolution.

Briefcases Stuffed with Cash

With a Romanian lawyer as Tenneco's agent, and supported by a Bucharest firm staffed by American and Romanian lawyers, we conducted negotiations over several months before acquiring each land parcel through the agent. In all, we paid the equivalent of more than $350,000 in cash—and lots of it. The largest note in local currency is the 10,000 Romanian lei. At that point, that 10,000 lei note was worth about $1.60, so we actually paid many owners with briefcases stuffed with cash.

Most owners were thrilled with this windfall. A few had it stolen by shameless family members or friends although thievery, robbery, and other crimes were considered uncommon in that part of Romania. Citizens were accustomed to a standard police method of shooting suspects first and asking questions later. This practice apparently had a salutary impact on the low local crime rate in Buchin and

Caransebes. Our people faced virtually none of the physical threats or violence there that always worried Tenneco managers in some parts of Latin America or Asia. Few Romanians trusted banks with their money. The common drill for the lucky ones with excess cash after paying rent and other bills was to convert the cash into German marks. Deutsche marks are a rock-solid currency compared with perpetually devaluing Romanian lei. With their marks in hand, Romanians often then would stuff the cash into their beds or bury it in nearby yards or farm plots.

A few of the Buchin landowners did refuse our first offers and threatened to stall the project. They wanted more money. The Tenneco name was known by some of them and as far as they knew, "teh-NOCK-o" as they pronounced it, was an oil company. We were still in the energy business at that time, but Tenneco's big integrated oil company—involved in everything from exploration and production to refining, transportation, and marketing under the Tenneco shield at service stations—had been sold in 1988. (See Chapter 2.) We, in fact, were operating and drilling a few wells at that time in the Gulf of Mexico through our Houston-based energy businesses, whose activity primarily was natural gas transmission and ranked as one of the largest natural-gas pipeline companies in the United States.

In the entire twentieth century, Romanians probably had never produced oil within 100 miles of this site in Transylvania. Still, these land owners suspected that our plans to build a wood products operation was a ruse. They figured that with Romania's old history as an oil producer, Tenneco's old oil-company image, the presence of a large, state-owned furniture manufacturing plant nearby and the fact that wood processing plants had never done good business there, what we really were up to was some secret oil discovery—on their land! "They truly believed that as soon as they sold the land, we would begin pulling rigs up to the site and start drilling," Griswold said. It took a long time to sort out.

A Squalid Outpost

For nearly a year until just before Christmas, 1996, Kelly's residential base was a grim, mice-and-roach-infested inn called the Hotel

Tibiscum. Its beds were barely a notch better than wood benches, with little padding. The Tenneco contingent eventually grew to 32 people, including spouses and other companions in the group, and nearly filled the place to capacity. Their neighbors were mostly other expatriates from the United States working in the region for Coca-Cola and Delta Air Lines, or Italian construction workers in town to assemble equipment in the plant. The 30-room Tibiscum was the best, and only, hospitality available for visitors to the larger town of Caransebes about 10 minutes down the road from our construction site in Buchin.

During those long months, the hard-driving Kelly served as the Tibiscum's de facto quality manager. Tenneco was generating much of the inn's suddenly steady and rising revenues, and Kelly insisted that the local proprietors improve the service. He bought a new dishwasher, and new linen and laundry facilities. He hounded the owners every day until they and their staff mastered these basic appliances. Phones sometimes were answered. Floors were swept occasionally. Daily laundry was delivered to the right room more often. Some rooms got new lighting, and televisions with satellite-linked Western programming. Kelly's Tenneco crowd ate virtually all its meals at the Tibiscum; a 6 o'clock breakfast, lunch at 11 A.M., and dinner at 6:30 P.M. They soon dined on much better food than the standard Tibiscum fare of fried pork and potatoes—and no vegetables. Supplies of their weekly rations were too big to handle for any food wholesaler in Timisoara, a city of 1 million people little more than an hour's drive away. Their foodstuff had to be trucked in along the nine-hour route from Bucharest.

First Links with the Neighbors

The arrival during 1996 of more Americans and Canadians and, subsequently, construction workers from elsewhere in Europe, aroused a mixture of suspicion and curiosity about Tenneco in Caransebes, Buchin, and other nearby villages. Kelly sought to lower some of this concern in practical ways. Food left over from the dinner meals at the Tibiscum was given away each night to 10 or so families that Kelly selected in an ad hoc rotation system developed to accommodate some nearby neighborhoods. When heavy construction equipment arrived, Kelly diverted a bulldozer to clear two new soccer fields in the town. A British unit of Tenneco Packaging shipped over two large boxes of soccer balls from the United Kingdom that were given to youth sports programs in Caransebes. English-Romanian dictionaries were given to the schools, where in some cases Kelly's daughter taught English to the students in the summer. When the plant began operating in 1997, Kelly periodically donated wood chips for firewood in volumes of five or six tons per delivery.

"I think the local politicians have seen we've become a part of the community," Kelly said. "At Christmas in 1996, the local parish priest joined all of us for a supper. A caroling group drove in from Timisoara to sing carols. They put on a folk dance for us. The local people have tried to repay us for our kindness in different ways, which is much appreciated. There are many people here who love us." Added Griswold: "Meeting people on their terms is very important in foreign operations; you have to work the local community. You have to have those people wanting you to be there."

I had learned this axiom very early in my military career. It was more than a decade after the end of World War II when I was first stationed in Germany as a junior officer. The American military by then had realized it had created many problems for its officers, soldiers, and their families by isolating them from the daily mainstream of German society. So an officer was assigned full-time to what was essentially community relations—attending town hall meetings with the burgermeisters and so on. This made a huge difference.

In a similar way, business executives making investments in poor, underdeveloped economies have to accept that there is going to be a social cost and be willing to pay a price. There is a cost to administering programs like distributing food, making better medical care available, providing social counseling, or supporting youth sports programs. This is one reason why we added 10 percent of "risk premium" to our requirement for potential profits when we first considered going into Romania. We need to do what we can to ameliorate some of the social problems wherever we operate. After all, these are communities where our employees live. You can't just take the key to the plant, lock the gate each day, say this is the place where we work, and forget about everybody on the outside.

Life Adjustments for Westerners

Our managers, all from the United States or Canada, had to make a new life for themselves in Buchin on the remote high plains of Transylvania. In some cases, the transition came easier because spouses and young or adult children came along. A modicum of entertainment was available: TV broadcasts received via satellite from Western Europe, and a video library of 900 movies. Other modern comforts like microwave ovens and telephones were supplied in the ten 1,200-square-foot, prefabricated bungalows that our small management team built in the final four weeks of 1996 as their little Levittown in the Carpathians. Each of the homes had two modest-sized bedrooms, a bathroom, a small living room, and a kitchen. The homes also had hot water for daily showers and cooking, something our Romanian workers considered a luxury. If the Romanians had running hot water in their homes, and most did not, it was only on a few days each week.

Our expatriate neighborhood was less than 100 yards from the always-humming mill on the grounds of the fenced-in Tenneco property. No Dunkin' Donuts™ or Cineplex Odeon™ movie house down the road. No hometown newspaper on the doorstep with last night's sports scores. The closest McDonald's™ restaurant, opened in 1997, was 100 miles away. There was no reliable health care beyond the plant gate; when time neared for a mother to give birth, or for vital surgery for one of our managers, off they went to Vienna where Tenneco had arrangements with some of the finest medical centers in Europe.

It is a peculiar life to most of us: long seven-day workweeks punctuated every 35 or 40 days with two full weeks on holiday. Some members of our team had lived this way for more than 20 years in different countries. They were foreign legionnaires of the global forest products industry, moving on every four or five years for new projects being bankrolled in distant lands.

"We had to get the right mix, a combination of Tenneco expatriates and Canadian engineers on contract who were hoping to become full-time employees," Griswold said. "This was a leadership team capable of building a major project on 28 acres off somewhere in western Romania, much different than what we needed to run a sawmill in Arkansas. They needed to know their jobs and be good at what they do because one screw-up could take the whole team out. And another thing: these people have to work, sleep, and operate together. They will have all the skirmishes, the family feuds, everything within the confines of the project."

In general, Griswold saw the typical American business personality as too brash and forceful to be truly effective in getting new business projects underway in foreign lands. "This is not to bash Americans, but Canadians, with their more easygoing style and work practices, are more easily accepted," he said. "So are the Scottish, maybe more so; I've found they mix very well. We Americans always want to focus down real tight. You can do that occasionally to make a point, to be tough and get a message across. But more than anything you just have to meet people on their own terms. Context is very important."

Good Business for Beech Products

Nothing we were learning about potential demand for the beech wood products was discouraging our team in Buchin from one of their biggest incentives for signing up with Griswold and Kelly: the chance for a substantial bonus. Major retailers in home furnishings and residential construction were lining up for our products. The first shipments left the plant in the first week of October 1997. It was shelving, stair treads, doorframes, wide panels for flooring, furniture, and interior decorating—all of it made from the smoothly sanded and specially treated beech wood. We also exported finished beech lumber from local sawmills. We shipped products to Germany, Taiwan, and China, with dozens of 18-inch square samples going to other prospective customers. There soon would be more orders than we could quickly fill, just as we had anticipated. One big contract was from a single Korean customer, who ordered 52 containers of furniture panels. So the first revenues from Romania were starting to roll in.

What we didn't anticipate was a production bottleneck of our own making. Finished products had to stay twice as long in the huge kilns just outside the plant to get the moisture content in the wood down to levels our customers wanted. We had underestimated the volumes of hot air required to heat the kilns, meaning the boilers that supplied the heat had too little capacity. This increased our costs because the wood had to sit in the kiln for longer periods. Eventually, we brought in more boilers to increase the capacity and get the wood moving through at a faster clip.

Otherwise, the world-class equipment we were pulling together was working well. The used sawmill equipment was bought in Vancouver, British Columbia, at 10 cents on the dollar, then refurbished. The kilns came from Italy. Remanufacturing equipment was purchased in North America, Germany, Italy, and the United Kingdom. The kiln building was shipped from Houston, Texas, and the power equipment came from Atlanta, Georgia. When complete, this would comprise the most modern colossus for making hardwood products in all of Europe. Even so, much of the equipment was portable, designed to be shipped out on quick notice if an ill political wind should blow our way.

Profile of Romanian Workers

For their part, our new Romanian colleagues were going to have to make all of this work on the plant floor. Few spoke English. Most had to adapt to disciplined work routines they had never experienced, such as rigid starting times and limited coffee or lunch breaks. Several had completed high school (95 percent of Romania's adults can read), but very few had the instincts or confidence to solve the simplest uncertainties in the workplace without specific direction. Most came to us from lives at the edge of poverty. Few had homes with running hot water, or televisions. Hardly anyone owned a car, had any savings, or ate an adequate diet. Many suffered from rotting teeth and gums. This was a consequence of a low-calcium water supply, no habit of toothbrushing, and the lack of even intermittent professional care. The continuing dental pain for some was so intense that they worked with bandannas tied tightly across their jawbones to relieve some of the discomfort.

Some of these new Tenneco employees had scrambled for a meager living in the ubiquitous black market of Eastern Europe, even venturing into war-torn Yugoslavia 50 miles away to sell goods in violation of the NATO trade embargo. Most lived in towns and villages in the western half of Romania, as far away as 60 miles or so from our site. It was a culture stew of Romanians, Germans, Hungarians, Jews, and Gypsies. This region became part of Romania only in the twentieth century after hundreds of years largely in Hungarian control. We had to be aware that, at some level, our workers brought with them each day the tensions, prejudices, and suspicions wrought from centuries of these ethnic rivalries.

Two-thirds of the Tenneco work force of 650 at the end of 1997 were women, most between the ages of 20 and 45. Much of the work at the plant then involved sorting and color-matching small pieces of wood that are glued into wide panels. Women enjoyed these faster-paced, sort-and-match tasks far more than men, who tended to prefer working with heavy machinery or going out into the forests cutting trees and hauling timber. Like most Western businesses trying to start in Romania, we were advised that bad work habits and attitudes were ingrained in most people over the age of 35 years. Sleeping on the job. No ability to identify or solve problems independently. No concept of being paid in relation to performance or output. That sort of thing. You don't have to look far in Romania to find an older person who yearns for the old days under Communism. Indeed, high inflation in the 1990s sharply reduced living standards for pensioners.

Under-35 Generation Is More Eager

But the younger generation, more aware through television of the economics, politics, and material prosperity in the West, is more eager to embrace the concept of "you work, you earn." They besieged us with job requests, initially at the rate of 200 per day after we opened the doors in April 1996. In all, we received 7,000 job applications in those 18 months, and another 3,000 in the six months after that. Most of these job seekers were younger than 40 years old. The average age of the first 500 hires was 27. Our average wage was about double the rate in the area, where many factories were rapidly laying people off. We paid $117 per month, not including all of the nonfinancial benefits, or about 850,000 lei per month, after a typical employee's first four weeks on the job (Figure 6.2).

The jobs we brought to Buchin were a godsend for many workers. They provide a regular income at above-average wages, technical training, and hope. One of the standouts among our first Romanian employees was Iulia Ilianu, a woman who typifies the young, talented people in the world's developing economies. Intelligent, focused, enthusiastic, and fluent in English, Iulia completed studies at the large university in Timisoara a few months before we arrived in Buchin. Raised by parents with professional occupations (her father is a dentist, her mother a biologist), she rushed to take advantage of the opportunities she expected to find with us in the workforce of a large global business. She was not disappointed.

When we hired Iulia as an assistant in human resources at the plant in the spring of 1996, she was put in charge of interviewing, screening, and helping to hire from the flood of job applicants.

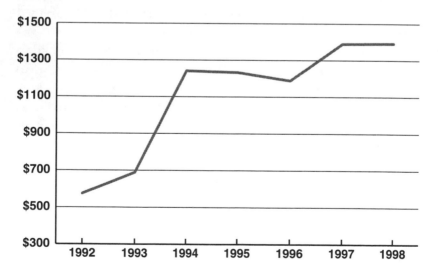

Figure 6.2 Average Nominal per Capita Income in U.S. Dollars for Romania, 1992–1998. (*Source:* WEFA Group/*Eurasia Economic Outlook*).

She was so successful that within 18 months, she was on her way to a conference of Packaging's human resources staff in suburban Chicago. Before her return flight to Europe, she spent a week at Walt Disney World in Orlando with her new husband, Gianni, a Romanian and head environmental and safety engineer for the Tenneco plant in Buchin. "I can't tell you how happy I was to have a chance to go to the United States," she said, sitting in her small office just inside the main gate of the Buchin plant. "I had been in Hungary and Poland, but never a Western country. This was something I wanted to do for my whole life, I can tell you that!"

Only 26 years old when she joined us, Iulia (pronounced YOOL-yah) became one of the most public faces of Tenneco management to the local community, perhaps at times even more so than Shawn Kelly. As each Romanian was hired, Iulia attempted to make the job requirements as clear as possible before the person's first day on the job.

Teaching Attributes of Leaders

On a wall near her desk, she hung in large print, in English and Romanian, the Tenneco Leadership Behaviors that we encourage in our employees all over the world. The list includes these guiding points: motivate your people, hold them accountable for superior results, face reality, communicate what is expected and why, listen to and involve your people, enlist cooperation, build effective teams, and so on. She covers each point with every new employee and explains how that person might apply the guidance in a specific job. To send the message that the company takes these values seriously and rewards people who champion them throughout the Tenneco organization, even Romanians in Transylvania, she gives each person a wallet-sized list of the Leadership Behaviors.

"We want to change the mentality, the concept of work in Romania," she said. "It is not easy compared with the way Romanians are used to. Many are used to going to a job to stay, to spend the day. Now they are realizing that when they go to this job, they go to work. And they realize that if you work, you are compensated. You have opportunity for advancement. You have opportunity for a better life."

During the day, Iulia often put those Leadership Behaviors into action through her own intuitive drill of Management by Wandering

Around. She goes into the plant, the wood-stacking yards outdoors, or the cafeteria on alert for rumors, gossip, or early warning signs of festering tensions. She is a Romanian in the management roles of counselor, adviser, and interpreter.

Unexpected Consequence: Wife Beating

One issue that caught us by surprise was wife beating. Iulia, Shawn Kelly, and other staff members noticed a few women appearing on the job with bruises on their arms and faces, or missing work a day or two at a time. Some had been hiding facial bruises with cosmetics. These bruises were, we learned, the result of beatings by often idle, unemployed, drunken husbands who awaited the women at the end of their workday. Some of these husbands felt threatened. They were embarrassed to be making a smaller (or no) wage. They had lost what they perceived as their status and authority. Their wives and, in some cases, even their children were less dependent. And some men began to wonder whether the cosmetics and new clothes their wives were buying were making them more attractive to other men.

One woman was beaten so badly, she was hospitalized for several days. She was forced to quit her job with us, divorce her husband, and take her two children to live with her parents in a distant town. "She was very, very sad to do this," Iulia said. "She was a good worker, very happy." One man sent a signed, handwritten death threat to his wife at the plant one day; it was handed to the local police.

"A lot of this is related to the mentality of men and women in Romania, and that cannot be changed so fast," Iulia explained. "After working here for so many hours, usually 11 hours a day, the women go home and are expected to take care of the kids, take care of the man, wash the clothes, prepare the food . . . everything! But when they get home they are tired and cannot do all of this. So sometimes the men get angry and sometimes they hit them." Moreover, Tenneco employees—whether men or women—usually have two benefits each day that might stir envy among spouses, other family members, or friends: a hot meal at midday and a hot shower before heading home. Medical and dental care also is far superior to anything available to most Romanians in the region.

On occasion, some of these battered women approached Tenneco supervisors with a desperate question, "Would it be possible for my husband to take my job?" The answer in the first few years was no because men usually were less adept at these specific jobs. We did change the basic work schedule to four days a week, from five. This gives them a work cycle of four days on, and four days off. We also sought counsel with local religious clerics and inquired with national politicians in Bucharest about possible legislative remedies. In both cases, the responses could be summarized simply as, "What is the problem that needs to be fixed? This is the way it is with a husband and wife in Romania." Local hospitals were only slightly more sympathetic.

These cultural and sociological problems raise a fundamental and, essentially, timeless business and philosophical issue: How far should modern industrial companies go in applying what in advanced technological societies are considered world-class standards and practices in vastly different economies and cultures? What happens when those standards and practices disrupt traditional values and relationships in those cultures? Who decides whether it is in the best interests of those cultures to adapt new ways? And, when it is relevant, who gauges and who bears the financial, political, and social cost of that change?

Our response to the wife-beating problem changed by 1999. We downplayed the benefits of Tenneco employment, partly because those benefits are more obvious than ever in the local communities. At the same time, we put more energy into educating the work force and their families about the long-term benefits of an improved living standard in the region. We were more flexible about employing multiple members of the same family, including husbands. We also were more attentive to possible signs of abuse, and established a care center at the sawmill site. It was doing a better job in caring for beating victims than the local hospitals.

Steady Job with Good Wages Matters Most

The process to hire the right people, then support them as they learn their job, kept turnover at low levels, as well as the hard fact that the area's high unemployment is estimated at as much as 80 percent. Ten percent of the work force left within the first year for a variety of reasons; they turned out not to be qualified, they didn't like the work schedules, or they broke work rules. The toughest ones included safety practices and theft. Theft of construction materials, tools, and other items became a problem before the Buchin site began operating in 1996. Before anyone was hired permanently for operations, Kelly laid down the law of zero tolerance. Anyone caught taking anything from the site, even if it was a tea bag from the cafeteria, would be fired on the spot.

After a few months of operation, after our workers had gotten a few monthly paychecks, our Romanian laborers were confirming that for them a Tenneco job was something special. Sandu Stoti, then 38 years old and a forklift operator at the plant, said that the big gossip about Tenneco making the rounds in cafes and shops in the nearby towns and villages was our pay and working conditions.

"Wages is the main problem" for most people, he said. "Everyone is interested in how much they can make. The salary here is at a premium that you never can get at another company." Most employed men in the region still worked for the government, making an average of $80 to $100 per month. Sandu said he was working seven days a week at the Tenneco sawmill, 11 hours a day, and glad to do it. He had worked for six years as a forklift operator at Mocars before being laid off in the early 1990s. He had tried for a few years but could not make much of a living as a street merchant, selling electrical parts, shoes, and clothes in Caransebes, so he peddled some of those goods on the black market in Serbia.

He and his wife had two sons, ages 16 and 13. Like most Romanians, the boys were getting fleeting images of Western living standards from Hollywood movies and other popular fare that Ceausescu had banned but were now available on Romanian television. For Sandu, this was bittersweet. His sons, he said, "probably have the idea that we don't have the possibility to make their life the same as the other children they see" on television.

"I am trying hard to work much more, to get more money, in order to show them that I can do more for them," he said. "Otherwise, there will probably be a time when they will say, 'you didn't do too much for us.' There was a time when we lived very bad because we didn't have enough money. Everything is so expensive. The older our boys are, the more they need, and the more they want. Our work is focused on them. We do everything for them." He was hoping within a year to have saved enough money to buy a bicycle for his younger son, and a second-hand car for his older one. He also was planning to add for the first time a bathroom, with toilet, sink and hot-and-cold shower, to his home.

Sandu was one of a few hundred people we hired who had worked in the nearby state-owned furniture factory, Mocars, where typical monthly pay was less than half of what we were paying. Mocars was a grim setting out of Charles Dickens dating to the 1880s, a place reputedly with few modern industrial safety practices. Some of our new employees had witnessed co-workers there killed or maimed in violent accidental encounters with the old machinery. Mocars, once broadly subsidized by Ceausescu's Ministry of Labor, also offered little job security. Its headcount was in a downward spiral, from 3,600 in 1992 to 200 in 1998.

Tina Padure, 38, who was hired after working 17 years at Mocars, was quickly promoted to supervisor on the sorting and finishing lines. She found much to her liking. Tenneco's modern machinery required much less physical exertion than in her previous job. Tenneco provided better technical and safety training and our work processes were more efficient and orderly. There was the daily meal, transportation and safety equipment, and the better pay. She summarized all of this quite simply. She and others wanted jobs at Tenneco because, she said, "we hope that coming to Tenneco will be better for us."

Romanians Want a More Open Economy

The Romanian people generally have been far ahead of the bureaucrats in wanting their society and economy to open up. They have demonstrated this view repeatedly at the ballot box, at local town meetings, and in their desire and willingness to work for us and for other global corporations. At one local meeting that could have resulted in fines and construction delays for us as the Buchin project took shape, local residents spoke out against the government and backed us against regulators who had refused to sign construction permits. Kelly recalled: "A couple of ladies got up and said, 'Look, our sons and daughters have to leave our community now to try to find work. Here is a large company coming in that wants to hire them. Now our families don't have to break up.'"

In an indirect way, we also helped modernize practices of Romanian cement makers. Most buildings are made of concrete, so this change had far-reaching benefits. The change was very simple; we taught the concrete mixers how to winterize the batteries that helped power their mixers. Romanian concrete suppliers had always shut down for the winter, for four months in most places. With batteries that could function in subfreezing weather, the mixers could work through cold days. "This was simply taking an existing capability we had and showing it to them," Griswold said. "It's that old saying, 'You don't know what you don't know.' In all kinds of international business operations, you need to lead by example. Role modeling is enormously important."

Taking on the Bureaucrats

Despite these small forward steps, Kelly had to fight many battles with Romanian officials over construction, safety, electrical power, and other issues. The local fire marshal protested once about all the structural steel that was framing the new mill. Not fireproof, he said. On another visit, he objected to the on-site fire truck and ambulance, both of which we had flown in from Tenneco mill locations in the United States. He asked, how did we know the truck or ambulance would start in an emergency? Throughout the plant, we had sensors to detect sparks built into our extensive ventilation and piping systems. The fire marshal asked, how do you know this will work?

One day, Kelly blew up at him. Kelly figured they were looking for any angle to shut the project down, if only for a while, just to flex their power against these foreigners. Kelly said, "If you shut me down, or you won't let any of my workers in, I'll bring in two jumbo 747s with 600 workers on board! They'll all be North Americans, and we'll all watch you sons-of-bitches on the other side of our fence. You're just a bag of wind. I'm going to kick you off this site if you don't shut your mouth!"

Months later, the fire marshal came again with stone-faced deputies by his side. The plastic-coated electrical wiring troubled him. It wasn't fireproof. The burly Kelly protested. This was high-quality wiring made by Pirelli, the Italian manufacturer, and standard in similar industrial projects in Germany. Doesn't matter, the fire marshal replied. Has to be fireproof. That's the law. "What law?" Kelly wanted to know. "Show me the law!" Kelly had seen bureaucrats pull this bluff all across the Americas: meet any resistance with an assertion about "the law." Kelly persisted, offering his visitor the opportunity to sample "all of the wiring you want," and handed him several strands. Then he invited the official to a lunch in the employee cafeteria. There, with none of the fire marshal's aides nearby, the Romanian tossed the wires into the trash. "I don't need this." And that was it.

In operating the business Kelly took on the role of an entrepreneurial owner/manager in a market economy. Many Romanian officials believe they must scrutinize any significant decision by a business and to find reasons to *reduce* your activity, not expand it. On occasion, Kelly would yield. The Tenneco project is in a designated earthquake region, a concern many Romanian officials take seriously. More than 1,500 people were killed in a 1977 quake that devastated Bucharest. The huge death count embarrassed the Ceausescu government. Construction standards were stiffened, with the practical effect of forcing builders to use more concrete.

Our plans at Buchin included a three-story, wood frame administration building with little concrete. It was not long until a needed construction permit was blocked. Kelly conceded this time, agreeing to add concrete stairwells at each end of the 200-foot-long building for more stability. "Our original plans for the administration building meet safety codes in North America," he said. "I'm not saying we're right all of the time, but I do choose certain areas where I'm not going to give. By not giving, you have to be right. This one was not worth a fight."

Others were. Romania's state-owned electrical power company, Renel, gave Kelly some major headaches. To hook our site up to their power grid, Renel declared that it would have to install what is called a T connection. They wanted $700,000 for the connection, their estimated costs to build the connection three miles from our site so that it could be hidden from the view of local townspeople and travelers. Renel also was irritated that Kelly had not cleared his operating plans with them long before construction began.

Kelly was angry and would not pay. We have other options, he said. We don't need you. We want the T connection to the Renel grid built on our site. We could build our own boiler unit as an in-house power plant. We could bring in our own power generators. We could do all of this ourselves and not pay $2 million a year to Renel to supply electricity. Didn't they get it? They were running the risk of losing the biggest customer they might ever have. Fuming, Kelly left the meeting. Aides at the American embassy told Kelly later that the stunned Renel officers said it was the first time any American businessman had ever walked out on them.

That didn't matter to Kelly. "Most anywhere else in the world, the power companies are at our beck and call, 'What can we do for you?'" Kelly told the embassy. "These guys would rather set up roadblocks and artificial deadlines. They don't look at the fact that we are going to employ 600 people or more. The concept of the time value of money, and of new jobs, income, and revenue is just not there."

Scaling Back

By the first months of 1998, we had kept open the spigot for Tenneco investment in Romania for more than two years, exceeding $40 million. We still were not generating a profit, and had growing doubts that we would make much headway toward our specific goal of reaching $30 million in operating income that year in Romania. As the year played out, our inability to consistently buy high quality beech timber from the local woodsmen and lumberjacks gradually shifted our ambitions to narrowing potential losses. We were unable to export many high-grade wood panels to the construction companies in Western Europe and Japan who were willing to pay the high prices that translated into a handsome profit. We had the solution to the problem in our original plans: Build roads into the regions with the highest quality beech timber and take greater control of the woodcutting.

During this period, economic conditions in Romania reversed course. The gradual improvement that began showing up in 1993 statistics now evaporated. After Constantinescu's rise to power, gross domestic output declined 6.6 percent in 1997, and another 5.0 percent in 1998, essentially wiping out gains from the previous three years (Figure 6.3). Living standards weakened, with real private consumption falling by 8.6 percent in 1998 from the 1996 level. Inflation soared by 152 percent in 1997, and 43 percent in 1998 (Figure 6.4).

This brought us to a crossroads early in 1999. Four years since we had begun our construction in Buchin and our negotiations in Bucharest, we confronted this question: With nearly $50 million invested, were we willing to ante up tens of millions more to retrieve the high-quality beech timber we needed for a chance to achieve a big payoff in the highest profit beech market? Two principles led our decision making. One, the classic definition of a fanatic is someone

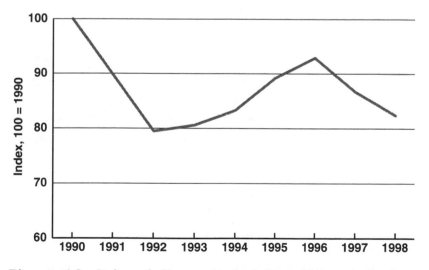

Figure 6.3 Index of Change in Real Gross Domestic Product in Romania, 1992–1998. (*Source:* WEFA Group/*Eurasia Economic Outlook*).

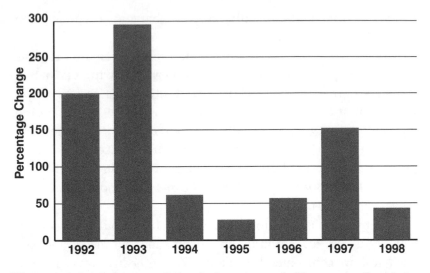

Figure 6.4 Consumer Price Index. Annual Change in Romania, 1992–1998. (*Data Source:* WEFA Group/*Eurasia Economic Outlook*).

who redoubles his efforts as he loses sight of his goals. And two, don't blindly fall in love with international projects.

Early in 1999, we scaled back panel production to roughly 25 percent of capacity, essentially eliminating manufacturing of our two highest quality grades. We laid off about 150 workers, mostly women on the panel production line, reducing total employment at the site to 450. We continued to mill mid-grade quality beech lumber in varying dimensions, as well as logs used for furniture veneer, and ship those products to Europe and Asia.

These changes were underway before the crisis in Kosovo began in March, but the 11-week war clearly wounded the Romanian economy as well. NATO's destruction of major bridges across the Danube, Yugoslavia's northern border with Romania, brought commerce to a halt along Europe's vital industrial waterway. A World Bank study indicated that the six nations surrounding Yugoslavia would lose on average as much as an additional 4 percentage points in economic output in 1999.

Meanwhile, reform in Romania is hard to find. Even what appears to be positive action can be discouraging when the facts emerge. For example, 70 percent of the loans at the largest bank in Romania, with

25 percent of commercial loans, were declared nonperforming early in 1999. *The Financial Times* reported (on February 23, 1999) that Bancorex, based in Bucharest, had lent hundreds of millions of dollars prior to 1998 to trading and import-export companies, many of them operated "by former members of communist Romania's intelligence service, the hated Securitate."

By mid-summer, our operations were close to breaking even, excluding our capital costs. At that point, we began actively searching in the European forest products industry for a partner to acquire a significant interest in the plant, or perhaps a buyer for the entire project in Buchin. The market for prime Romanian beech panels remained appealing, but we were not going to put any more big money into supplying it by ourselves. With the initial skepticism within the company about the high-risk project now proven correct, the board of directors properly was seeking some return of the considerable capital already committed.

More Points of Caution

During a particularly difficult stage of the Italian campaign during World War II, General George Patton was approached by some of his officers. They complained about the hardships their soldiers faced. "What would they rather be doing," Patton said to them, "shoveling manure in Missouri or making history here with the Seventh Army?"

Our investment in Romania carried a lot of risk. It was the largest of its kind by a U.S. company in an economy that had been Stalinist and stagnant for the last half of the twentieth century. Making history is never easy, as Patton pointed out. If our presence subsides, or ends, soon, many of our Romanian colleagues will find themselves prepared to identify and seize new opportunities ahead. They confronted difficult conditions along with us, and they are at the forefront of making the new history that most Romanians want for themselves and their country.

Leaders cannot avoid risk and, certainly, they should be evaluated on how their collective risks play out. This reminds me of a simple, but harrowing combat lesson I received of the necessity at times of being forced to weigh trade-offs of mortal risks and make an instant choice.

When I was a high-ranking officer in Vietnam in 1969, I often spent hours explaining to my colleagues future movements of U.S. and allied South Vietnamese troops in an area near the demilitarized zone at North Vietnam's southern border. It was a dangerous place, and raiding North Vietnamese soldiers occasionally turned it into a war zone, usually at night.

One night, just after darkness fell, as the helicopter I was seated in lofted upward, a map detailing the size and movements of our troops suddenly soared with a gust of wind out one side. I ordered the pilot to immediately get that chopper back on the ground. "We're not leaving without that map!" I said. My pilot complied, knowing that the loud sounds of the chopper might already be drawing North Vietnamese mortar fire or foot soldiers in our direction. In a few minutes that seemed like hours, I had the map in hand and we were aloft again. Yet when we were no more than fifty feet into the air, a volley of orange-flaring missiles speeded toward us. One caught and damaged the tail rudder blade. The crash landing injured neither of us, but the helicopter could not fly. We had to find our way back to safety on foot. In a few hours, we found our way to a dirt road and heard friendly voices in the distance moving our way. So the story ended with us temporarily losing a helicopter (it was recovered later), but retrieving a map that in the enemy's hands could have led to death or crippling wounds for hundreds of soldiers of the command. It was a decision I never regretted even while knowing how close my pilot and I might have been to our own deaths.

In a few years, our abbreviated Romanian operations should return an adequate profit while continuing to employ 400 workers. In still another few years, should Romanian politicians find more unanimity and urgency in policies to develop their immensely valuable beech forests, the plant could operate at full employment, generate abundant foreign currency, and reap attractive profits. Those chapters can still be written, but for now, our Romanian legacy bears the scars of an emerging market risk not rewarded.

Here are the broad conclusions we have drawn from our experiences in Romania and elsewhere about managing a significant project in a distant developing country.

Appropriate Initial Investment

Carefully consider the optimal amount for initial investment. In 20-20 hindsight, the plans for the Romania project were too ambitious, too optimistic. The appealing economics of assembling and shipping panels made from Romania's high-quality beech persuaded us from the outset to build a large sawmill and manufacturing plant. This required a large initial investment to get the plant operating, raising the pressure to generate higher revenues to cover our costs and produce the rate of return we wanted. We also had a steeper learning curve for operations than we anticipated. We had the expertise in sawmill operations. Still, it took us several months before we could adjust to handling the varying grades of beech timber, which our managers previously had not encountered.

A more cautious approach would have been to begin where we are now, operating as a sawmill for beech timber. The initial cash investment would have been lower, with less machinery, simpler processes, and fewer employees. It also should have reduced the disproportionate amount of executive and management time the project has required. We should have had fewer political and bureaucratic approvals after establishing high-level contacts with government leaders.

Limited Human Resources

Corporations from the modern industrialized west enter projects in developing countries with limited human resources. Most U.S.-based companies are woefully short of managerial talent, except for those that have been active in global markets for decades. Many times I've looked at attractive global investments. We have the capital, the technology, the machinery, the markets, and the distribution. We just don't have the right people, so we have to pass on the opportunity.

Recruiting local managers to run a project usually is a mistake. Local managers are more unprepared than people with experience in modern industrial economies. They know the language and the culture, but often they lack sound judgment on routine trade-offs that come with running a business. Even the best-qualified locals in a project usually prefer having a more experienced manager in charge, which surprised us. The locals figure they learn more rapidly that way, the business has a better chance to succeed, and the new jobs added to the local economy become more lasting and stable. As they learn necessary management skills and the business issues, they will be able to begin running these projects and the expatriates will move out.

The developing countries are not prepared either. The head of a prestigious business school in the northeastern United States estimates that China needs to graduate 300,000 MBAs per year to meet the development goals for their economy. China now is graduating about 1,000 MBAs a year. In the United States, the figure is about 100,000 a year.

Unintentional Consequences

The law of unintended consequences from introducing change into a culture always applies. Generally, workers in our plants and government officials in developing countries have much different and more complex agendas and goals than we do. In many countries, there is no concept of profit. A decade after the fall of Ceausescu, this continues to be true of many high-ranking Romanian officials. But it is not just Romania. We see it in India and China, too.

U.S. companies inevitably want to bring in new technology to increase productivity by reducing input costs, meaning employees. It is especially difficult to reduce factory head count in formerly socialist economies like China and India, but Western Europe is also a challenge. Social benefits there are the big issues, much more than wages. For example, in Germany, after months of negotiations with government and union officials, Case Corporation finally agreed to pay approximately $170,000 per employee to close a large plant in Neuss. In countries with a long history of a paternal socialist government, all profit is seen as fair game for the welfare state.

Efficiency-minded businesses too often begin operating in direct conflict with some of the most cherished or deeply inbred values of these countries. Wherever you operate, you have to come to terms with the indigenous value systems, or eventually you are going to fail. Sometimes these values will violate your sense of justice and human rights. The profusion of wife beating was a disturbing consequence of the improved pay and working conditions we brought to economically depressed Romania. The same problem has been reported throughout Central Europe, as male unemployment rose and women attained more independence and money in new political democracies and new market economies.

Stability—*the absence of change*—turns out to be one of the most prized values in developing countries. The basic elements of Schumpeter's "creative destruction" are the most threatening aspects of global capitalism in developing countries where jobs and stability are welcome, and productivity and profits are rarely understood. The American notions of downsizing, reengineering, and restructuring are inherently destabilizing in these cultures. Many executives and government officials in the West are showing a tendency to lose their optimism as predictable circumstances of resistance have occurred. We must make pragmatic and necessary adjustments in each situation. We continue to make ours in Romania. But we should not neglect the long-term perspective. American companies have an unprecedented opportunity to make economic history, by bringing more modern technologies and improved living standards to millions of people.

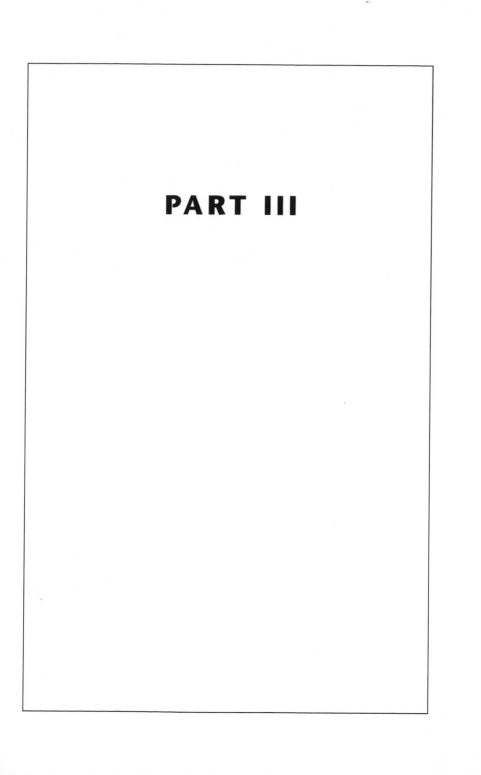

PART III

CHAPTER 7

Public Policy: Winning in Congress

BETWEEN 1993 AND 1996, TENNECO MOUNTED TWO RELATED campaigns to change policies favored by the Navy, the Pentagon, Congress, and at times the White House. We naturally were acting in Tenneco's interests in each case. But our ability to weave our corporate cause into broader political and economic policy issues under debate in Washington was a key factor in our success.

Every business has many constituent groups: customers, employees, investors/owners, suppliers, communities, government officials, and the news media are considered the most universal. Our objective was to approach each of these groups as a distinct set of customers, each with its own set of needs, wants, and traditions. We couldn't ever give away the store, but we wanted to be respected by each group as professional and effective. Over the long haul, this reputation is a huge strategic asset for companies that invest in achieving and maintaining it. In Washington, we were quickly developing the talent and the tools we needed in 1993. We did it by hiring people with a sophisticated understanding of federal government processes, and through existing relationships we had with many elected and appointed people holding the power that controlled those processes.

We knew from the start that these campaigns would stir up adversaries among existing business, political, and government allies. We also knew as Tenneco's new leaders that we would be putting our managerial judgments and political instincts on trial. The direct role I took would enable me to capitalize on Tenneco's size and prestige and, if I were successful enough, to enhance that prestige and the company's reputation. There also was the risk that any highly publicized failure would have the opposite effect on the company—and on my career.

An Aircraft Carrier and More Submarines

The goal of our campaigns was to ensure an appropriate flow of business to Tenneco's Newport News Shipbuilding. The first effort was to win approval from divided Navy leaders and uncertain White House and Congress policy makers for the federal contract to build a new nuclear-powered aircraft carrier, the largest warship in the Navy fleet. This would be the "product" with the highest price tag of any program in the federal budget, and the biggest sales contract of the decade for Tenneco. The second part was to reverse a Navy directive to force Newport News Shipbuilding out of the submarine business. This was a staggering prospect for the nation's largest shipyard, which generated about 40 percent of its revenues and more than 10,000 jobs from submarine construction activity during the peak of the Cold War in the 1980s.

When I came to Tenneco, it was obvious that military shipbuilding did not have the prospects to meet our new criteria for Tenneco's future growth. The Cold War had ended. The Soviet Union was breaking apart, and its military was in shambles. Defense spending in the United States was under siege by the Democratic-controlled Congress and by the new Clinton White House. Even most Republicans, except for a few outspoken defense hawks, agreed that the United States could remain the world's lone military superpower with fewer troops, bases, and materiel, including warships.

We had to think hard about how we could get Newport News back into the tough business of global commercial shipbuilding. Prospective competitors in Korea, Norway, Japan, and elsewhere were heavily subsidized by their governments, but we had seen tantalizing estimates for a significant rise in worldwide demand for ships soon after the millennium. Meanwhile, we had to make certain we entered bids for and won every Navy contract possible for Newport News.

Pressures to rein in expanding federal budget deficits were rising. Curbing the deficit, which reached a historic high of $292 billion in 1992, was the cutting edge of Ross Perot's populist attacks against George Bush. In November, Perot's candidacy caused Republicans to split their votes between him and Bush, allowing Clinton to claim the White House with only 43 percent of the votes cast, and just 24 percent of 187 million eligible voters. The Clinton victory inspired a brief revival of political debate over a "peace dividend," but this soon faded because there really was only one mandate from the 1992 election. With $3 trillion added in just 12 years to the total federal debt of $4.1 trillion, it was long past time for Congress and the White House to limit government spending.

The budget cutters' prime focus was on defense spending, so the future of Newport News Shipbuilding was among our most urgent concerns. White House and Congressional approval to begin funding for the next aircraft carrier was absolutely critical for the shipyard and for Tenneco. A new carrier would represent by far the biggest single order any of our businesses would compete for in the 1990s, more than $4 billion. Combined with the restructuring and prospective sale of the Case farm and construction equipment business, securing that contract for the new carrier amounted to the highest priority for keeping Tenneco's recovery on course.

Sentiment to Delay Building a New Carrier

Early in 1993, Newport News was anticipating a commitment by Congress within the next two years to spend a total of $4.4 billion for the new aircraft carrier that this shipyard expected to build. It expected to see some of that money in the fiscal 1994 budget so that purchase orders could be made for steel and other parts for construction. By late spring, though, first signals from President Clinton's Pentagon about its priorities for ship construction in the approaching fiscal year were not promising. In fact, the outlines of a potentially disastrous situation for Tenneco and Newport News Shipbuilding were starting to take shape.

We learned that some senior Pentagon and Navy officers planned to delay a request for initial funding for the new carrier for eight years, to 2001. The Navy's view was that the hundreds of companies involved in assembling, making parts, and supplying services for nuclear-powered submarines and aircraft carriers would not suffer from that funding delay as long as they continued work on nuclear-powered submarines.

This would be a blow to Tenneco and Newport News Shipbuilding. Delayed funding for the new carrier would create a huge problem by straining cash flow and further crimp our resources for rebuilding the company. For Newport News, losing $3 billion of revenue for the next seven years could trigger a retrenchment in operations to the lowest level since the 1930s. Meanwhile, it would be a boon to Newport News's lone rival in nuclear shipbuilding, Electric Boat. Navy submarine contracts would remain on schedule through the 1990s at Electric Boat, the only shipyard other than Newport News capable of making submarines. Based since 1900 in Groton, Connecticut, Electric Boat is a division of one of the nation's largest defense constructors, the General Dynamics Corporation.

In favoring Electric Boat, the Navy's priority was to reserve a portion of its share of the Pentagon budget to complete construction of the first two Seawolf submarines and add a third Seawolf. The Seawolf was a powerful, advanced technology invention for Cold War intelligence gathering. Its political support had faltered under George Bush. Moreover, high cost overruns on the first two Seawolf prototypes, from a projected initial budget of $1.5 billion to actual costs exceeding $2.5 billion, had aroused growing political opposition to the program. Then, too, the Seawolf's ultimate military mission—to outrun and destroy Russian submarines armed with ballistic missiles—had withered with the collapse of the Soviet Union.

Undaunted, and in addition to seeking full funding for three Sea-wolf submarines, the Navy advocated a $70 billion program for 30 so-called New Attack Submarines. These were to be faster, smaller, more versatile, and less costly than the Seawolf, the Navy's prescription for the United States to control any suboceanic foes well into the next century. The first two Seawolves were under construction at Electric Boat.

Submariners are a strongly unified brotherhood within the Navy. They share both a heroic legacy and an impressive record for innovative technology and decades of superb safety performance. Brought to life by Admiral Hyman G. Rickover to track and counter Soviet naval power during the Cold War, nuclear-powered submarines were for four decades among the West's more secretive and effective weapons of military intelligence gathering and counterespionage. More than 170 were built before new orders slowed to a near-halt during the Bush Administration. Newport News was a respected participant in the submariners' military legacy, innovative technology, and safety record, but it could not compete with Electric Boat for emotional ties among Navy officers who served on submarines. All the submarine officers were trained at the Navy base near Electric Boat. As a result, submariners' budget priorities had an edge over aircraft carriers as the new administration debated policies about future Navy force strength in the spring of 1993.

The Pentagon's inclination to put submarine funding ahead of a new carrier also was politically consistent with candidate Bill Clinton's preelection policies. Clinton's view then was that the Navy could get along in the post-Cold War era with 10 carriers, down from 14. To implement it, the Navy would have to retire five aging carriers during the next 15 years before a new one would be needed in 2008. Since it takes six or seven years to add a new carrier, from the first orders of steel and other materials to the final sea trials under Navy command, construction on a new carrier would not be necessary until 2001.

Yet there were many military, budgetary, and industrial management issues suggesting this was a very bad idea. First, Navy statistics showed that morale problems rise and reenlistment rates fall for carrier crews when carrier missions away from home ports extend beyond six months. With fewer carriers, mission lengths were likely to rise. Second, the Navy would have more difficulty fighting two major regional conflicts at the same time.

Third, Newport News estimated it would save the Navy $500 million if it began construction in 1995, compared with 2001. Much of the savings would come from not having to recruit and train thousands of skilled workers after the turn of the century to replace those at the shipyard and at all carrier suppliers who would leave for other jobs after losing work on a postponed carrier. At Newport News alone, more than 130 different types of welding specialists were needed to build a nuclear-powered carrier. Also, hundreds of construction and supplier facilities would not have to be mothballed.

Defense Secretary Les Aspin, the Undersecretary of Defense for Acquisition and Technology, John Deutch, and other senior Pentagon policy makers faced a difficult choice. The political mood in Congress might allow enough money to begin funding a third new Seawolf submarine or a new nuclear-powered aircraft carrier, but not both. And there were fewer federal dollars available for building new ships in 1993.

With these facts before us, we had to act. In taking on our biggest customer, the Navy, as well as the Pentagon, the White House, and many members in Congress, we would be putting on the line a huge amount of our credibility as Tenneco's leaders. This would be especially true inside Tenneco, where failure in this high-cost, high-stakes campaign would be very visible and damaging for us from the shop floors to the boardroom.

Backroom Setback by a
Rival in Submarines

We soon set about doing everything we could to make sure the President, senior White House policy makers, key members of Congress, and, of course, the military budget drafters at the Pentagon understood why funding for the new carrier should remain on track, and not be delayed. We also organized a very public attack against the Navy. It would be like pouring salt into an open wound. Emotions between executives at Newport News and their counterparts in the Navy still smoldered two years after Newport News had sued the Navy—unsuccessfully.

The lawsuit was prompted by Navy maneuvering that persuaded Congress to rescind its decision to award a $2 billion contract for a second Seawolf class submarine to Newport News, and give the contract instead to Electric Boat. That was a bitter pill for Newport News, for two reasons. First, Congress's reversal on the second Seawolf was a testament to Electric Boat's superior political moxie and resources in Washington. And, second, the upshot of the decision was that Newport News would be shut out of new submarine orders for at least another five years.

We had no choice but to push hard to get Newport News into some future submarine program at the same time as we campaigned for the new aircraft carrier. The Congress also had to come up with an answer to this very complex problem: More than solely submarines and aircraft carriers, what is the future role of all naval power in an era when the United States stood as the world's lone superpower? Moreover, what is the appropriate size and strength of the total U.S. armed forces in this new geopolitical era?

As this analytical work and debate unfolded privately in the first months of the new administration, interest groups jockeyed to influence the Defense Department's conclusions. Air Force officials argued that a few B-2 stealth bombers (at $2 billion per plane) would be a better buy than a new aircraft carrier, and that B-52 bombers based in Florida could launch deadly cruise missiles in the Middle East as effectively as any carrier-based fleet of warplanes. When completed and approved by Defense Secretary Aspin, the Pentagon's "bottom-up" review would become part of the Administration's federal budget proposals for the 1994 and 1995 fiscal years. Aspin expected to announce the results by September 1, a month before Clinton's official budget proposal would go to Capitol Hill. We had to scramble, even though the debate on the defense budget ultimately would not be resolved for another nine months.

In June, the submarine admirals gathered for the Navy Submarine League's annual conference along with the leaders of the submarine construction industry. Their message for Pentagon policy makers and Congress was to continue funding to complete a second Seawolf submarine. The admirals also wanted to preserve investments in the industrial equipment and skilled labor for building submarines. Even though the Navy conceded that a third Seawolf no longer had a practical military purpose, the Navy wanted it built at Electric Boat. Their logic was that this was the only way to keep the submarine industrial base alive until construction on a new submarine class could begin in 1998.

Attacking Our Biggest Customer

Knowing this spectacle was taking place, we seized an opportunity to challenge the submarines-first crowd within the Navy hierarchy and attract some valuable news coverage for our differing views. We invited ourselves onto the site of the League conference, a hotel in Alexandria, Virginia, for an unusual news conference in which we signaled that we were prepared to fight for Newport News's stake in future submarine work as well as for the new carrier. At the conference and in many one-on-one interviews with reporters, Mike Walsh and Pat Phillips, president of Newport News Shipbuilding, protested what we saw as a plan to elbow aside our proposal to fund the new carrier and end our 35 years in building submarines. Mike asserted it would be more economical for taxpayers if new aircraft carriers and submarines were built in one location, Newport News, because the set of skills to build a carrier includes 80 percent of the skills, technology, and supplies to build a submarine.

In fact, we estimated that if the next carrier and next four submarines were built at Newport News, the savings compared with splitting the work between the Virginia and Connecticut yards would be between $1.5 billion and $2 billion. As Mike told the reporters, the Pentagon's plan to separate future construction of nuclear-powered submarines from nuclear-powered aircraft carriers "defies logic, common sense and the facts." He added: "We are apprehensive it will produce a self-fulfilling conclusion, and the conclusion will be wrong and costly; which is that the industrial base can be preserved only by building additional submarines" (Tenneco News Release, June 8, 1993).

Our Rival Also Faced Serious Troubles

This argument was a shot across the bow of the Navy, as well as Electric Boat and its corporate parent, General Dynamics. Electric Boat had strong political connections with President Clinton not only in Connecticut's two Democratic senators—Christopher Dodd and Joe Lieberman—but also other Senators and House members from across New England. The largest employer in Connecticut, Electric Boat was struggling to avoid its own demise, and those politicians naturally were closely engaged in its cause.

Electric Boat's work force had declined to about 17,000 in 1993 from a recent peak of 21,500 in 1991. Those employees were working to finish construction of the first two Seawolf submarines as well as the Navy's last orders for the Los Angeles class and Ohio class Trident missile models, seven in all. Without a third Seawolf, and at least a five-year wait before construction could begin on the new Centurion class submarines, Electric Boat officials feared their yard would be forced to close.

But on September 1, when Les Aspin announced the Administration's defense budget proposal, Electric Boat was celebrating. Our rival was picked to build the third Seawolf, and as the sole builder for the new submarine class. Newport News would get sufficient funding to begin purchasing material for the new aircraft carrier. But the Pentagon also continued to hold to its early view that would shut us out of new submarine work, a serious blow.

One of the most effective Democrats working for Electric Boat's cause on Capitol Hill, Joe Lieberman wasted no time in congratulating the Administration for seeing things his way. Appearing before hundreds of Electric Boat employees at the Groton shipyard, Lieberman shouted, "I don't know about you, but I feel like yelling a little bit! It is a victory for the people at EB and Connecticut and our nation's security" (*New London Day*, 9/2/93, p. A10).

A Shared History in the Navy's Rise to Global Primacy

In the spring of 1993, Newport News Shipbuilding was the only shipyard in North America capable of designing, constructing, and repairing both nuclear-powered aircraft carriers *and* nuclear-powered submarines for the U.S. Navy. In turn, the Navy was the shipyard's only customer. This symbiosis had served both organizations well during the military buildup of the Ronald Reagan presidency. But it also contained the seeds of turmoil in an inevitable downturn in defense spending that began under George Bush.

Fluctuations in the construction pace for warships were nothing new at Newport News. The shipyard had undergone four great expansions in the twentieth century as a result of the Navy's rapid increase in warships during World War I, World War II, the Vietnam War, and the final act of the Cold War in the 1980s. Each of the first three expansions was followed by major downturns in Navy spending and shipyard employment, and it was certain to happen again after the 1980s.

More broadly, the Navy's grand history in the twentieth century has been closely interwoven with the people, ships, and legends of Newport News Shipbuilding. Newport News has delivered more than 260 ships to the Navy, starting in 1897 when three small gunboats built at Newport News joined the Navy fleet—the *Wilmington*, the *Helena*, and the *Nashville*. The *Nashville* saw combat action two years later in the Spanish-American War when it fired the first shots at sea aimed at Spanish ships. Those three Newport News ships were the seventh, eighth, and ninth to be completed at the yard since the complex was brought to life in 1886 by Collis P. Huntington, one of the most original and wealthy organizers of large-scale industrial enterprises at that time.

Huntington established his fortune in the 1860s as one of four legendary founders of the Central Pacific Railroad. The Central Pacific's track across the west was joined with the Union Pacific Railroad at Promontory Point, Utah, in 1869 to create the nation's first transcontinental railroad. Huntington's vision was not only to establish the nation's premier shipyard at Newport News, but also for the broad, deep waters at the mouth of the James River to be developed into a large international shipping harbor.

By 1907, Newport News Shipbuilding was well established as a prime Navy shipbuilder. When President Theodore Roosevelt pushed the United States out of global political isolation and toward command of the seas with his launching of the Great White Fleet, 7 of the 16 battleships came from Newport News. A generation later, the Virginia yard was building many of the aircraft carriers, battleships, destroyers, and cargo ships that proved essential in U.S. victories in Europe and the Pacific during World War II. It was from the deck of the U.S.S. Hornet, a Newport News-built carrier, that Jimmy Doolittle led 16 B-25 bombers on a daring, surprise attack on Tokyo in April 1942. After receiving news of Japan's surrender in 1945, James Forrestal, the Secretary of the Navy, praised the shipyard in a letter to its president. "Among the companies which gave our fleet the power to attack, yours has been preeminent," he wrote. "On this day of final victory, the Navy sends you its sincere thanks."

Nonetheless, the shipyard and the Navy had a 100-year tradition of conflict in all aspects of ship contracts. There were disputes and disagreement over the designs, standards, and quality for new ships; new technology, costs, and billings; construction schedules; the advancing arts, sciences, and strategies of naval warfare; and the practical limits of the Navy's budget. There also were continuing conflicts with Congress and the Pentagon, the two institutions that ultimately defined the terms for these debates. Tenneco jumped into the fray in 1968 when it acquired Newport News Shipbuilding at a time when Navy orders were strong during the Vietnam War but the shipyard's finances were ailing.

Behemoths That Project Military Power

For the past half century, the aircraft carrier has been unrivaled at projecting U.S. military power at strategic positions around the world:

- Some 70 percent of the world's population can be reached by warplanes launched from U.S. Navy aircraft carriers situated as far as 100 miles from the nearest coastline.

- Navy fighter planes launched after World War II from U.S. carriers have dropped bombs into Korea, Vietnam, Lebanon, Libya, Iraq, and Yugoslavia.

- Since 1974, presidents have called carriers to special military or diplomatic missions 70 times, including crises or flare-ups during the Clinton years in the Balkans, Iraq, Taiwan, Somalia, and Haiti.

- In the spring of 1999, carriers with U.S. warplanes flying NATO missions over Yugoslavia were situated in the Mediterranean Sea and the Persian Gulf, and another was active in the Sea of Japan.

We felt that the new carrier would play a critical role in the Navy's strategy of projecting force from the sea. Identified in 1993 only as CVN-76, this new aircraft carrier represented for Newport News an opportunity to generate a total of more than $3 billion in revenues over six years. (The name CVN-76 was derived from Navy alphanumeric coding. C was code for "cruiser" in 1920, and the first carrier was judged to have cruiser functions. V meant "lighter than air." Thus, CV became the symbol for aircraft carrier. N later was added to specify "nuclear powered." The "76" identifies the specific hull.)

Nearly another $1 billion of the ship's total cost would go to suppliers of nuclear propulsion equipment. A contract for CVN-76 would preserve 5,000 jobs at the shipyard, plus another 120,000 among 4,000 suppliers of steel, machinery, and other materials and equipment from across the country. At the same time, a new contract would only slow reductions in jobs and operations already underway at Newport News. Employment already had dropped to 22,000 from a peak of 30,000 in 1985.

Frustration, Caution, and Calculated Response

So when we learned about the Pentagon's plan to separate future submarine and carrier work and to delay the CVN-76, our anger over the setback on submarines was immediate. Yet we had to be cautious about how we expressed it. We did not want to endanger the administration's advocacy for immediate funding for a new carrier, so mainly we let close political allies in Virginia vent our dismay.

"I think it's a particularly, singularly bad idea, and bad precedent," Herbert Bateman, a Republican representing Virginia's Hampton Roads district in the House, told the local *Virginian Pilot* newspaper (September 2, 1993). "It's an incredible waste of money, and they recognize that it is the most expensive alternative they could have recommended."

We also made it clear in other ways that we were not going to go quietly. Our head of communications at the shipyard and the Navy's previous chief communications officer, Jack Garrow, told the *Newport News Daily Press* (September 2, 1993), "We would not concede being out of the submarine business at this point. We'll certainly be talking with people, and we'll be looking forward to working with the new administration and Congress on these matters."

In fact, we had been active on the Hill, at the White House, and in the Pentagon at an increasing pace for several months. We trailed Electric Boat after a late start in getting our message out. But this was only the first phase in an effort to represent the Newport News cause at each relevant point of influence in the political process. Our programs soon evolved into a good illustration of how a corporation legitimately can work the Washington process to change policy and procure a high-profile government contract. It also is a vivid example of how a skilled team of specialists in government and politics can provide a company with an important competitive advantage.

Knowing Whom to See, What to Say

The three top officers of Tenneco, Mike Walsh, Ted Tetzlaff, our top lawyer, and I came to these positions with very specific knowledge of government's continual impact on big business. We knew how to work effectively with public officials and bureaucrats. Our combined experience in federal government was more than 20 years.

Mike was an assistant for a year to the agriculture secretary in the Johnson administration, then after Yale Law School worked 12 years as a public defender, federal prosecutor, and U.S. Attorney in California. I spent half of 1968 in the Pentagon analyzing and writing about the Vietnam War, then four years drafting legislation and managing domestic policy issues in the Nixon White House. Ted, also a Yale Law graduate, was an administrator of the federal Legal Services poverty law program for two years, a legislative aide in Congress, and a staff lawyer for the congressional impeachment hearings in 1974. We shared strong convictions about how to protect and advance Tenneco's business interests wherever they intersected with government. There was a great deal we had to change.

Tenneco had bankrolled one of corporate America's biggest political contribution programs during the 1970s and well into the 1980s, legally (then) ferrying members of Congress hither and yon in its fleet of company-owned aircraft and contributing heavily to Republican candidates. Democrats rarely got a nickel. The amount the company handed out for election campaigns in the early 1980s was tops among all corporate Political Action Committees (PAC). But as oil prices went into descent and Tenneco's financial fortunes waned, company political contributions dropped below $100,000 in 1991. The company's Washington staff had retreated to a very low profile.

Mike, Ted, and I knew in the summer of 1992 that this inactivity and administrative disarray in Washington were serious problems threatening to become worse, with gathering political clouds threatening the survival of Newport News. The three of us were unusually well connected in Washington, beginning with Mike and Ted's first-name relationships, respectively, with the President and Hillary Rodham Clinton. Mike was one of a handful of corporate CEOs to endorse Clinton over Bush in the 1992 election, and Ted had worked with the First Lady on the Watergate hearings staff in 1974.

For my part, many of my relationships with several Senators and House members were forged in the early 1970s, when I was deputy director of the Nixon administration's Domestic Council. Negotiating with powerful members of Congress and their staffs on legislation including revenue-sharing, transportation programs, social welfare budgets, and governing policies for the District of Columbia was one of my main responsibilities. A centrist Republican, I naturally considered myself better established with the Republican side of the aisle on Capitol Hill than Mike or Ted, but I also was on a first-name basis with many Democrats. More broadly, the three of us had a pragmatic understanding of the policy-making culture in Washington that probably was as sophisticated and experienced at the time as any corporate leadership team in the country.

Overhaul, Revival at the Political Beachhead

Still, we needed an experienced corporate lobbyist to revive and lead our office there. We wanted someone who knew public policy machinery, understood best corporate practices for the right ways to influence that machinery, and had experience in one or more of Tenneco's six industries. We also needed someone who could hit the ground running, with good working relationships on Capitol Hill and in the White House, as well as the Washington think tanks, law firms, and communications specialists. We recruited a government-relations executive, John Castellani, who knew several of our industries because of his work as a vice president at TRW, another multi-industry corporation that had big operations in defense, aerospace, and automotive parts. Moreover, he had led public-policy development in energy and technology for the National Association of Manufacturers during the late 1970s after beginning his career at General Electric.

The Washington office we handed to him had four serious problems. First, policy specialists in our different businesses (e.g., natural gas pipelines and nuclear-powered aircraft carriers) rarely coordinated policy positions and political plans among themselves. On occasion, they even had opposing views, which baffled the elected officials and industry lobbying groups. This too often left the impression that Tenneco was a company that didn't know what it wanted.

Second, the government relations group often missed or was too late to influence political and legislative issues that had a real impact on Tenneco businesses. This often was related to the third failing: a lack of continuity in relationships with likely natural allies for our businesses in both parties in Congress, as well as in the administration, foreign embassies, and trade and industry groups. Finally, the office was not consistently active or effective in practicing political preventive medicine. It did not assemble and present the facts and arguments that might have headed off regulations, policies, and laws that hurt Tenneco businesses.

We had to find ways to exploit Tenneco's large and diverse geographic and industrial presence, not continue to be hobbled by it. To start, we brought onto our staff industry specialists who understood a Tenneco business and its public policy issues. For example, an expert on the people and processes of environmental regulation focused on our chemicals and packaging businesses; from an industry trade association we recruited an experienced lobbyist on natural gas pipelines; from the Commerce Department a specialist in international trade issues, and so on.

Next, these industry specialists had to become a team focused on the public-policy priorities we set for the company. They had to share facts, insights, and hunches on our priority issues, such political trends on federal labor laws, the environment, workplace safety, international product standards, and others. They also had to be certain that whenever we were going to take a stand for or against any policy position, we had to agree on one Tenneco view before calling on an elected or appointed official. Any internal policy conflicts had to be identified and sorted out ahead of time.

Reviving a Moribund Political Action Committee

We also had to raise more money volunteered from Tenneco employees for political contributions. Federal laws prohibit businesses from requiring employees to make political contributions. We had to sell the need to participate in the political process and the potential benefits of Tenneco's PAC to our senior managers. We also established a small committee, with representatives from each Tenneco business, to determine which political candidates we would support in state and federal elections, and how much Tenneco would contribute to their campaigns. There rarely was a dispute about who should get the money.

Our goal was for managers to pledge donations equal to 1 percent of their salary. Mike announced this program with such zeal to the 400 managers at our Leadership Conference late in 1993 that he pledged to contribute 5 percent of his salary. That amount, of course, was the highest of anyone there and would have equaled more than two-thirds of the entire collections of the Tenneco PAC for the year. Sitting in a front row, Ted Tetzlaff immediately corrected Mike, noting that federal law restricted an employee's contribution to $5,000, or about 0.5 percent of Mike's salary. So this quickly turned into a rare Mike Walsh pledge that he withdrew in less than a minute.

The campaign quickly proved a financial and political success. In 1994, donations to the PAC surged nearly fourfold, to $326,000 from $85,000 in 1993; then to $450,000 in 1996, with nearly half of 9,000 eligible salaried managers participating. And we had a presence in elections important to our businesses. In 1994, we supported 103 Democrats and 88 Republicans in House of Representative campaigns; 171 of these candidates were victorious, or 91 percent, including all eight running in open seat contests. In the Senate, 23 of our 25 candidates won, including seven Democrats and 18 Republicans. We committed $286,000 to those campaigns, and another $55,000 to 80 races in three states: Texas, Ohio, and Pennsylvania. In the 1996 federal campaigns, 237 of 259 candidates we supported with an average of $1,569 won seats in the House, and 24 of 36 won in the Senate, with an average Tenneco contribution of $4,653.

It is common sense to identify and support your allies in politics just as in any business endeavor. There is no shame or embarrassment for a business to give campaign money lawfully to the candidates who hear you out on issues and who are likely to agree more often than not with your priorities and positions on public policy. I never knew what difference these contributions made for a candidate in any specific race.

Five Essentials for Effective Lobbying in Washington

Effective political work in Washington begins with five nonpareil essentials:

1. Good relationships with decision makers: the elected officials and their staff.

2. A keen understanding of their political priorities, motivations, and allegiances.

3. Broad support among constituents who elect these officials.

4. Timely, accurate information.

5. Courage to fight for your programs and issues.

Little PAC money was available to us in the fall of 1993, and comparatively little had been contributed in recent campaigns. Still we were confident about the case for Newport News. We also were committed to pouring all of the required energy and resources into winning the fight.

We put together a team of outside lobbyists in the summer of 1993 to help us cover three of the four essentials: relationships, understanding, and information. The group included former members of Congress, former staff officials in the Reagan and Bush administrations, former members of or advisers to congressional subcommittees for Armed Services and Defense Appropriations, as well as Washington lawyers and grassroots lobbyists. This talent and experience did not come cheap, a fact I was reminded of whenever our Washington office submitted its sky-high expenses. I once told Castellani, "You're the only corporate officer I've ever known who consistently exceeds an *unlimited* budget."

They met every Tuesday, Wednesday, and Thursday at 7:30 A.M. in our Washington office. They traded information about the latest twists and turns on Capitol Hill and in the administration regarding the carrier. Above all, they tracked voting positions of every member of the House Armed Services Committee and the Defense Appropriations Committee, more than 100 representatives in all. It was in these two committees that we would face the biggest challenges to CVN-76. If we could win here, our prospects would be good for approval by the entire Congress and ultimately the Clinton White House.

We entered the CVN-76 campaign secure with our good relationships with the Virginia delegation on Capitol Hill. If anything, they became even more vital advocates and advisers for our strategy and tactics within Congress. The Newport News shipyard, for several years the largest private-sector employer in Virginia, was well understood and supported by the two U.S. Senators, Republican John Warner, a former Navy Secretary, and Democrat Charles Robb, an important ally for us in communications with President Clinton.

In addition, all four members of the House of Representatives from the Hampton Roads region in southeast Virginia were vital partners: Norman Sisisky, Owen Pickett, and Robert Scott, all Democrats, and Republican Herbert Bateman. They were disturbed by the shrinking defense budget's impact on future contracts and lost jobs at the shipyard. They all shared our goals to at least get partial funding for the new carrier in the federal government's fiscal 1994 budget, and to get us back into future submarine business as soon as possible.

Identifying Allies, Expanding Grassroots Influence

I'm not giving away secrets to say that hiring experienced lobbyists and getting knowledgeable executives into face-to-face meetings with powerful members of Congress are good ways to influence lawmaking in Washington. These simply are "club dues." General Dynamics in particular excelled at this insider's game. So we knew we would have to reach further to identify any advantages in Tenneco's larger size and comparatively greater breadth of businesses.

We soon focused on three groups that turned out to be enormously effective allies:

1. Unions that represented large numbers of Tenneco workers, especially those at Newport News.

2. Suppliers of the equipment and material needed to build the carrier, led by big steel companies and located in 43 states.

3. Our other five Tenneco businesses, which included manufacturing operations and thousand of employees who voted in 35 states.

These tactics emerged from posing two related questions: What single item or material would be ordered in largest quantities for building the new carrier? And, which of the many skilled trades among the 22,000 workers at the shipyard was most prevalent? The answer to the first question would tell us who outside the shipyard would have the greatest business interest in the carrier's construction. The answer to the second would suggest where we would find the biggest support for the carrier among organized labor in Washington. The answers were simple: steel and steelworkers.

A modern aircraft carrier is expensive, at about $4.5 billion, and very big:

- A new carrier requires 47,000 tons of structural steel and 95,000 tons of steel products altogether.

- It includes 900 miles of electrical cable.

- The flight deck covers four and a half acres.

- From the base of the keel to the tip of the control tower, a carrier is nearly 25 stories tall.

- If pointed skyward from street level at 34th Street and Fifth Avenue in New York City, the carrier's bow would reach as high as the 86th floor observatory of the Empire State Building, nearly 1,100 feet.

Overall, Newport News estimated it would have more than 4,000 suppliers for carrier materials, with Bethlehem Steel in Pennsylvania likely the largest. As for labor, the United Steelworkers of America represented 7,000 of the shipyard's 14,000 hourly workers, and virtually all of its unionized workers.

The Steelworkers' biggest concern was stanching job losses, and their leaders and rank-and-file members recognized they had a huge stake in CVN-76. Judy Boyd, the international union representative at Newport News Shipbuilding, told the *Virginian Pilot* newspaper, "There were real strong signals and evidence that if the carrier were not funded in 1995, we'd be facing a major layoff." Boyd was an effective advocate for the carrier in dozens of meetings with lawmakers and congressional staff members. She and a welder from the shipyard, Alton Glass, aided the cause with their message of what delay or cancellation of CVN-76 would mean to thousands of shipyard workers.

This story also got through to the Congressional Black Caucus. Robert (Bobby) Scott, one of those local members of Congress most committed to our side, was an African American in his first term representing a district that included the city of Newport News. The shipyard not only was the biggest employer there, it paid some of the highest wages in the region along with good medical and retirement benefits. More than half of the hourly jobs were held by African Americans. Some were from families whose primary livelihood had been linked to the shipyard's fortunes for three or more generations. Many also were graduates of the shipyard's highly regarded Apprentice School, a four-year program for high school graduates that combines academics and training in 18 shipbuilding crafts such as millwright, electrician, welder, and sheet metalworker, along with an income.

Scott was an effective advocate for CVN-76 not only within the Black Caucus, but also among the large class of first-term members of Congress, where we also had a lot of work to do. Many of its members, whether liberal, moderate, or conservative, were eager to cut defense spending. Liberals wanted to apply the "peace dividend" to increases for education, jobs training, social welfare, and other domestic programs. The priority for moderates and conservatives most often was reducing the federal budget deficit.

Scott and our other Virginia politicians in Congress were persuasive in voicing military and economic reasons for the carrier. They met individually with nearly every one of the 535 members of the House and Senate. Scott also arranged informal sessions for me and Mike Walsh, the two top shipyard executives, Pat Phillips and Bill Fricks, and others in our camp to talk with many members, several of whom had seats on the House Armed Services and Defense Appropriations committees. When the roll call for votes came later in the fall, most of them were on our side.

Navy regulations require the shipyard to keep extensive records. We were able to mine those records to help our grassroots lobbying, saving precious time. Working with a Washington-area political consulting firm, Direct Impact, we assembled a plan for suppliers of parts and equipment for two carriers already under construction to campaign aggressively for CVN-76 with letters and phone calls to their senators and congressmen. This involved more than 4,000 businesses with 120,000 jobs in 43 states. Many of these business owners and employees were eager to join us. If construction of the carrier were delayed until 2001, many of these businesses would go bankrupt. Those who could avoid bankruptcy still might have to lay off craftspeople trained specifically for work related to aircraft carrier parts and supplies.

Box Plant Managers Help
Sell an Aircraft Carrier

We also sent out a message for help to all plant managers in the five other Tenneco businesses around the country. Tenneco box plant managers in Georgia called House Speaker Newt Gingrich in Atlanta. Managers of Tenneco auto parts factories in Michigan knocked on the door of Senator Carl Levin. Managers of Case tractor plants in Wisconsin called freshman Senator Russell Feingold, and so on. One day we had a political briefing in Washington for managers of 44 of our packaging business's box plants. I told them, "While you're here, let's go see your congressman." They would go in, introduce themselves and say, "before I tell you about my plant and our products, I want to tell you about CVN-76." This was a hands-on lesson for our managers in grassroots political action, putting the spotlight on an oft-neglected part of any plant manager's job.

Managers of corrugated box plants, egg carton factories, and paper mills might have seemed unlikely advocates for an aircraft carrier. But they were well briefed and credible. Just as the shipyard's suppliers were doing, they lobbied for the carrier across the country. They were very effective, at times inspiring awe or ire. One day, a congressman from Wisconsin grabbed John Castellani at a

Washington gathering and asked with some urgency, "How do you *do* this?! I want to do this. I want to do this when I run for office!"

Two Democratic senators from Nebraska, Robert Kerrey and J. James Exon, warmed to the cause of CVN-76 after we pointed out among other things that Tenneco was Nebraska's largest employer in the auto industry. Exon said with a smile, "Now we get to talk about something other than grain futures or beef exports." Our logic was that what is good for Newport News is good for Tenneco. What is good for Tenneco is good for the 1,500 Tenneco employees at our auto parts plants in the Nebraska towns of Cozad and Seward, or a box manufacturing plant in Omaha. What is good for those auto plants is good for families of the employees and the economies of these towns, and so on. Even our well-informed Virginia delegation did not know that one of our largest distribution plants for automotive exhaust systems was in the state's Shenandoah Valley, in Harrisonburg.

But some on Capitol Hill perceived us as shameless conspirators against fair play. One day an irritated committee chairman called Castellani on the phone. "I've got five letters on CVN-76," he fumed. "I had my staff person call every one of them because I figured it was some ruse. It turned out they all knew what they were talking about. They knew the issues. I don't know how you do it." The congressman wanted John to call off the effort because it was eating up a lot of his staff's time and, as he put it, "wasting taxpayer money." We kept pressing ahead.

Backroom Politics and the CEO

THERE ARE CERTAIN THINGS THAT ONLY THE CEO CAN DO FOR HIS OR her company in the political arena. This chapter describes my role pressing and bargaining in Washington for defense contracts that were vital to the future of Newport News Shipbuilding and Tenneco, and to the economic stability of the Hampton Roads region of southeast Virginia.

Understand the Arena before Entering

You can marshal all the experienced, talented staff available for vital projects, but when it comes down to the big decisions and the big commitment, the CEO has to be a visible, persuasive ambassador. This is the one person that a president or vice president wants to see, or a senator, a member of Congress, a cabinet secretary, or some foreign dignitary or official. They usually prefer, of course, to bargain with a perceived equal on the scales of power and prestige, someone able to make an agreement on the spot and quickly execute a bargain. They also want to gauge a chief executive's sophistication on a given issue and his depth of commitment to a position, whether favorable to them or hostile. This is one of the reasons why the Business Roundtable, which is comprised only of chief executives, has a unique influence in the hierarchy of associations of business leaders.

You should have a good understanding of how any politician you are about to meet developed his or her power base, how much is owed to whom. There is no better guide to predicting how much flexibility any politician might have on a given issue. Business leaders with little experience in government or the political process often are naïve and ineffective in working with elected or appointed government officials. There inevitably are limits or restrictions on what any politician can do. Politicians who know or at least sense that you understand this can become important allies.

Sometimes this means the CEO has to park his ego back at the office, or at least lower the decibel level a few notches. You have to understand the political motivations of these elected and appointed officials. If you have to wait in a senator's anteroom for half an hour, you don't take it as an insult; you realize that a senator's staff routinely carves his schedule into 15-minute blocks and overbooks it. Senators are always running 20 minutes late.

My years in official Washington—at the Pentagon and on the White House staff—included many trips to Capitol Hill to talk with representatives and senators about political issues, to testify for or against legislation, and to join in hundreds of luncheons, banquets, and testimonials. I enjoyed the atmosphere of power and politics. Even though I had been away from any official capacity for 20 years, many of the former administration officials and junior members of Congress I had worked with in the early 1970s were by the early 1990s among the nation's more influential decision makers.

Probably more than most CEOs, I was a known commodity on the Hill. I was often welcomed like a member of the lodge when I called for an appointment or a request. To be sure, the fact that we were reviving Tenneco's political contribution machinery and becoming more active in campaign contributions got us onto the daily calendars of elected officials and provided opportunities to make our case on any given issue.

Delays on Carrier Budget Vote

The final vote by Congress on the 1994 federal budget was delayed for weeks, well into November. A big reason was the wrangling over which defense programs would take the biggest spending hit. Political horse-trading revolving around CVN-76 was active and intense. The budget for the Central Intelligence Agency, the new free-trade agreement with Mexico and Canada—NAFTA, and competing defense projects such as the B-2 bomber and other shipbuilding programs all were forces that came into play. One day John Warner told me only half in jest, "If I added up all the things that I have traded for this aircraft carrier, I would have to support every other bill that comes out on the floor."

We believed by early November that support for CVN-76 was strong in both political parties and both houses of Congress. We had met with all 56 members of the four key committees for defense spending in the House and the Senate. The last significant hurdle in our attempt to get at least partial funding for the carrier into the 1994 budget was Ronald V. Dellums, the Democrat from Oakland, California. Dellums, in his first months as chairman of the powerful House Armed Services Committee, was enjoying the new prestige and putting his stamp on military policies and procedures. His Democratic predecessor on the House military panel, Les Aspin, had moved into the Pentagon as Bill Clinton's new Defense Secretary.

A Maneuver and an Insult

An African American who had been in the Congress since the early 1970s, Dellums had overcome some hardball tactics by more senior politicians in his first years on Capitol Hill. Once an outspoken foe of the Vietnam War, Dellums, a liberal, now was in position to alter the military priorities of the Reagan-Bush years and put more federal money into social spending programs. So he was angered by a failed attempt to push full funding of $3.4 billion for the carrier into the 1994 budget. The dapper, courtly Dellums was insulted, seeing this as a direct challenge both to his new authority and also a test of wills. His key adversary on this issue, John Murtha, a gruff, blunt-spoken Democrat and former Marine from Johnstown, Pennsylvania, was in effect another Newport News ally seeking complete funding for the carrier. But it wasn't hard for me to understand Dellums's reaction.

Murtha was a leader of the steel-industry caucus in Congress, and certainly an advocate for thousands of workers in his district and region who stood to benefit from steel orders for a new carrier. He also was chairman of the House subcommittee for defense appropriation, a formidable position from which to shape final proposals for the Navy's next budget. But it was not quite so formidable as the position of the chairman of the House Armed Services Committee. Dellums and Murtha exchanged harsh words during these few days, with Murtha at one point bragging that he could gather enough votes to override any effort Dellums might attempt to block Murtha's move for the carrier. Not so. In addition to Dellums's hard feelings, Murtha's overture to seize full funding for a new carrier also drew the ire of rival shipyards that were seeking Navy dollars for their own projects. Within days, other representatives on the subcommittee blocked Murtha, and his proposal for CVN-76 funding was pared to $1 billion.

Watching this unfold, we realized fences were being broken that we needed to mend. Newport News Shipbuilding invited Dellums to a tour of the yard, but could do no better than hosting one of his staff members. President Clinton personally called Dellums, asking him to soften his opposition to carrier funding in the 1994 budget, but Dellums resisted. The Clinton call was partly related to his effort to win congressional support for the North American Free Trade Agreement (NAFTA), the proposal to reduce tariffs and other trade barriers between Mexico, Canada, and the United States. Labor unions and their leaders were bitterly opposed to the pact, and Clinton needed to pursue every vote on the Hill to get it passed. His lobbyists knew how badly the Virginia delegation wanted the new carrier to be funded, so the President's favor of a call to Dellums was at least partly intended to move the Virginia delegation behind NAFTA.

Finally, a solution was worked out that got at least some federal money onto the table. A sum of $1.2 billion for the carrier was included as an addendum in the appropriations budget for Navy Sealift cargo ships in the 1994 fiscal year. This compromise was a good step, but not a guarantee. Appropriations make money available for federal spending, but the money cannot be released from the Treasury until that specific spending is *authorized*. Four committees, two each in the House and the Senate, still would have to authorize spending the $1.2 billion.

Ron Dellums, as chairman of the House Armed Services Committee, was in a position to block authorization of funds for the new carrier. We still had work to do to erase any lingering impression Dellums might hold that Murtha had been our stalking horse in challenging his authority, and also to soften somehow Dellums's opposition to the new carrier, whether that opposition might be personal, or philosophical, or both.

Playing the CEO Card

Soon after becoming Tenneco's chief executive early in 1994, I emphasized for all our key allies in politics and government that even though Mike Walsh could no longer be engaged, CVN-76 remained one of Tenneco's highest business priorities. I soon met in Washington with the Virginia delegation, the Secretary of the Navy, top Navy admirals who were influential in budget recommendations for new military vessels, and senior aides to the President. I also made certain that I paid a personal visit to Ron Dellums. He had just gone on record at a public hearing of the armed services committee that the Navy's military rationale for adding CVN-76 was unconvincing. He also was opposed to authorizing the $1.2 billion for the new carrier that had been parked in the Sealift budget account.

These positions did not surprise me. I had first met Dellums and other members of the Congressional Black Caucus through my White House assignments that covered important government issues in the District of Columbia. At that time, the Executive Branch had governing authority over the district and, as deputy director of the Nixon Domestic Council, I was the principal liaison between the D.C. mayor's office and the White House. Dellums came to Congress in the early 1970s as "a commie pinko Afro-topped bell-bottomed dude from Berkeley," or at least that is how he described himself 25 years later in a 1998 interview with the *Washington Post.*

This was a knowing, concise self-portrait. A former Marine who became a dedicated antiwar activist during the Vietnam War, Dellums made President Nixon's "enemies list," an aptly named document that surfaced during the Watergate investigations. In the 20 years between then and his elevation to the chairman's seat on the House Armed Services Committee (the name subsequently was changed to the House National Security Committee), Dellums regularly opposed new weapons programs such as the B-1 and B-2 bombers, and higher military spending generally. Still, he had agreed to meet with me.

Establishing Substantive Common Ground

Our conversation was scheduled for 20 minutes. It began awkwardly when the congressman pointedly recalled what he phrased as Murtha's attempted "end run" around Dellums's House committee on the budgeting process. But we soon were deep into a consideration of how to appropriately gauge the optimum level of defense spending in the post-Cold War world. This was very familiar ground for me. My Ph.D. dissertation examined military planning and spending in the United States during two decades of peace between World War I and World War II. I had been an Army officer for 21 years, including tours in Germany in the North Atlantic Treaty Organization (NATO) and in Vietnam. I ran the prestigious National Security Seminar course at West Point. And at Tenneco I was now a top executive of a major defense contractor. I wove each of these substantive points of reference into the discussion, and we talked cordially for an hour and a half. But as I walked away that afternoon, I was uncertain how Dellums would vote on CVN-76.

I knew going into the meeting that he favored delaying funding for the new carrier until 2001. He believed that the construction schedule for new carriers should be slowed to one every eight years from the current pace of one every four. When he reiterated that opinion in our meeting, I conceded at first that this change could be managed over time. The problem was how to retain specially trained workers at the yard who would have nothing to do in the interim. If they had other ships to assemble, it could be feasible. If not, the shipyard would have to lay them off by the thousands, because there would not be enough work. That ultimately would prove more costly because the Navy would need to have these workers replaced and new hires retrained for nuclear-powered carrier work every eight years.

Clarifying Our Commitments and Risks

I offered a compromise. Support funding for a new carrier now and give Newport News time to develop a commercial business, to again make ships for private industry. We already had plans underway to install $70 million of new technology in steel fabrication to speed the construction process and reduce costs for the shipyard in the future. Sharply reducing costs was the only way the shipyard could become competitive with the nationally subsidized shipyards of Korea, Japan, Norway, and elsewhere.

Newport News already had begun to work its way back into the market for tankers and other commercial vessels. Our research indicated that demand for new ships could rise significantly early in the next decade. New international political pressures for double-hulled ships, increasing international trade, and replacement of aging fleets all were encouraging factors. Moreover, if we could get our costs down to compete effectively for non-Navy business, the Navy would benefit when we applied these new efficiencies to more productive methods for building Navy ships. Finally, with a new source of orders from big shipping companies and lower construction costs, Newport News Shipbuilding could keep its work force intact if the Navy did slow carrier construction to an eight-year cycle.

My argument to Dellums was that Tenneco was investing in the country's biggest shipyard, pursuing new business, and improving productivity—all of which would benefit the Navy and U.S. taxpayers. Tenneco was not sitting on its hands, hoping for a bailout in the form of a contract for some marginally useful ship just to keep jobs for our workers, and revenues for our business. That, I told Dellums, was how we viewed the Navy's support for construction of the third Seawolf submarine at Electric Boat.

Avoiding Potential for Hostile Fire

Well, the Congressman heard me out, but he never changed his mind. He never voted for any of the money we wanted for the new carrier. But he also didn't use his considerable powers to block our way. He could have maneuvered to have the $1.2 billion allocated for the carrier in the Navy Sealift budget shifted to some other Navy program. He could have advocated spending money for B-2 bombers instead of the carrier, as the Air Force was hoping. Instead, in May, during the House Armed Services Committee's conference to outline its defense budget for the 1995 fiscal year, Dellums permitted Norm Sisisky to offer an amendment that endorsed full funding for the carrier. Indeed, the committee then approved $2.3 billion for Newport News, precisely the amount needed in addition to the $1.2 billion that had been authorized in the 1994 budget for the Navy Sealift.

Dellums could have been a tough adversary that day. He never told me why he took the path he did, choosing neither to endorse our funding proposal for CVN-76 nor to oppose it. I was left to conclude that his decision evolved possibly from the credibility of our arguments, the depth of our private discussions, and the deference I displayed in devoting whatever time he wanted that one afternoon to explaining them. We never discussed the issue again. Four years later, in 1998, Ron Dellums resigned from Congress and returned to live in the Oakland area.

Final funding for CVN-76 was included in the $244 billion defense appropriation bill that Congress approved and Bill Clinton signed into law for the 1995 fiscal year. By the summer of 1999, the hull of this new carrier, christened in 1996 as the *Ronald Reagan*, was nearly complete in the shipyard's Dry Dock No. 12. The carrier is on schedule for delivery to the Navy in 2002.

Submarines: Going against a United Opposition

As important as this new aircraft carrier was for the Navy, Tenneco, Newport News Shipbuilding and its workers, plus 120,000 employees in the shipyard's supplier network for aircraft carriers, we still had more delicate business and political negotiations ahead to get Newport News Shipbuilding back into the submarine business. The submarine business in the 1980s had contributed 40 percent of the shipyard's total revenues, generally between $600 million and $800 million a year, and directly supported 10,000 jobs. That made it equal in importance to the aircraft carrier program for the shipyard's strategy and future outlook.

The restructuring of the entire operations at Case Corporation and preparations for selling a portion of Case stock to the public were in full gear in the spring of 1994, near the time of Mike Walsh's death. Yet the shipyard's rising vulnerability to losing all future submarine construction work had been an increasingly urgent matter throughout the previous winter. Mike had thrown down the gauntlet to the Navy, Congress, and Clinton Administration less than a year earlier, publicly demanding a reassessment of their inclinations to delay construction of a new carrier. Now, with money for the carrier authorized for the 1994 and 1995 defense budgets, it was time for me to lead another charge on Capitol Hill, this time to reverse the Navy's maneuvers to block Newport News from building new submarines.

The Congress, the Navy, the Pentagon, the White House, and General Dynamics' Electric Boat division were unified in wanting all post-Cold War construction of nuclear-powered submarines consolidated at Electric Boat's historic yard in Groton, Connecticut, with no role for Newport News. Some Navy officials, including the top political appointee, Navy Secretary John Dalton, and the most senior Navy officer, Jeremy (Mike) Boorda, the Chief of Naval Operations, wanted assurances of support for their position from us during the private discussions about giving their endorsements to funding the new carrier.

They wanted no one from Tenneco or Newport News to oppose their efforts to persuade Congress to approve money for building a third Seawolf submarine. If we would agree, then the Navy would support funding for the carrier in the 1995 defense budget. Their point was that Newport News Shipbuilding could have the carriers, but should stay out of future submarine work. In the Navy plans, nuclear-powered carriers would be built only in Newport News and nuclear-powered submarines would be built only at Electric Boat, the original builder of submarines for the Navy since 1900.

Submarine Work Was a Major Line of Business

There was no way we could accept this. Tenneco had invested $1 billion into advanced construction facilities at Newport News in the 1980s, with $300 million devoted to more modern and efficient production methods for submarines. After all, the reasoning was, this was going to remain a major line of Tenneco business. The evidence available at the time certainly supported that logic, and the huge investment. Beginning in 1960 and through 1994, Newport News built 53 submarines, including 29 of the modern Los Angeles-class submarines. The idea that military and political powers in Washington would cancel future submarine work at Newport News had been unthinkable to our shipyard executives—until the Navy's new budget priorities emerged in 1993.

Separately, several of us in Tenneco's senior management group realized that the shipyard might well be operating as an independent company within a few years. With defense budgets tightening, Newport News Shipbuilding was not likely to have sufficient opportunities to increase revenues and earnings in line with our corporate targets. We said as much in the spring of 1994 in the annual report mailed to all of our shareowners. In that report, we omitted the shipyard from the list of core businesses we designated as having the best opportunities to meet those growth targets: automotive parts, packaging, and nonregulated energy.

If Newport News were going to become an independent company, it had to be in the best possible shape to stand on its own financially, with solid footings in its strongest businesses. The strategy included design, construction, and repair work for the Navy's most advanced aircraft carriers *and* submarines, as well as the reentry into international markets for double-hulled tankers and other large commercial ships.

A Tenuous Bargain

Around that time, I told John Dalton that we at Tenneco would "keep our heads down" and not publicly oppose Electric Boat's bid to get $3 billion for the third Seawolf included in the fiscal 1995 defense budget. But I would not concede all future submarine work to Newport News's rival. My first priority, I said, was securing funding for the new carrier. But I also wanted to keep our options open to bid on the next class of future submarines, a program projected at $70 billion over the next 20 years.

We wanted the Navy to have a bidding competition between Newport News and Electric Boat for the first four prototypes of these smaller, more economical vessels known in the Navy as the New Attack Submarine. Newport News calculated that it could save the Navy more than $10 billion if all of the 30 submarines were built there in Virginia, and not at Electric Boat in Connecticut.

John Dalton was furious. He doubted my integrity, saying I was reneging on an earlier promise to yield all future submarine construction to Electric Boat to get the Navy's backing for CVN-76 at Newport News. He also accused us of hiring consultants who were actively lobbying against the Seawolf, which in his mind would have been another violation of the CVN-76 deal. We had once used these consultants Dalton had named to lobby for Navy contracts, but they no longer were on our payroll. I told him that if those consultants currently were working against the Seawolf, someone other than Tenneco or Newport News was paying them. It was not only the Navy top brass we had upset in pursuing a role in the New Attack Submarine program. We also were jeopardizing Tenneco's relationships with some powerful members of Congress, the defense hawks who viewed themselves on most issues as willing agents for Navy policies and priorities.

The Navy officials' anger usually was triggered by our periodic, behind-the-scene efforts to erect a political roadblock whenever they sought funding for the Seawolf or the New Attack Submarine programs. The strategy of our congressional allies was to put a political fence around this money. This would prevent Seawolf money from being authorized in any spending bill until the Navy agreed to two things: include CVN-76 in its spending priorities, and allow Newport

Tense Confrontations and Disputes

News to bid competitively against Electric Boat on the New Attack Submarines.

Votes in various committees and subcommittees on the Hill and other administrative maneuvers were fairly common throughout the second half of 1993. It was no secret to the Navy. In fact, we typically would inform their legislative officers on the Hill of what we were doing, and why. These legislative aides were savvy politicians in their own right who did not take our opposition to the Seawolf personally. We routinely would tell them in advance that a political ally of ours on one of the key House or Senate defense committees intended to block or oppose a favorable funding vote that the Navy was seeking.

Tense Confrontations and Disputes

Senior Navy officers, however, were enraged that one of their largest shipbuilders would dare to attempt this. The head of the Navy's nuclear propulsion program and ruling paterfamilias for the Navy's submarine heritage, Vice Admiral Bruce DeMars, gave me an earful of obscenities over the telephone one day in 1995 that would have made his most bilious sailors turn pale. He demanded that we halt our strategy of holding the Seawolf money hostage. He wanted Castellani fired. Subsequently, his boss, the Chief of Naval Operations, Admiral Boorda, called Castellani and told him we would never see a nickel for CVN-76 until our political team relented in opposing funding for the new submarines. John replied, "Admiral, I can't believe the Chief of Naval Operations is threatening to sabotage his greatest warship over a dispute about who is going to build the next submarines." Boorda slammed down his phone.

Our communications with DeMars in particular often were contentious. It was DeMars who authored the first drafts in 1993 of the Clinton administration policy on how the Navy's shares of military forces should be reshaped for the post-Cold War era. It was his show at the Navy Submarine League that spring that we had crashed in a very loud way, presenting DeMars with a rare public challenge. From this start, DeMars's policy preferences seemed to favor Electric Boat and to be at odds with the interests of Newport News. His agenda was to save Electric Boat and keep its submarine suppliers in business by making funding for the third Seawolf a priority, and then to add the New Attack Submarine program exclusively for Electric Boat before the end of the decade.

We countered first by adopting an argument similar to the one that DeMars was using for the Seawolf, to preserve the industrial base for nuclear-powered aircraft carriers. In brief, this logic holds that a lengthy delay or interruption in spending for a program can seriously weaken or disperse the unique network of labor skills and technology in privately owned businesses—the particular industrial base—created to support the program.

Political Fence and a Quid Pro Quo

The next piece of the strategy was for the Virginia delegates in Congress to vote down any attempts to put Seawolf funding into the defense budgets unless the Navy had agreed to our quid pro quo on CVN-76 and future submarine work. This political fence effectively and consistently denied funds for the Seawolf. The Navy was going to have to deal with us on our two issues. We were very clear with the Navy top brass that we would not back down until Newport News was allowed to compete for contracts on the new submarines.

For more than two years, this strategy never faltered because we were able to march in lockstep with the Virginia politicians in Congress. DeMars was checked at every turn, and he deeply resented it. This standoff came to a head in the spring of 1995 when, in our view, DeMars made a political and tactical miscalculation. He tried to force us to write a letter to Congress in favor of the third Seawolf. He vowed privately that, if we refused, he would block any future attempts by Newport News to bid on any new Navy ships other than aircraft carriers.

We did refuse, again, and when we fired another political shot across his bow, DeMars soon backed down. This occurred when some of our Virginia allies on the House Armed Services Committee called the submarine admiral on the carpet during a public committee hearing with news reporters in the audience. One of the Virginia politicians, privately informed of the Admiral's broadside against me, bluntly asked DeMars if he had threatened the chairman of Tenneco. "No," the admiral replied. "I had a frank conversation with the chairman of Tenneco." That same day, before the same committee, the president and chief executive of the shipyard, Bill Fricks, implicitly criticized DeMars when he characterized the idea of maintaining two construction yards for nuclear vessels as "both counter-productive and very expensive."

A Good Relationship Framed on Common Concerns

Burning bridges with powerful federal officials carries risks, especially when one of them can influence billion-dollar orders from your biggest customer. That is where we stood with DeMars. Yet the support of the Virginia delegation continued to make us bulletproof politically for the debates and maneuverings still to come. It also helped that Admiral Boorda, who outranked DeMars, and I had a casual relationship and mutual respect that helped both of us through these rough spots and kept the conversation open and usually civil.

We had this relationship because of our involvement with a new association in Washington. This group, the Council for Excellence in Government, brought together business leaders, senior government officers, elected officials, and scholars to identify ways to transfer appropriate business practices into the management of government agencies. The idea was that perhaps the public sector could use some of the new methods and ideas that U.S.-based business had developed in the past 20 years to improve operations and services in response to intensifying global competitive pressures. Our occasional meetings provided an informal setting for business executives to meet with important government officials on matters not directly involving some business issue.

As it happened, Boorda and I were teamed together in a group working on military personnel issues. I pointed out one day that there was a problem with the Navy's pay schedules; people who were poor performers yet had more years of service made more money than better performers with fewer years of service. This is a huge problem, bad for morale, which still exists. But we worked on it together. Partly as a result of having that shared agenda, Boorda and I always were able to discuss the political differences we encountered amicably, and could agree to disagree. His tragic suicide in 1996 was a great loss for the Navy and for the country.

Quiet Proposal for a Shipyard Marriage

Privately in 1995, we explored with Dalton and Boorda and other Pentagon officials the outlines of a deal in which Tenneco would buy Electric Boat from General Dynamics and merge its operations with Newport News Shipbuilding. This was a period when a flurry of mergers was underway in the defense industry, and shipbuilders were part of the action. There was logic to a combination of Newport News and Electric Boat, and the possibility had been a topic of speculation for several years in the industry, the Navy, and the news media. Some Tenneco executives had scouted out the possibility of General Dynamics acquiring Newport News Shipbuilding and marrying it with Electric Boat in 1987, just prior to Tenneco's decision to sell its oil business.

The offer we sketched for the Navy and the Pentagon was to transfer thousands of engineers to Electric Boat's operations in Groton from Newport News, then continue all the design activities for submarines at that location. We also would retain the Quonset Point site in Rhode Island where Electric Boat had an additional 3,000 employees making large steel framing rings for new submarines. In turn, the main manufacturing site at Groton would be scaled down, and the majority of submarine construction then would occur at Newport News.

To execute the plan, the Pentagon would have to allow Tenneco to reduce assets at Electric Boat more gradually than otherwise would occur as we closed facilities and laid off employees in Groton. A more rapid write-off likely would be too staggering to Tenneco's short-term earnings, and thus make the deal unworkable from our view. We also requested approximately $400 million from the Pentagon in accelerated payments on existing contracts to help cover initial, higher costs associated with the combination. Most of the money would be used for severance payments to workers who would lose their jobs. We figured the Navy would save $10 billion on the New Attack Submarine program if this consolidation was carried out, but the Navy insisted the savings would be $2 billion.

We never found much enthusiasm for this or any similar type of deal. I wasn't surprised. That strong personal attachment so many high-ranking Navy officers have for Electric Boat and its 100-year history provides a powerful incentive to keep Electric Boat in business. DeMars, of course, was Electric Boat's most ardent standard-bearer behind the scenes in Washington. When the *Washington Post* reported later that summer that "the Navy believes Electric Boat is the world's best submarine builder," the newspaper would have been more accurate in saying "DeMars believes Electric Boat . . . "

Rumblings of a Political Backlash

We also realized the deal would have severe political opposition, perhaps more than we could overcome. Political repercussions from a Newport News-Electric Boat merger would have been severe for the Connecticut and Rhode Island members of Congress. Thousands of blue-collar jobs would have been lost in regions surrounding New London, Connecticut, where unemployment was rising. When in fact rumors of a possible merger began to leak in Congress, the Democratic representative from the New London area, Sam Gejdenson, was incensed. He accused me of a "rapacious" guile to steal taxpayers' money. This was a reference to the $400 million we sought from the Pentagon, an accusation that I considered ill informed, to put it mildly.

A Newport News-Electric Boat combination would carry a lot of future risk for Tenneco. No doubt a final job count after the marriage would have favored Newport News, but we also would have preserved and invested tens of millions of dollars in the design operations in Groton. Part of that would have included transferring thousands of high-paying technical and professional jobs into southeast Connecticut from Newport News. I thought Gejdenson was incredibly shortsighted not to understand this.

Despite this and related disputes and the many harsh words exchanged with Gejdenson, DeMars, and others we crossed swords with on the Hill and in the Navy in these years, I always understood that the opponents were fighting on a political battleground, not a personal one.

There is no underestimating the survival reflex in politics, even if you know and admire the politician who senses a threat to his power base. When Jack Reed, one of Rhode Island's U.S. senators, heard of the Newport News-Electric Boat rumors, his reaction was almost as strong as Gejdenson's. A Democrat, Reed had been one of my students and a faculty colleague at West Point. He was top-notch, and I had recommended him 20 years earlier for acceptance into Harvard Law School. In a few years, Reed had become a Harvard Law graduate, a status that I'm sure provided him a pretty fair foundation for his future political career. Yet when he heard of a possible deal and my role, he called to ask "what the hell" was going on. "Just relax, Jack," I told him. "Quonset Point will still be there. You won't have to worry about it." He said, "Okay, that's all I want to know." And that was the end of it.

Some sketchy details of the merger proposal were leaked several months later to the *Washington Post*. We never commented on the story, which was published, but speculation about a merger of these two yards soon faded away. I'm convinced a merger would have been the right conclusion from a conventional analysis of the business, economical, and technical issues.

Politically, though, I knew that trying to arrange this kind of a deal was going against big odds. But it was something that had to be explored with the right people and at the right time. In February 1999, the tables were turned when General Dynamics offered to buy Newport News for $1.4 billion and merge it with Electric Boat. Two months later, Defense Secretary William Cohen ruled against the proposal on the grounds that the combination would reduce competition on bids for future Navy ships. This time, it was the Virginia delegation, led by Senator John Warner, that voiced the loudest objections. Litton Industries' subsequent attempt to buy Newport News Shipbuilding also was rejected by Secretary Cohen in July 1999.

A Gingrich Intervention

When the Newport News-Electric Boat merger idea was ruled out in 1995, we put together a different proposal to keep up the pressure to get Newport News back into submarines. If we really believed we could outdesign and outduel Electric Boat in building submarines more efficiently, we needed the chance to prove it. What if we could persuade this Congress, the first Republican-majority Congress in six decades, to apply the principles of free enterprise in big government spending programs? If so, why wouldn't they respond to a competition between the two shipyards to build the first vessels in the New Attack Submarine program?

Interviews that Newport News conducted with average voters indicated that the public in general was cynical about political disputes. Opponents hurl charges and countercharges that involve billions of dollars, but the facts are too complicated for most people to sort out. That was the same response we got to our conviction that Newport News could save taxpayers $10 billion if it built the new submarines, and not Electric Boat. In this era of an $8 trillion national economy and a $1.7 trillion federal budget, voters couldn't get too excited about a $10 billion dispute among Navy contractors.

But the notion that the Navy would not permit competing bids for this contract struck a nerve. This was un-American, they told our researchers. It was wrong. We figured that logic would have a great appeal to Newt Gingrich, the Georgia Republican and then the most powerful member of Congress as the new Speaker of the House. Gingrich was very aware of the New Attack Submarine debate. He favored the program as a way to contribute to a strong national defense, but it also presented a problem because the submarine program was a big-ticket item in the federal budget he was determined to cut. Politically powerful Senate Democrats in the Northeast, including Ted Kennedy, Chris Dodd, and Joe Lieberman, supported Electric Boat as a national treasure. Meanwhile, influential Republicans and Democrats on budget and defense committees such as John Warner and Chuck Robb solidly backed Newport News.

We knew Gingrich wanted this submarine built, but that he also was trying to find a compromise among two warring factions of

Republicans in the House: the defense hawks and the federal budget hawks. Defense hawks generally supported Pentagon funding requests. Budget hawks instinctively were more challenging and resistant to those requests, especially in the lengthening aftermath of the 1989 fall of the Berlin Wall.

If we could get Gingrich to agree to force the Navy to open the door again for Newport News, we would have our victory. On June 8, Representative Herb Bateman and I met with the Speaker in his office to explain our position. I proposed a "shoot-out" between the two shipyards, with each yard building a prototype of the Navy's approved design for the New Attack Submarine series. This, I argued, would encourage both sides to deliver their best technology from the outset—not only for inside the submarine, but also in the design and construction methods. I told him Newport News would be the clear winner, and that Congress confidently could award the entire contract to Newport News.

Gingrich didn't necessarily agree that Newport News had the superior capability, but he immediately embraced the idea of the shoot-out. Instead of one prototype from each yard, he and a senior member of the House Armed Services Committee, Duncan Hunter, a California Republican who headed that panel's military procurement subcommittee, conferred right there and quickly agreed that the proposal should be for *two* prototypes from each yard. Well, fine with me.

Back in the Submarine Business

That, essentially, is how we got Newport News back into the submarine business. It took dozens of our key players at Newport News, in Washington, and in our corporate headquarters to get to that point. They logged thousands of long hours and were determined to win. Within weeks of that meeting, the House and Senate approved bills framing a compromise on the submarines. That compromise soon became part of the 1996 defense budget. Electric Boat would build the first and third prototypes of the new Attack Submarine; Newport News would build prototypes 2 and 4. Both yards then would compete for a winner-take-all contract for all future vessels in the New Attack Submarine program. In turn, the Virginia Senators, Warner and Robb, dropped their opposition to adding $1.5 billion to the 1996 budget for completion of the third Seawolf. On February 10, 1996, President Clinton signed the defense authorization bill into law.

The political game in Washington is never over. Newport News in the late 1980s completed all the design work in blueprints to create the new Seawolf, only to have the Navy reverse a congressional decision and have all Seawolf construction awarded to Electric Boat. The Cold War ends, and suddenly the Seawolf's mission to seek and attack Russian submarines is obsolete. Newport News is pushed out of all future submarine construction work in 1993, then recovers to near-equal footing in 1996 to compete for the next new class of submarines. To quote Churchill, as I often do, the lesson here is "never, never, never give in."

The uneasy ceasefire among the Navy, Electric Boat, and Newport News continued late in 1996 when Newport News was separated from Tenneco and became an independent company. Within a few months, though, the Navy asserted that it did not have the money to build the four prototypes for the New Attack Submarine. Unstated was the Navy's long-standing aversion to prototypes, and also its concerns that Newport News might well defeat Electric Boat in any head-to-head competition. It asked Newport News and Electric Boat to scrap the planned competition and work together instead on plans to reduce costs and still get the four submarines built on schedule.

That arrangement became formal late in 1997. Newport News now is designated to build the bow and the stern, while Electric Boat has the engine room and the electronic control systems. Completed modules then will be shipped between the two yards by barge along the Atlantic Coast between southern Virginia and southeastern Connecticut.

The many-layered episodes that brought construction work on CVN-76 and the first New Attack Submarine into Newport News demonstrate the great political resources that companies can tap if those resources are properly identified, supported, and put into action. In Tenneco's case, these resources were alliances within the

Pentagon and the Navy, a large number of workers, the impact of those workers and their jobs on local and regional economies, business leaders and government officials in those same economies. These all are sources for support and activism on behalf of their interests, as well as your own, in Congress.

Big Successes, Imperative Results

Our victories in Congress with Newport News Shipbuilding between 1993 and 1996 were vital to advancing our strategy for Tenneco. They provided billions of dollars in new Navy contracts that will continue well into the next decade. They built a new momentum at Newport News that enabled it to plan more confidently for its independence and to operate as a stable, solid company. And they contributed significant shareowner wealth: Tenneco shareowners received new common stock in Newport News Shipbuilding, which nearly doubled in market price after it was first traded in December 1996. Tenneco's own corporate debt was lightened by the transfer of $600 million of debt to the balance sheet of the new Newport News Shipbuilding corporation.

None of this would have been possible if we had sat on our hands in 1993 and accepted much of official Washington's dour vision for Newport News. When you understand and have confidence in the process of government and your ability to credibly influence policy debates, you have the power to change the politics and policies that support and strengthen your business. These are tremendous strategic advantages.

CHAPTER 9

PUBLIC POLICY: NUDGING THE FED

THIS CHAPTER LOOKS AT HOW BUSINESS LEADERS CAN HELP SHAPE THE economic environment in which they operate. If war is too important to be left to the generals, the economy is too important to be left to government economists. We all benefit from a full exchange of information, and business leaders often have access to early indicators of future trends. The economic policy process works better when business leaders get involved.

In the autumn of 1995, many business leaders were hoping to persuade Alan Greenspan and other policy makers at the Federal Reserve Board to discard old ideas about the relationship of inflation, productivity, unemployment, and economic growth. I was one of them. And from the day my one-year tenure began that September as chairman of the National Association of Manufacturers (NAM), I had a central role in what was perhaps the biggest organized attempt the private sector ever made to influence economic policy in Washington.

The century-old NAM is the nation's biggest industrial lobbying organization, sponsored by nearly 14,000 companies, large and small, or about 85 percent of the manufacturing sector of the economy. The sector collectively employs 16 percent of the nation's labor force and generates 21 percent of total gross domestic product.

Put simply, one purpose of our campaign was for the Fed to shift the focus of its monetary policies to support a faster-growing economy, rather than its past focus predominantly on warding off inflation. This would improve business conditions and create more jobs and national wealth. Some doubted our plans, assuming that the Fed did not welcome overtures from the White House or Congress regarding its monetary policy, and was even less responsive when the business community knocked at its door. We proved the doubters wrong.

Two Cheers for Low Inflation

Economic growth during the first three years of the Clinton Presidency averaged 2 percent a year, a weak pace for the first years after a recession. Yet many economists and government policy makers were satisfied because in 1995, for the fourth year in a row, inflation was running at 3 percent or below. This was the first period since the mid-1960s that inflation had been so well tamed.

Any wage earner whose purchasing power was eroded steadily through the 1970s and into the 1980s would agree that subduing inflation was a major achievement. Inflation in the United States hit a staggering, post-World War II peak of 13.5 percent in 1980, the year that Ronald Reagan swept into the White House with a pledge to cut taxes and scale back the size and role of big government.

Reagan delivered on both counts, yet he was no inflation fighter. With $4 trillion added to the federal debt between 1980 and 1995, the task of beating inflation largely was left to the Federal Reserve Board and the tight monetary policies of Paul Volcker, the Fed chairman from 1979 to 1987, and his successor, the current chairman, Alan Greenspan.

By mid-1995, the financial markets had become conditioned to the Fed's likely response to indicators that had once accurately forecast renewed inflation—such as falling inventories of manufacturers' goods, or rising commodity prices. Bond prices would fall and yields rise when traders anticipated that the Fed soon would raise rates after such indicators were reported. The markets often were correct.

High Costs of Low Inflation, Slow Growth

This low-inflation policy had costs. High interest rates hampered business investment, idled a higher percentage of the work force and kept a lid on economic growth. Moreover, I was convinced that continued sluggish growth would make it difficult for the nation to absorb the high investments and operating costs that the new economy developing from computing and communications technologies soon would require, as well as the costs of traditional federal entitlement programs such as Social Security and Medicare.

Faster economic growth is the best path to the wealth we will need to meet these costs. On the bright side, growth also is the source of all the things most Americans want: more jobs; higher wages and benefits; more tax revenues to fight crime, better education, and abundant health care and pensions. More growth equals higher living standards.

By mid-1995, after the seventh move by the Fed within 12 months to raise interest rates, I was irritated because these preemptive strikes against unseen inflation had gone too far. Growth in the U.S. economy in the second quarter that year came nearly to a halt, advancing by only 0.4 percent. The fusillade from the Fed in continually raising rates had left the economy in a drowsy state. The slowdown was hitting most businesses, including Tenneco.

Many business leaders, Wall Street bankers, prominent economists, and, at least in private discussions, some high-ranking White House officials agreed with me that the Fed had erred by putting the brakes to an economy that was not at risk of generating higher inflation. Unemployment was down from a recent peak of 7.5 percent in 1992, but still unnecessarily high in mid-1995 at slightly below 6 percent. Borrowing costs, as measured by the Federal funds rate—the short-term rate manipulated by the Fed to control the money supply—had doubled to 6 percent in the unusually brief period since early 1994. Yet inflation was below 3 percent.

Bully Pulpit in a White House
Election Year

When I became chairman of the National Association of Manufacturers in September 1995, I stepped into a bully pulpit with the potential to reach an ever-widening audience. The 1996 presidential election season was almost underway, and campaigns would move into full throttle by the following February when the first state primary contests were held in Iowa and New Hampshire.

Presidential campaigns provide the best times to influence policy in Washington. All the candidates for Congress or the White House are looking for the voters' hot-button issues. Under the heat of an approaching election, they often are more receptive to policy positions that can help them work their way onto the front pages and local and national news broadcasts.

This is why I had agreed a few years earlier to accept the chairman's post for the one-year term starting in the autumn of 1995. It was a time-consuming commitment requiring travel across the country to direct meetings and deliver speeches. It added many commitments to a calendar already crowded with the important meetings, travel, and events you would expect for the chief executive of a corporation with $11 billion in revenues at that time and operations in 35 countries. Yet I usually had some flexibility in my Tenneco schedule, and made sure that was communicated months in advance to officials at the NAM. If I was in Chicago, for example, to meet with executives of Tenneco Packaging or Tenneco Automotive during the same week as the NAM's big annual trade show, we would arrange for me to speak at the lakefront McCormick Center and meet with reporters to advocate NAM policy positions. I often traveled to Washington on Tenneco matters, and many times conducted NAM business in Congressional offices, at the White House, or elsewhere the same day before returning that night to Connecticut. My rule was never to miss an important Tenneco event if a conflict ever arose. This same practice also worked well when I was chairman of the Business Roundtable.

The main point is these activities can help your company not only in making or renewing important relationships in government or trade association leaders, you also develop better ties with key players in your industry or market. This can stimulate new sales contracts or cooperative deals such as joint ventures, or even prepare the way for major mergers or acquisitions.

In this opportunity with the NAM, I knew any impact we could make to change conventional thinking at the Federal Reserve about limits on economic growth would help each of our Tenneco businesses in the long run. Our sales increases for automotive parts to new-car manufacturers and of paperboard packaging products, among others, tracked the rate of the nation's real economic growth, as measured with the effects of inflation removed, with a few percentage points of extra growth for the Tenneco products factored in. For paperboard, each 1 percent increase in gross domestic product translated to a 20 percent increase in the volume of orders.

"That kind of thing ripples back into your revenues, into your earnings; and your earnings really determine how much cash you've got to reinvest," I later told to an *Industry Week* reporter (September 16, 1996). If "you aggregate that across an entire economy, you are beginning to look at the generation of a tremendous amount of cash for reinvestment, which in turn not only builds the companies, but also maintains—and in some cases will create—jobs."

My closest allies in this campaign included several experienced and successful Washington insiders and corporate leaders: Felix Rohatyn, the investment banker and adviser to Democratic administrations since the Kennedy presidency; Paul Allaire, chairman and chief executive of Xerox; Jack Kemp, the long-time congressman, advocate of supply-side economics and 1996 Republican vice-presidential candidate; Paul O'Neill, chairman and CEO of Alcoa and a former White House colleague of mine; and Jerry Jasinowski, president of the NAM and former economic adviser in the Carter administration.

The Growth Orthodoxy of 2.3 Percent

The basic formula for estimating real economic growth, with no inflation, is derived from anticipated increases in a nation's labor force and in its productive use of labor and capital, which is measured by a worker's output per hour. The orthodoxy in Washington in 1995 was that economic output could not rise faster than 2.3 percent a year without triggering inflation. In the mid-1990s, the U.S. population was growing at 1.1 percent, and official government statistics gauged the trend in productivity improvement since the 1970s at an annual rate of 1.2 percent. It was as simple as 1.1 . . . plus 1.2 . . . equals 2.3.

We argued that the Fed had not focused adequately on the new facts of rising productivity, and also that the government's methodology for measuring productivity was outdated. We were managing our companies in a new period of lowered costs, higher spending on technology and new products, and an inability to raise prices. One Tenneco mill making paperboard, for example, improved its productivity by 9 percent in just three years. This was accomplished without adding a single dollar of investment, or trimming the number of workers. It was achieved solely by using new processes, new management, and electronic control systems, on the same equipment.

Our view was that the old economic models had missed these changes, but the continued use of old models at the White House, the Office of Management and Budget, the Congressional Budget Office, and the Federal Reserve Board unnecessarily restricted economic growth. The old models lowered expectations of what was truly possible.

Those of us in large corporations were seeing these improvements continually in our businesses and industries, especially in manufacturing. The manufacturing sector had achieved productivity gains of 3 percent for several years. We also knew that the service sector, aided by rapid advances in computers, telecommunications, and other technological innovations, was becoming more efficient, but in ways that still were hard to measure. We saw and read about the competitive pressures, the new innovations and lower prices, and our counterparts running these service-sector companies confirmed our impressions from the outside. We were convinced the economy could grow at least by 3 percent a year, and maybe 3.5 percent, without rekindling inflation.

We focused our arguments on three truths, among others, that the Fed considered fundamental for gauging the potential for faster economic growth without higher inflation: (1) rising productivity is a precondition for faster growth; (2) little or no pricing power is a precondition for little or no inflation; and (3) a decline in borrowing by the federal government is a precondition for lower interest rates.

Many Issues Fit under the Growth Umbrella

Through speeches, news releases, interviews, and appearances in the business news media, and anticipated private meetings in the White House and with Alan Greenspan, I moved ahead to execute the strategy we had developed at the NAM. One goal was to raise the growth issue to the top of the agenda in the 1996 presidential campaign.

The first news coverage of our plans to challenge the candidates to take a stand on economic growth policies signaled that we had an issue that could make an impact on the national political dialogue. *The New York Times* (September 24, 1995) carried a news story the day after more than 100 directors of the NAM unanimously approved the campaign, with the headline, "Manufacturers Challenge Economic Policy." A brief reference to that article noted on the front page, "American manufacturers, disagreeing with policymakers, declared that economic growth could be a robust 3.5 percent without risking high inflation."

We thought the topic of economic growth should have broad appeal. It was a wide thematic umbrella under which many topical economic issues simmered: corporate downsizing, foreign trade imbalances, hourly wage stagnation, rising taxes, costly federal regulations, climbing stock prices, and unending debates over federal budget spending and interest rate policies at the Fed.

There also was an intriguing undercurrent to our confrontation: having recaptured from Japan the title of "world's most competitive industries" that American business executives lost in the 1980s, we now were taking on the wise men and women at the Fed who were applying the slow-growth gospel.

In fact, it was not just the Fed that was holding back growth. I often said the Federal Reserve was doing a tremendous job under Alan Greenspan of "managing to the wrong target," meaning a growth rate of 2.3 percent, when the target should have been 3 percent or higher.

Monetary policy was just one element of the policy and legislative changes we sought in Washington to ease the road to higher economic growth. Among our other goals were a balanced federal budget, lower taxes, an easing of the high costs of regulations and liability laws, and reduced trade barriers.

I listed this menu for growth reforms a few days later in my first speech on the growth theme at the National Press Club in Washington. And I included Fed policy among them. "I am one of those who believes the Federal Reserve is fighting the inflation wars of the past," I said, "not taking into account changes in our economy like the lower rate of natural employment, productivity increases, and higher capacity."

Manufacturing as the Engine of Growth

The next day, the NAM issued results of a survey of its 20-member executive committee. By a margin of four to one, most executives intended to add jobs in their businesses rather than cut them. It was another chance to underscore the growth theme.

"Manufacturing continues to be the engine of growth for this economy," I said in the NAM news release. "Industry is translating impressive productivity gains into job creation despite the Federal Reserve's unnecessarily tight monetary policy. . . . Increasing our annual growth rate by just 1 percent would be enough to balance the budget in seven years without any of the Draconian methods being considered today."

"Washington still doesn't get it," I concluded. "This is the largest economy in the world . . . Yet too many of our leaders think it's just fine to allow the economy to putt-putt along at a growth rate of 2.5 percent. Washington needs to embrace a progrowth agenda, which includes balancing the budget, lowering interest rates, reforming the regulatory and legal systems, and promoting exports and job training."

One of the leadership lessons West Point instills in cadets, and I practiced at Tenneco, is that "action creates opportunity." Two weeks later, opportunity in the form of a year-long series of endorsements and coverage in major news media began in a big way.

Business Week published the first of what became its own series of cover stories and editorials on rising worker productivity and the consequent prospects for faster growth in the American economy. The magazine backed our cause, which opened doors to more high-level media interest and helped in arranging private talks with powerful figures in Washington.

"Policymakers should heed the words of the National Association of Manufacturers, the folks who make things in America," the editorial said.[1] "[The NAM] recently declared that its members can sustain a 3 percent to 3.5 percent growth rate without inflation, but can't because of the stranglehold of Washington policy."

A Talk with Greenspan

In December, Greenspan agreed to meet in his office with me and with Jerry Jasinowski, president of the NAM and leader of its full-time Washington staff.

The conversation was focused on how manufacturers were achieving significant leaps in output after revamping operations and re-training workers. It was a new economy in terms of managerial methods and practices, and in terms of increasing competitiveness and industry capacity that made it very difficult in most markets for businesses to raise prices.

I described, for example, how many of our factories were operating at times above 100 percent of capacity as originally designed because of major changes in processes. Much of this was related to a change in philosophy that gave factory workers a bigger voice in creating new techniques, improving safety, and raising efficiency.

At the strategy level, I explained that our automotive parts business now often built plants next to auto assembly sites of big customers such as the Chrysler Corporation. This proximity slashed transportation costs, improved coordination, and sharply reduced inventories because we could ship new parts to the assembly lines within two hours of a call from a customer's purchasing manager.

---

[1] "Sign a Contract for Growth." *Business Week,* October 9, 1995, p. 166.

In the prevailing slow-growth orthodoxy, economists like Greenspan studied inventory levels for signs of approaching inflation. Low or declining inventories indicated that manufacturers were operating close to full capacity to fill orders, and soon would be raising prices. This was less often the case, I said, because just-in-time manufacturing techniques now were widely used in industry.

Jasinowski described how thousands of other manufacturers had been improving productivity by shaking up their organizations. They were getting better ideas by including employees in designing work processes to reduce waste, raise output, improve safety, and develop new products more quickly. They were equipping and training their work force with advanced tools and techniques in the battle to become the lowest cost producer and market leader in their lines of business. He pointed out that the impact of all this activity clearly was improving productivity in U.S. manufacturing.

Concurring, but Looking for Data

The Fed chairman was attentive and asked a question occasionally as we moved through the discussion. I don't recall his exact words, but when we had finished he told us in essence, "I think you are right. But my problem is these improvements are not showing up yet in the economic data. So we don't have the empirical evidence to act."

As Jasinowski and I departed, we sensed for the first time that Greenspan was thinking seriously about a shift in his approach to these issues. "It was a major turning point," Jasinowski recalled later. Greenspan had been more restrained at a similar discussion with manufacturing leaders a year earlier, he said.

This restraint was understandable. Greenspan had invested more than 30 years in learning, applying, and adjusting conventional methods for analyzing economic statistics. Financial markets had been convinced that, since succeeding Paul Volcker in 1987, Greenspan was an inflation-fighter par excellence and that he also had a deft touch in guiding interest rates to keep the economy growing, but not too fast.

But even before our meeting at the end of 1995, he clearly had been exploring whether economic growth could in fact accelerate above 3 percent without forcing prices higher and bringing on a slowdown or a recession. On the same day that NAM directors had gathered in September to embrace the faster-growth theme, Alan Greenspan—while testifying before the Senate Banking Committee—provided a signal that he might one day agree with our position. "It is a mistake for a central bank to look at a growth rate and say that if the economy moves up to that rate, we are in danger," he said.[2]

Throughout 1995 and much of the presidential election, the Clinton administration was cautious about endorsing a faster growth rate. The head of the National Economic Council, Laura D'Andrea Tyson, officially agreed with the Fed's concept that 2.3 percent was the optimum level for G.D.P. growth in statements to reporters and in private meetings with business executives gathered at NAM headquarters or at the White House. Tyson was knowledgeable and attentive while taking in our productivity stories but, like Greenspan, she said in effect, "We're just not seeing it yet in the numbers."

But behind the scenes we knew the issue got a regular hearing in the administration. After all, it was James Carville's inelegant distillation of the national mood, "It's the economy, stupid," that had kept the Clinton camp focused and eventually triumphant over George Bush in 1992. Yet economic growth was languid in Clinton's first term. Bob Dole and Jack Kemp, the Republican opposition that emerged in 1996, took dead aim at the economy in the fall of 1996, getting no discouragement from us. Indeed, Kemp, a tennis-playing friend of Jasinowski's, addressed our NAM board meetings and enthusiastically echoed our views months before Dole tapped him as his vice-presidential running mate. When the debate over growth moved onto the front pages and became a top campaign issue late that summer, we were delighted, knowing full well that Alan Greenspan also was watching.

Clinton should have done more after his second White House victory to ease regulatory burdens on business, reform taxes, and reign

---

[2] Mike McNamee, with Christopher Farrell, "The Great Growth Debate." *Business Week*, October 8, 1996, pp. 160–161.

in the outrageous, ongoing scandal that masquerades as product liability law while lining the pockets of thousands of trial lawyers. All this would improve conditions for economic growth. Yet Clinton's steady record on trade, achievement of a federal budget surplus while Democratic left-wingers pushed for more spending, and appointment of sophisticated thinkers on economic policy were admirable policy decisions. Certainly, the economy's surge has been the crowning achievement of his second term. It may also have been the principal factor in his ability to complete it.

Felix Rohatyn, one of the most influential Democratic businessmen for the past quarter-century as managing director of the investment banking firm, Lazard Fréres & Company on Wall Street and one of my closest business advisers for much of that time, orchestrated private meetings in the Oval Office with the President and his economic staff in the winter of 1995–1996. The tone on both occasions was cordial, and the colloquy focused. We departed encouraged. High-ranking advisers in these meetings subsequently encouraged the President toward our views on productivity, job creation, and global industrial competitiveness. Indeed, there were times on the campaign trail when he adopted parts of our rhetoric on faster growth, usually its virtue of creating more jobs.

The President attended both of these Oval Office meetings as well as his chief of staff at the time, Leon Panetta; Treasury Secretary Robert Rubin; Commerce Secretary Ron Brown, who died tragically in April with 34 others in a plane crash in Croatia; and Alexis Herman, then a White House liaison to business and Labor Secretary in Clinton's second term. Felix (appointed U.S. Ambassador to France in 1997) and I were there with George David, chief executive of United Technologies; Bernard Schwartz, chief executive of Loral Inc.; Paul O'Neill, chief executive of the Aluminum Corporation of America (Alcoa); and, Paul Allaire, chief executive of Xerox Corporation.

The shift in monetary policy by the Fed was glacial. It was vaguely evident when the Fed lowered rates twice early in 1996. The average growth total for all of 1995 was reported at 2.3 percent, the optimum noninflationary rate in the eyes of traditionalists.

Later in the year, Alan Greenspan resisted widely reported pressures from traditional thinkers within the Fed to raise rates as growth accelerated above 3 percent. They were wary that gradually declining unemployment soon would trigger a new wave of inflation.

Stronger Than Even We Expected

Today most analysts and other Fed watchers agree that Alan Greenspan has led the other members of the Federal Reserve's policy-setting Federal Open Market Committee to a new appreciation of how advances in technology and managerial process lifted productivity improvements in the 1990s. In turn, and parallel with the fiscal policies of the White House and Congress that eliminated the federal budget deficit in 1998—faster than hardly any of us could have imagined—the Fed gradually abandoned its rigid limits and has enabled the U.S. economy to grow at a faster pace.

I will leave it to Alan Greenspan and others at the Fed to comment on how persuasive our efforts in 1995 and 1996 proved to be. Certainly, those of us at the NAM were only one section of a nationwide chorus that included many like-minded allies in Congress and the White House, as well as economists, essayists, and editors. And Greenspan himself was the major force for change within the Fed. To the extent our role was influential, I attribute it to the facts and logic we assembled and presented, not only to the Fed but more broadly within the policy-setting machinery of public opinion and private negotiations with government officials.

Greenspan's changing views benefited not only the U.S. economy but also the entire global economy. If growth continued through the end of 1999 at the average rate since 1996 of nearly 4 percent, the economy will be $500 billion larger, at $8.6 trillion, than if the old dogma of 2.3 percent had prevailed and the economy remained on that track through the same period. This continuing strength provided a growing market for exports from Asia and Latin America that contributed to slowing the staggering economic reversals that swept those regions in 1997 and 1998, and their gradual recoveries in 1999.

The Longest Economic Expansion

Everyone has a stake in the debate over the noninflationary pace of economic growth. Higher growth creates more jobs, more income, more wealth, larger tax revenues for government, and higher living standards. The $500 billion of higher output during the past four years has provided more aggregate revenue for businesses, more income for workers, and greater wealth overall for the nation. Through July 1999, 10 million new jobs were created from the start of 1996.

A landmark seems certain to be set in February 2000 when the recovery that began in April 1991 enters its 107th month. This will set a record for the longest economic expansion in the nation's history. The current record of 106 months was set between 1961 and 1969, an era when the federal debt grew sharply to finance Lyndon Johnson's Great Society programs and the Vietnam War. LBJ had rejected his economic staff's advice to raise taxes, choosing instead the path of political expediency by ordering the Treasury Department to print more money. The decision set the stage for the soaring inflation and stagnating economy of the 1970s.

In contrast to those times, the federal budget now has a mounting surplus and the U.S. economy again is the most competitive, productive, and innovative in the world. We have no shortage of worries, yet our current prosperity shows few fundamental signs of ending soon. One of the biggest reasons is that the Fed has established a new kind of credibility among business leaders as well as the financial markets. It balances concerns of potential inflationary factors in the economy against the evidence of a continuing rise in productivity.

Instead of taking away the punch bowl when the economic party gets going, the Fed now is more content to leave the bowl in place, adding water occasionally if the punch seems to be getting too potent.

In testimony before Congress early in 1999, Greenspan gave one example of why his thinking has moderated. As we had counseled four years earlier, he now views the economy of the 1990s as distinct from that of the 1970s and 1980s. In those two decades, he said, companies typically raised their prices when labor costs increased. Now, he said, competitive pressures typically rule out price increases, so companies look hard at how to reduce costs. Cutting costs keeps inflationary pressures low. Applying new technology and reinventing work processes is the most common and effective method today for cutting costs, which often improves productivity.

More Fed Agreement on Rising Productivity

If manufacturing continues to raise productivity by more than 3 percent a year, and productivity overall in the economy improves at a pace of at least 2 percent a year, the U.S. economy will have the essential ingredient to continue a strong advance averaging near 3.5 percent.

The Federal Reserve governors have not abandoned their responsibilities or desires to keep inflation in check, but more of them now are speaking publicly about fundamental changes in the nation's productivity. Some of their recent speeches read much like our pleadings in 1995 and 1996.

"Unemployment has been very low—lower than most economists thought it could remain for long without igniting inflation," the Fed's then-vice chairman, Alice Rivlin, told her audience in Buffalo, in October 1998 "Wages have been increasing, but not so fast that the rise caused rapid escalation of costs," she said. "Productivity increases have been offsetting compensation growth, keeping profits growing. . . . Most remarkable of all, inflation has been falling and not showing any clear evidence of accelerating again."

Six months later, speaking to a Business Roundtable symposium in Washington, Rivlin analyzed why tight labor markets no longer are necessarily harbingers of inflation or lower productivity as unskilled workers are brought into the labor force. "Recent experience suggests that, in the context of intense global and domestic competitiveness as well as the continuing revolution in computers and telecommunications, tight labor markets provide incentives for managerial innovation, skills acquisition, and higher productivity, leading to higher growth with little inflation."

Because Rivlin embraced our views with fewer qualifications in her public remarks than any other Fed governor, including Greenspan, her resignation in June 1999 was a disappointment. Yet even some of the most conservative members of the Federal Reserve have come around to the view that productivity has surged and that these gains can be sustained.

In a speech in April 1999, William Poole, president of the Federal Reserve Bank of St. Louis, concluded, "It is increasingly reasonable to believe that the United States has turned the corner on productivity growth." He put the figure at close to 2 percent, or nearly twice the conventional view on the Fed in 1995. Lawrence Meyer, a staunch old-liner, softened and adopted a similar stance in September 1999.

In his July 1999 Humphrey-Hawkins testimony, Greenspan provided a perceptive yet still-cautious account to Congress of the improvements in business processes and productivity in the 1990s. Computer automation and other labor-saving equipment were major factors, but not the only ones, he said. "Business restructuring and the synergies of the new technologies" also have contributed. In turn, new technology has made businesses more flexible and "enabled firms to adjust quickly to changing market demands." All this described significant changes at Tenneco through the 1990s, as he and I had occasionally discussed over the past four years, and as recently as the Business Roundtable's annual meeting in Washington a month before these hearings. The Fed chairman told Congress that productivity increases were "more than 2 percent" in recent years, and averaged about 2½ percent in the past year.

His biggest concerns for symptoms of rising inflation were the threat of increasing employment costs, and its relation to the shrinking pool of available workers. Immigration is the best solution to these worries of a dwindling labor force. No industrialized nation in the world is better equipped than the United States—culturally, politically, or geographically—to assimilate immigrants into its future labor force.

Testing a New Level for NAIRU

It seems amusing to recall that just four years ago my colleagues and I were ridiculed by economists and many in official Washington as heretics in the temple, *their* temple. We asserted that the economy could sustain average growth above 3 percent, unemployment below 5 percent, while keeping inflation in check below 3 percent. The prevailing view then was that whenever the rate of unemployment dropped below 5.5 or 6 percent, inflation inevitably would rise unless the Fed increased interest rates to slow the economy. This was the doctrine of the nonaccelerating inflation rate of unemployment, or NAIRU.

That old calculus of NAIRU now is thoroughly discredited. Perhaps even we were too cautious. For nearly three years, the U.S. economy has grown at a rate of 4 percent, unemployment has remained below 4.5 percent, and inflation has averaged less than 2.5 percent. The unemployment rate fell to a 29-year low of 4.2 percent in March 1999, while the annualized rate of inflation for the same month was 2.4 percent. In August, the trend continued to hold, with unemployment at 4.2 percent, and consumer price inflation for the first eight months of 1999 averaging only 2.4 percent despite resurging oil prices. (See Figures 9.1 and 9.2.)

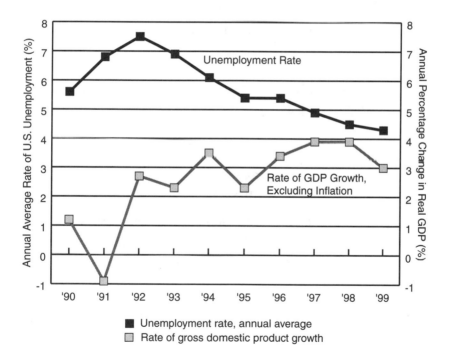

Figure 9.1 The jobless rate hits a 29-year low as economic growth soars above 3.5%. (*Source:* Commerce Department, Bureau of Labor Statistics.)

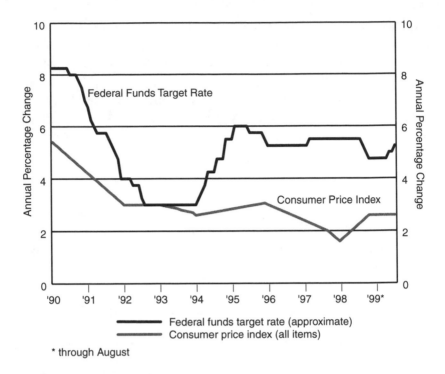

Figure 9.2 The Fed holds steady after '95 and inflation remains in check. (*Source:* Federal Reserve Bank of New York, Bureau of Labor Statistics.)

Business Leaders
Understand the Changes

Is the nonaccelerating rate of unemployment now in the range of *4 percent*? This arcane question gets to the heart of a vital matter of public policy. Each 1 percent swing in the level of unemployment now is equal to the loss, or gain, of nearly 1.4 million jobs. I think the 1990s could well be the era in which surging productivity in the United States reduced the nonaccelerating rate of unemployment to nearly 4 percent.

Several economists speculate that the floor for the noninflationary jobless rate now is below 4 percent, and that the continuing economic expansion soon will test their view. *The Wall Street Journal* reported in March 1999 that large portions of the United States already had unemployment rates below 4 percent. About 55 metropolitan areas were below 3 percent.

James Annable, chief economist of the First Chicago NBD Bank, theorized in August 1996 that the nonaccelerating rate was at least as low as 4.5 percent. In the prior two years, as the Midwest's 12-state manufacturing sector left the "rust belt" era of the 1970s and 1980s far behind, unemployment in the region averaged 4.5 percent. In a remarkably prescient op-ed article for *The Wall Street Journal,* Annable said that in the debate over faster growth versus inflation:

> The economists are wrong; the business leaders are right. . . .
>
> Business leaders understand the magnitude of the continuing changes in the economy . . . This process of cost rationalization has spread throughout the whole country, substantially altering the U.S. economy. . . . Most notably, efforts to improve cost efficiency have helped push up corporate profits as a share of national income, reversing a two-decade decline.
>
> If Washington doesn't mismanage the process, today's rationalization will provide the foundation for the best sustained performance of the U.S. economy since the 1960s. Like the '60s, this new golden age will be characterized by strong profits, low inflation, modest unemployment, rising financial-asset prices, rapid investment, robust productivity gains and a resumption in the growth of real wages and living standards. Books will be written, and read widely in Europe and Japan, on how to manage like the Americans.[3]

Krugman and the Two-Percenters

Many economic traditionalists attacked the optimistic conclusions in this and other faster-growth essays and speeches that appeared throughout the 1996 election campaign, as well as editorials in *Business Week, U.S. News, The Wall Street Journal* and other news media. However, I can think of none so consistently and loudly dismissive of the case for faster growth at that time than Paul Krugman, whose clever harangues appeared regularly in influential publications including *The New York Times, Fortune, The Economist* and *Harvard Business Review.*

---

[3] James Annable. "No Need to Fear Lower Unemployment." *The Wall Street Journal,* August 21, 1996.

Krugman, a prolific and engaging writer, is a high-profile economics professor at the Massachusetts Institute of Technology. He was a leading polemicist in the camp of vocal "two-percenters" who opposed many policies we believed would promote continued economic growth above 3 percent. His dismissal of the facts and logic of an emerging new economy with potential for faster growth amid low inflation extended well into 1999.

In the July–August 1997 issue of the *Harvard Business Review* he asserted, "We would like to believe that the economy can grow much faster if only the Fed would let it. But all the evidence suggests that it cannot." By the spring of 1999, however, even Krugman seemed to be in retreat. "The economy is flourishing, with unemployment at a 25-year low," he wrote in *The New York Times* magazine (May 23, 1999; Section 6, pp. 24–26). "Yet so far inflation is quiescent. . . . This is partly because exceptional productivity gains have made it possible for companies to pay higher wages without raising prices."

He goes on to expresses surprise that workers have remained "remarkably diffident" in not demanding higher wages, even as competition for good jobs has fallen with the jobless rate. Here, like many other business analysts, Krugman overlooks or undervalues important changes in the workplace that raised the significance of nonwage rewards for employees in thousands of companies in the 1990s. These include healthcare benefits and training programs, as well as cash payments and stock grants linked to meeting business performance objectives. In many companies, workers' job satisfaction has risen. This is especially true, as we witnessed in Tenneco, when front-line workers are given more training, responsibility, and authority to improve product quality and plant safety. This includes the power to shut down assembly lines when a machine malfunctions or taking a role in purchasing new equipment they will operate.

Faster Growth and Work Force Disruption

Rapid economic change presents inescapable social costs. Thousands of 50-something machinists and other factory workers have lost jobs in the past two decades that are gone forever. Many of these middle-aged workers in the industrial economy are not sufficiently computer literate to qualify for the thousands of unfilled jobs being created in the growing knowledge-based economy in electronics, telecommunications, and Internet-related products and services.

This is one reason the government needs to join with the private sector in managing the social costs for the transition to this new economy. We must continue to provide safety-net programs such as unemployment insurance for the inevitable dislocations that jolt portions of the work force and create or prolong economic hardships for the poor. The costs also must include training and retraining programs for jobs requiring twenty-first-century skills that have never existed, and for investments in the education system to prepare students for the new work world. Corporations should be budgeting 3 percent of their total costs to training and retraining employees, roughly double the average among manufacturers.

Faster economic growth, aided by the best-managed fiscal and monetary policies we have seen in Washington for decades, is the biggest reason the federal budget produced a surplus in 1998 for the first time in 29 years. Faster growth is the best path to creating the resources we need to meet the continuing social costs for the transition to the new economy.

Factors Influencing Rates of Growth

Several factors have contributed to a faster growing U.S. economy in the second half of the 1990s, including some that are temporary and others that are favorable long-term trends. Cheaper oil, excess global production capacity related to economic weakness in Japan and elsewhere in Asia, and surging payments into the U.S. Treasury fed by rising capital gains tax receipts all could prove temporary.

Favorable structural trends include a more experienced and ethnically diversified work force; the dominance of U.S. companies in fast-growing electronics, computing, and communications industries; the world-class status of U.S. research and higher education;

and efficient capital markets that supply investment for enterprises with potential for fast growth and high returns.

Several variables in the global economy that are not now major obstacles to growth in the United States could come into play:

- Rising commodity prices.

- A retreat from liberalizing the rules and practices of international trade.

- Rising interest rates.

- Currency crises in emerging market economies.

- Rising political tensions between the United States and its important trading partners in China, Japan, and Europe.

- Regional, protracted armed conflicts in which the world's major military powers become engaged, such as the Kosovo War that flared after a decade of Serbian aggression throughout Yugoslavia.

Meanwhile, the serious problems that roiled most of the economies in Asia and Latin America appear to have been contained. This suggests that government officials in the major industrial nations of the global economy and financing system have improved their understanding of the global economy and the impact of the lightning-quick movements within the world financial system.

Why Accelerating Productivity Matters

The lengthening period of economic growth above 3.5 percent in the United States may not be sustainable at quite so high a rate in the decades ahead. Asia is recovering from its worst post-World War II setback, and Europe, led by Germany, soon should resume a more normal pace in economic growth. This worldwide expansion could accelerate demand and prices for commodities like oil, copper, and grain, which Fed policy makers seem unlikely to ignore without raising interest rates.

But we also could see productivity gains in the future that surprise everyone. From World War II to 1973, when the United States was the world's dominant industrial power, productivity grew at a

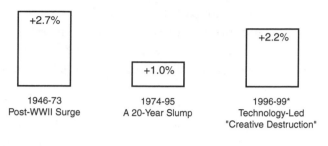

Average Annual Productivity Increase

+2.7%

+2.2%

+1.0%

1946-73	1974-95	1996-99*
Post-WWII Surge	A 20-Year Slump	Technology-Led
		"Creative Destruction"

*through June

Figure 9.3 Reasserting U.S. economic innovation. (*Source:* Bureau of Labor Statistics.)

rate of 2.7 percent. It is conceivable that we could not only return to that level, but exceed it. (See Figure 9.3.)

The productivity gains from computing technologies in the next decade could prove astounding. In his recent book, *Business @ the Speed of Thought,* Bill Gates describes how digital tools for collecting and delivering key information throughout an organization continue to become more advanced and easier to use. Smart companies are evolving their own communications systems to speed information in real time across the functions of knowledge management, business operations, and all aspects of sales and customer service.

Wal-Mart Stores, Dell Computer, International Business Machines, Cisco Systems, and Enron, among many others, demonstrated in the 1990s how aggressive applications of information technology can give companies leadership positions in their markets. Looking ahead, Gates, the Microsoft co-founder and chairman, declares that "business is going to change more in the next ten years than it has in the last fifty."[4]

That is a stretch, considering what large corporations achieved in the 1990s. But companies entering the digital era at accelerating

[4] Bill Gates, with Collins Hemingway. 1999. *Business @ the Speed of Thought,* p. xiv. New York: Warner Books.

speeds clearly have unprecedented opportunities to reduce costs even further and deliver higher quality products and services for their customers. Michael Dertouzos, director of the M.I.T. Computing Lab, estimates that a majority of U.S. economic output, or 60 percent, is now performed as office work. He forecasts that in the next 25 years, at least one-third of that work will be conducted over the Internet.[5]

Two prize-winning *Wall Street Journal* reporters, Bob Davis and David Wessel, also described favorable conditions for a continuing rise in productivity. In a 1998 book, they drew a convincing parallel between the lift that electric power gave the U.S. economy at the beginning of the twentieth century, and the faster productivity gains we have begun to reap from rapid advances in developing and applying computing and communications technologies.

"Two lessons are clear," Davis and Wessel wrote in *Prosperity: The Coming 20-Year Boom and What It Means to You.*[6] "New technology enhances productivity and growth, and it takes decades for powerful innovations, like electricity or computers, to fulfill their potential. The good news: after thirty years of experimentation, America is on the cusp of a computer-powered productivity surge. . . . "

What does higher productivity suggest for the United States? The answer for what remains the world's largest economy, with an output of more than $9 trillion of goods and services, is huge in terms of the real potential for economic growth. Assume an annual productivity growth in the range of 2 percent for 10 years. That would add more than $1 trillion to the size of the U.S. economy in 10 years, compared with productivity growth near 1 percent and economic growth at 2.3 percent.

This scenario also is possible: If growth in the United States could be sustained at the current rate of 3.9 percent even through 2005, the economy would be larger by $1.6 trillion at that point than if growth had averaged 2.3 percent in the same 10-year period starting in 1996.

---

[5] Alan Murray. "The Outlook." *The Wall Street Journal,* May 24, 1999, p. A1.
[6] Bob Davis and David Wessel. 1998. *Prosperity: The Coming 20-Year Boom and What It Means to You,* p. 26. New York: Times Books.

Fifty Years of Faster Growth

If we could sustain for 50 years the growth rate at 3.5 percent—again, less than the average since 1996, the output in the U.S. economy in the year 2050 would exceed $40 trillion. Compare that with an output of $25 trillion if the long-term average rate is limited to an average of 2.5 percent, a level that many traditionalists still consider the most optimistic.

On an individual level, the implications are staggering for potential living standards. Using 1996 as the launch point, a 3.5 percent average growth trajectory would raise average per capita income, after inflation, to $112,000 in the year 2045. That is more than half-again the total we would get with 2.5 percent growth, or $69,000, and *more than 5 times greater* than the 1995 average income of $20,000 for each American.

This is not some fantasy. Most corporate leaders agree with me that the faster growth of 3.5 percent can be sustained. We know it can be achieved if our successors continue to reach for high standards, and make the hard choices to change and adjust. The new Internet economy is only at its dawn. It will unleash countless new waves of creative destruction in the economy. This upheaval will speed innovation, reduce costs, and generate productivity in ways that in a few years will make what we accomplished in the 1990s seem prosaic by comparison.

Large corporations have growing cadres of tested leaders and managers who now are better equipped to manage the chaos and pressures that are commonplace in their industries. To be sure, Darwinian forces will continue to sort out winners and losers in every market. But the forces of change will prevail.

Economic historians will come to judge the 1990s not as some golden era when good luck happened to smile on the U.S. economy. They will see the 1990s as a period when business leaders and productive, innovative employees reclaimed the potential for economic growth in America, and alert policy makers in Washington helped open the path for them achieve it.

AFTERWORD

MUCH OF THIS BOOK HAS BEEN ABOUT LONG-SHOT SUCCESSES: THE restructuring of Case Corporation into a profitable, durable, and well-managed global manufacturer; victories in Congress that established a solid base of current and future revenue for Newport News Shipbuilding; and the emergence of a faster growing, low-inflation economy that has benefited businesses and workers not just in the United States but around the world.

There also has been tragedy, frustration, and disappointment. Mike Walsh's struggle, public and private, against brain cancer was heroic and inspirational. To be candid, it also placed a huge emotional and professional burden on our efforts to accelerate successful change at Tenneco. We probably will never know or understand just how much that burden affected us. The premature end to Mike's Olympian life was a great loss. The ambitious Romania project will find success in some form and in time, but under whose aegis is unclear. Talks with prospective buyers or joint venture partners that I noted in Chapter 6 remain underway.

Successes, Setbacks, and Strategy

Every company has ups and downs. From 1993 through 1995, Tenneco's opearting income exceeded $1 billion despite our operations overall becoming smaller and changing at a rapid pace. In subsequent years, orders from new-car manufacturers continually set records, and Tenneco's specialty and protective packaging operations expanded rapidly.

Yet those successes were not enough to overcome setbacks in linerboard as prices collapsed in 1997 and especially in the retail market, or aftermarket, for auto parts that spiraled into a nosedive in the final months of 1998. The cash we needed to continue buying higher-margin, faster-growth businesses fell far short. Without more acquisitions, we could not rebuild our scale to the level we projected.

An advanced information technology center in Lincolnshire, Illinois, a shared services center near Houston, Texas, and other big ticket administrative programs carried out between 1994 and 1998 were designed for a larger organization. Without the scale of business activity to comfortably support this new cost structure for information technology and administration, we could not achieve the gains projected for these state-of-the-art programs.

These setbacks caused me to re-examine the judgments we made and the strategy that evolved early in 1996. Were those judgments correct given our options, or did we err? Would it have been better then to divide all four Tenneco businesses into separate companies in a kind of "Big Bang" explosion, rather than keeping together the two manufacturing organizations—Automotive and Packaging—as cornerstones for rebuilding a more focused multi-industry company? If I knew then what I know now about each of their markets, would we have done things differently?

My answer broadly is that the course set in 1996 fundamentally was correct. The most vexing, unexpected problem has been very weak retail, or aftermarket, sales of replacement parts for exhaust systems (including mufflers) and ride-control (including struts and shock absorbers). As I'll describe shortly, I am confident that the right programs and people were in place late in 1999 to improve results in this business.

Shipbuilding, Energy, and the Government

Thinking back on our strategy sessions in late 1995, shipbuilding did not fit our growth projections in nonregulated markets, mainly because the U.S. Navy was its dominant customer. Its future would depend more on the vagaries of the federal budget than its markets or internal management. Unlike other areas where cost savings dropped directly to the bottom line, 88 cents of every dollar saved from new processes, technology, and other efficiencies at the shipyard benefited the Navy because of defense contract requirements, not Tenneco shareowners.

That said, Newport News Shipbuilding had solid support in Congress through the summer of 1999 for the funding of CVN-77, the first in a new class of advanced aircraft carriers. Also, Newport News and Electric Boat began their construction work in 1998 on the first of four new attack submarines. The keel laying for the first of what the Navy hopes will be 30 of these submarines, the Virginia, was celebrated at Electric Boat's Rhode Island assembly yard in September 1999.

Concerns about government regulation and intervention also applied at Tenneco Energy, operator in 1996 of the nation's third largest pipeline for natural gas transmission. As with Navy ship-building, many cost improvements made in the regulated pipeline had minimal impact on improving profit margins. Congress did allow competition into that business in the early 1990s with the "un-bundling" of natural-gas products, transportation and services through Order 636 of the Federal Energy Regulatory Commission. Yet we were skeptical as to how long it would be until federal officials again changed the rules. Even Order 636 worked to our detriment by limiting the amount of high returns we could achieve in the interruptible transportation markets. I would not be surprised by some major changes in the rules again within the next five years.

Tenneco Energy, however, was on its way in the mid-1990s to operating or developing several international projects with attractive prospects. Most were retained or expanded by El Paso Energy after the 1996 merger, even though El Paso's strategy had been to focus primarily on North American markets. We concluded in 1996, correctly I believe, that the international projects would be jeopardized if separated from the regulated business. And we did not want to invest further in regulated markets.

Grading the Six Businesses

We already had concluded by the spring of 1994 that long-term prospects varied for each of the six industries in which Tenneco still competed. We graded the six businesses against our criteria for higher profit margins, faster earnings growth, and lower risk. Specialty packaging, auto parts, and nonregulated gas in international markets rated highest, at high opportunity, low risk; followed by paperboard packaging (moderate opportunity, moderate risk); chemicals and shipbuilding (low opportunity, low risk); and regulated natural gas and farm equipment (low opportunity, high risk).

We used the discipline of Economic Value Added (EVA)* in much of this work. EVA was adopted by many large blue-chip companies

---

*EVA is a registered service mark of Stern Stewart & Company.

in the 1990s. The basic point is to ensure that the full cost of capital, both debt and equity, is included among all other costs required to estimate potential future returns. We examined all lines of business to see if they would generate returns sufficiently greater than the costs of their capital. Outside advisers agreed with and helped shape our conclusions. While the fundamental assumptions have held up, some detailed assumptions about timing and degree may have been wrong in setting the strategy.

When market values for natural-gas pipeline companies rose substantially in the final months of 1995, the sale or merger of the energy operations became more timely. Commodity businesses typically are too expensive to sell at the peak of a market price cycle. At the bottom of the cycle, buyers are more skeptical, harder to find, and less willing to pay a fair price. Timing is best when prices have risen from a bottom, with prospect of heading much higher.

The prospect of mounting a sale or merger of the energy business also made it a good time for us to pursue a tax-free spinoff of shipbuilding. El Paso merged with the "old Tenneco," and shipbuilding was spun-off directly to Tenneco shareowners.

Packaging, Automotive, and Strategic Choices

While the timing was good in 1996 to separate shipbuilding and energy, it was not for Tenneco Packaging and Tenneco Automotive. Packaging was in a major acquisition push in the consumer and protective businesses, buying three packaging businesses, Mobil Plastics, Amoco Foam, and a unit of Dutch-based KNP BT, for a total of $2 billion from mid-1995 through mid-1997.

We looked closely at selling the paperboard business, but the strong linerboard pricing of 1994 and most of 1995 began to weaken after topping $500 per ton. Selling businesses when revenues are in retreat is a bad way to get the price you want. We had to wait until the paperboard prices hit bottom and began an upturn before we could sell.

We analyzed paperboard again in 1997, but could not pursue buyers until after linerboard prices began a slow recovery late in 1998 (after falling below $300 per ton in 1997) and gradually worked their way above $425 by mid-1999. We sold a majority stake in the paperboard business for a good price early in 1999. Tenneco's remaining interest was set to be sold in what we anticipated would be a favorable initial public offering in late 1999. Through these combined transactions we expected to receive more than $2.7 billion for the paperboard business, or about 12 percent more than our advisers projected a year earlier.

As for Tenneco Automotive, it also was an active acquirer in the mid-1990s. Most of this activity was outside North America, primarily in Europe. Its largest customers, the world's biggest car manufacturers, were expanding in Europe and Asia, where most future sales growth was anticipated, and we needed to join them to stay competitive. In 1996, our auto parts executives were immersed in strategy, acquisition and integration issues and problems, a bad time to add making the transition to an independent public company.

Meanwhile, the robust U.S. economy spurred domestic car sales above 15 million vehicles per year, increasing orders for Tenneco Automotive's exhaust systems and ride-control components. Automotive posted new records in revenues and operating income in 1994, 1995, 1996, and 1997 increasingly on the strength of rising sales to the auto manufacturers.

Big Challenges in Auto Parts Replacement

Problems in the auto-parts replacement market, however, accelerated from nagging to serious in the two years after we created the new Tenneco late in 1996. In the first half of 1999, replacement parts contributed just 30 percent of Automotive's total sales, compared with 46 percent in 1996.

Why the sharp decline? As we had anticipated, improvements in the quality of original equipment parts in the early 1990s lengthened the useful life of those parts and reduced replacement sales. In particular the introduction of stainless steel exhaust systems sharply reduced revenue growth in replacement markets. Our plans to meet that challenge included expansion into international markets with higher projected growth rates. We also intended to exploit our traditional strength with wholesale parts distributors by introducing innovative new products that would command high profit margins. We wanted to take advantage of our strength in original equipment engineering to reinforce our position in the aftermarket.

Afterword

We were unable to execute as planned. First, major parts retailers were consolidating, reducing the number of potential high-volume customers for us. One large distributor, a major customer of ours, went out of business. The bigger retailers were in better position to reduce their inventories and negotiate tougher pricing for us. They did, and that crimped our profit margins. Second, we were slow to deliver the stream of innovative replacement parts we needed. Third, although we recognized that aftermarket sales in developing regions would lag behind original equipment sales in developing markets, weakness in international markets delayed the timetable even further.

We kept working to reverse those problems, and to sustain stable leadership. In the last two years, Tenneco Automotive twice had to replace both its president and chief executive and its senior executive for the global aftermarket.

The setbacks in the aftermarket and especially our difficulties in adjusting to the changes were disappointing. The downturn hit hard in the final quarter of 1998, just as we were preparing to separate the two businesses. The aftermarket problems complicated and ultimately scuttled our discussions late that year and early in 1999 with prospective buyers for that business.

Unable to attract offers we considered fair for the business, we instead took the course to create two independent companies.

Stock Price Impact

The weakness in Tenneco's common stock price tracked our problems in the aftermarket, especially in the third quarter of 1999. While the value of the Standard & Poor's index of 500 large capitalization stocks rose 4.35 percent for the year, the gain masked the double-digit downturns in many big-company stocks, including ours. The low point for Tenneco was late in September, with the price down more than 50 percent for the year, and two-thirds from the recent high mark in April 1998.

Even absent the faltering stock price, I knew 1999 was going to be tough on morale. At Tenneco headquarters, my leadership team prepared to break apart the corporation we had worked to build. This was particularly tough because these were all the "best and the brightest" that Mike and I had recruited or promoted years earlier into the adventure and challenges at Tenneco. Executive vice presidents and mail handlers alike began searching for jobs to replace ones they would lose at headquarters before the year's end.

The weakening stock price was another jolt. Through the decade, we adopted a number of programs to get Tenneco stock into the hands and portfolios of all employees. The goal was to encourage them to think and act as co-owners, and focus on ideas and activities to increase earnings and the stock price. When the stock price tumbled, employees and retirees with substantial amounts of their personal savings in Tenneco shares were hurt.

As the price fell, the impact effected 38,000 employees on Tenneco payrolls, tens of thousands former employees and retirees, as well as the large investment institutions and many thousands of non-employees who owned our stock. The stock options held by thousands had no value because the purchase price for each series was higher than what buyers could pay for Tenneco shares in the open market.

Throughout the ongoing partitioning, restructuring, and downsizings at Tenneco in the 1990s, my firm policy was to not engage in shortsighted slash-and-burn tactics. Aggressive cost-cutting often is overdone, at too high a price. It inflicts long-term damage on employee loyalty, disrupts internal processes, amplifies customer dissatisfaction, and stirs political reactions that can damage international trade and prospects for economic growth. Thousands of jobs were eliminated within Tenneco companies during the decade, even as thousands of new ones were created. For those who lost jobs, we maintained fair severance programs at every rank.

Rising Prices Followed Earlier Deals

Stock price certainly is one measure of how a company is performing, especially for those outside the company. But long-term results often vary from current conditions and speculation about short-term performance. Shareowners in three of the four Tenneco companies sold, merged, or spun off between 1994 and 1996 saw significant price increases within 12 to 18 months after those transactions. Indeed, the equity value of the four companies, collectively, more than doubled by October 1, 1999 from their initial market price, beginning with the first sale of shares in Case Corporation by Tenneco in June 1994.

Afterword

Here is the tally through September 30, 1999:

- After our initial public offering of 29 percent of Case for $19 in 1994, Case's shares traded as high as $72 in 1998. Tenneco sold its final stake in Case at $53.75 in 1996. Case's acquirer, New Holland, agreed to pay $55 per share in cash late in 1999.

- Newport News Shipbuilding, which traded around $16 on the day of its spinoff from Tenneco on December 12, 1996, closed the 1999 third quarter at $32.31.

- El Paso Energy, trading near $23 when it merged with Tenneco Energy late in 1996, closed the 1999 third quarter at $40.25. (The El Paso Energy price was adjusted for a two-for-one stock split that occurred in 1998.)

- Tenneco sold all Albright & Wilson shares at 150 pence in March 1995. Those shares traded as high as 205 pence within a year before tumbling to 57 pence after currency crises jolted Asian economies in 1998. Rhodia has stated it intends to complete its takeover of Albright & Wilson at 163 pence per share early in 2000.

Post-Tenneco Outlook

I am confident the Packaging and Automotive businesses are in positions to thrive competitively and to do well for shareowners as independent companies, just as these other businesses have.

Tenneco Packaging has successfully integrated its big acquisitions, a worthy case study in its own right in savvy human resource management and manufacturing logistics. Most of its markets are growing faster than the U.S. economy. It has an unusual breadth of product lines, providing a "one-stop shopping" appeal for many large customers, including several prominent manufacturers and distributors.

Its speed in product innovation has accelerated. More than 80 new products or product-line extensions were introduced in 1998 in consumer products and food/foodservice packaging. In all, it developed more than 500 custom product applications in 1998. In foodservice packaging, it has leading market share in the U.S. and Canada in four of its five major product categories based on unit

volume. In protective packaging, products contributing an estimated 80 percent of sales hold the No.1 or No. 2 market position in
North America, based on revenues.

Tenneco Automotive's largest customers are Ford Motor and
DaimlerChrysler, which collectively represented more than 22 percent of sales in 1998. In all Automotive's products were on six of
the 10 best-selling cars in the world and eight of the 10 top-selling
trucks in 1998. Its own analysis puts it among the top three suppliers in the world to auto manufacturers for emission control and ride
control products and systems.

A major restructuring of the aftermarket business, begun late in
1998, included the closing of two plants and five distribution centers. This restructuring was on track for completion in mid-2000.
Automotive's new leaders accelerated the pace of developing new
products for the replacement market, including a premium shock
absorber, heavy duty mufflers, and shock absorbers specially made
for recreational vehicles.

Meanwhile, Automotive believes it continues as the world leader
in market share in the global aftermarket for both emissions control
and ride control products. The Monroe® name in ride-control and
Walker® in exhaust systems are two of the most recognized brands
in the automotive parts industry.

Just as important, Automotive is recognized as a systems integra-
tor. As auto manufacturers push for more efficiency in their operations to reign in costs, systems integrators have increasing appeal as
suppliers. Automotive in 1999 supplied modules for 28 vehicle plat-
forms worldwide.

High Standards, Hard Choices

One of Tenneco's most talked-about advertisements in the 1990s
featured a large photograph of a rugby player diving headfirst
through a mud puddle, straining for yardage, with the ball clutched
in his arm. The headline read: "We don't look for people who never
fail. We look for people who never give up." That still is the standard by which I judge myself and others.

When I was a first-year cadet at West Point in 1953, we all had to
compete for several weeks in boxing matches. Whenever I visit that
boxing room at the gym, those memories come flooding back. That

was a place to confront your fears. The sign on the wall I most remember is still there. It says, "When the going gets tough, the tough get going." Folklore has it that this now familiar, over-used phrase originated in that gym at West Point.

I think I've learned the most in my life when the going has been the toughest. And the essence of what I've learned in those times is that you must set high standards, you will have to make hard choices, and you never, never give up.

Appendix A Book Timeline.

Year	Critical Events
1991	Tenneco debt crisis; loss for year exceeds $1 billion. Mike Walsh recruited as CEO; corporate bankruptcy averted through $3 billion of asset sales and cost reductions. **[Chapters 1 and 2]**
1992	Dana Mead joins as Tenneco president and chief operating officer in April. Adds positions of Case chairman and CEO in September. Symptoms detected, tests begin for unidentified Walsh illness. **[Chapters 1 and 2]**
1993	Walsh discloses brain tumor, vows to remain as CEO. Four-year Case restructuring begins at projected cost of $920 million; Tenneco sells $1.1 billion in new equity to fund Case plans. Political campaign begins for Congress to approve construction of new aircraft carrier at Newport News Shipbuilding and to approve the shipyard's re-entry into Navy submarine bidding competition. **[Chapters 2, 3, and 7]**
1994	Seriously ailing Walsh resigns as CEO in February after surgery, dies in May; Mead succeeds him as CEO, then chairman. Tenneco sells more than 50% of Case stock by year-end, starting at $19 per share; Newport News wins Congress approval for new carrier. **[Chapters 4 and 8]** First acquisitions and investments completed under new Tenneco strategy to accelerate earnings and increase profitability, mainly in automotive parts and specialty packaging. Purchase of leading maker of auto exhaust systems, Germany's Gillet Group, is first of 35 acquisitions to follow through 1997.
1995	Congress returns Newport News to Navy submarine competition. Construction begins in Romania on wood products venture. Mead endorses policies for faster economic growth as chairman of nation's largest industrial lobbying organization, National Association of Manufacturers. **[Chapters 8 and 9]** Tenneco sells chemicals unit, Albright & Wilson, plus additional Case stock, for more than $1.1 billion; completes $1.3 billion purchase of Mobil Corporation's plastics business, bringing Hefty® consumer products and brand.
1996	Romania project begins operations, but ties with government officials weaken after President Ion Iliescu, who welcomed Tenneco investments, is defeated. Economic growth becomes a focus of U.S. campaign for President. Greenspan warms to growth policies as G.D.P. rises 3.4% for year, inflation holds at 3.0% and jobless rate stays at 5.4%.

Appendix A   *(Continued)*

Year	Critical Events
1996	Final sales of Case stock nets $53.75 per share, for total of $2.1 billion, and overall benefits of $4.2 billion to Tenneco from $920 restructuring. Big acquisitions include $310 million deal for foam products unit of Amoco Corporation and $328 million for auto-parts maker, Clevite. Newport News Shipbuilding spun off to Tenneco shareowners. Tenneco Energy merged into El Paso Energy. Tenneco corporate offices moved to Greenwich, Conn., from Houston.
1997	Expansion of Romania project continues, with shipments of first beech products to Western Europe. U.S. economic growth expands by 3.9%, and jobless rate drops below 5%. **[Chapters 6 and 9]** Shipments to major auto assemblers and consumer packaging markets strengthen, but paperboard and box prices weaken and retail demand for Tenneco auto replacement parts slumps. Europe-based operations in protective and flexible packaging acquired for $380 million from Dutch-controlled KN Koninklijke KNP BT.
1998	Romania jobs peak at 700 at Buchin manufacturing site; sawmill operations struggle, government policy disarray continues, and project remains unprofitable. U.S. economic growth strong at 3.9%; jobless rate falls to 4.5%, inflation drops to 1.6%. **[Chapters 6 and 9]** Continued weakness in paperboard and auto replacement parts offsets strong demand from auto assemblers and consumer packaging markets. Stock price declines. Intention to proceed with final separation of Tenneco businesses announced.
1999	Exports of high quality Romanian beech halted; project scaled back to sawmill operation with 450 jobs; loss is narrowed but partner or buyer sought to keep project operating. U.S. economy on brink of beginning record 10th year of unbroken expansion; G.D.P. growth tops 3%, jobless rate at 29-year low of 4.2%, and inflation continues below 3%. **[Chapters 6 and 9]** Plans for final Tenneco break-up approved. Majority stake in paperboard business, renamed Packaging Corporation of America, sold to private investors, with balance to be sold in public offering late in year. Tenneco Packaging to be renamed and spun off as independent public company. Tenneco Automotive to become lone public company bearing Tenneco name. Mead to retire as Tenneco CEO and chairman, becoming non-executive chairman for new packaging and automotive com-panies through March 2000.

Appendix B   Historical Highlights for Six Tenneco Operating Companies (through September 1999).

JI Case/Case Corporation
- Founded 1842.
- Acquired by Tenneco in 1967 through Kern County Land Company acquisition.
- Separated via initial public offering in 6/94 as new public company, **Case Corporation.**
- Acquisition by **New Holland,** controlled by Italy's Fiat S.p.A., pending in 9/99.

Albright & Wilson
- Founded 1851.
- Acquired by Tenneco in 1970–78.
- Separated via initial public offering in 3/95 as new public company.
- Acquisition by France's **Rhodia** specialty chemicals group pending in 9/99.

Tenneco Gas/Tenneco Energy
- Founded 1943 as Tennessee Gas and Transmission Company.
- Original business leading to organization of Tenneco conglomerate in 1966.
- Renamed **Tenneco Energy** in 11/95.
- Merged with **El Paso Energy** in 12/96.
- **El Paso Energy** acquisition of **Sonat** pending in 9/99.

Newport News Shipbuilding
- Founded 1886.
- Acquired by Tenneco in 1968.
- Separated as new public company via spinoff to Tenneco shareowners in 12/96.
- Separate acquisition offers from **General Dynamics** and **Litton Industries** rejected by **Defense Department** in 5 & 7/99.

Appendix B   *(Continued)*

Packaging Corporation of America/Tenneco Packaging

- **Ohio Boxboard Company** and **American Box Board Company** founded separately in 1903.
- Merger of **Ohio Boxboard, American Box Board** and **Central Fiber Products Company** creates Packaging Corporation of America in 1959.
- Acquired by Tenneco in 1965.
- Renamed **Tenneco Packaging** in 11/95.
- Majority of paperboard segment sold to private investor group in 4/99. That segment renamed **Packaging Corporation of America.** Folding carton unit sold to Caraustar Industries in 6/99.
- Tenneco's sale of remaining interest in new **Packaging Corporation of America** via initial public offering pending in late 1999.
- Renaming of Tenneco Packaging and spin-off as independent public company to Tenneco shareowners pending in late 1999.

Tenneco Automotive

- Founded 1888 as **Economy Spring Company,** forerunner of **Walker Manufacturing Company.**
- First shock absorber by **Monroe Auto Equipment Company,** formerly Brick Blast Manufacturing Company, introduced in 1926.
- **Walker Manufacturing** acquired by Tenneco through Kern County Land Company acquisition in 1967.
- **Monroe** acquired by Tenneco in 1977, forming **Tenneco Automotive** with Walker.
- Restructuring as independent public company, retaining **Tenneco Automotive** name, pending in late 1999.

Appendix C Tenneco Key Data.

	1991	1993	1995	1997	1998
Revenues (in billions)	$13.6	$13.3	$8.9	$7.2	$7.6
Operating Income (in millions)	($147)	$1,169	$1,369	$764	$741*
Assets (in billions)	$18.7	$15.4	$13.5	$8.3	$8.8
Employees	89,000	75,000	60,000	49,000	48,000
Net Income per Share	($6.09)	$2.44	$4.16	$1.85	$1.89*
Operating Divisions	Tenneco Automotive	Tenneco Automotive	Tenneco Automotive	Tenneco Automotive	Tenneco Automotive
	Packaging Corp. of America	Packaging Corp. of America	Tenneco Packaging	Tenneco Packaging	Tenneco Packaging
	Tenneco Gas	Tenneco Gas	Tenneco Energy		
	Newport News Shipbuilding	Newport News Shipbuilding	Newport News Shipbuilding		
	JI Case	JI Case			
	Albright & Wilson	Albright & Wilson			
	Tenneco Minerals				

* 1998 operating income does not include a pretax restructuring charge of $100 million; 1998 net income per share does not include an after-tax charge of 38 cents per share related to the same restructuring charges.

ACKNOWLEDGMENTS

WE SKETCHED THE FIRST CONTENT OUTLINE FOR THIS BOOK SHORTLY AFTER Tenneco became solely a manufacturer of auto parts and packaging late in 1996. We began the project to stir more feeling of cohesion in the fast-changing organization with 20,000 employees—40 percent of our workforce—who had been with us early in 1997 for three years or less.

Much of the general public still thought Tenneco was an oil company. A book about the new Tenneco could mine a storied corporate history, project our strategy and management values, and help change that misleading oil-company image.

However, in July 1998, when we made the decision to separate these businesses, we had to consider whether to scrap this project, shelve it, or recast it and continue.

We chose the third option. Instead of a collection of case studies of our management principles in action, we focused on five major crises and leadership challenges. Our goal was to make these accounts useful to current and past Tenneco employees and families, as well as managers, students and scholars of business and economics, and general business readers. Rather than a book of "how to" leadership maxims, we decided to let it take the form of a CEO's journal—based on what I might have written each day to describe what we did.

My co-author, Tom Hayes, carried much of the responsibility to organize, research, and write the manuscript. His skills kept my time on the project at a minimum throughout 1998 and 1999 when my focus more than ever was on Tenneco's performance, strategy, and structure. Jim Golden, leader of our innovation programs, was a superb in-house editor. A Harvard Ph.D. and author of nine books on economics, Jim improved every draft with wise and rigorous critiques.

Dr. Kenneth D. Wells, Dr. Victor A. Levin, Dr. Robert G. Grossman, Dr. James D. Cox, Lyn Emerich, and Dr. Jean Herzog graciously described the science and chronology of efforts to cure and comfort Mike Walsh during his tragic illness. Joan Walsh provided indispensable counsel and consent in reconstructing Mike's story. Ted Tetzlaff, Dr. Peter T. Flawn, Ambassador Felix Rohatyn, and Jack Lascar contributed insights about business challenges that arose from Mike's illness and how we managed them.

ACKNOWLEDGMENTS

Executives of Tenneco or its operating companies during the 1980s added perspective on events in Chapter 2. I am honoring their requests and those of a few other sources who asked not to be identified by name. Paul Griswold, Dave Brush, Shawn Kelly, and Dolores Muniz eased the complicated logistics of Tom Hayes's journey to Romania late in 1997. Paul and Shawn provided extensive interviews and site tours in Buchin, as did Dick Buerlich and Iulia Ilianu. Iulia translated local employee interviews.

John Castellani, a Tenneco executive vice president, was a rich source of anecdotes, analysis, and ideas for the chapters on Washington. So were Sheryl Shelby, Ted Austell, and Sally Painter. Ted and Sally also added memorable stories and perspectives about Romania. John monitored the book's progress, strengthened its research, reviewed every chapter draft, and resolved production issues. Mike Petters, Mike Hatfield, and Brenda Roth, all of Newport News Shipbuilding, fortified the lobbying chapters with research, interviews, and anecdotes. Jerry Jasinowski and Laura Brown Narvaiz made the extensive archives of the National Association of Manufacturers available and helped reconstruct events in the economic growth debate.

Jeanne Glasser, our editor at John Wiley & Sons who first suggested the project, was flexible and supportive, especially after the book's theme changed and production schedules were redrawn. Nancy Land and Pam Blackmon and their staff at Publications Development Company prepared the final manuscript with professional skill and optimism. Stacy Dick, Bob Blakely, Barry Schuman, John Howard, Dr. Kimball Kehoe, and Dick Robinson, among others, offered valuable ideas and corrections to various drafts they reviewed. Chris Gable, Kara Smith, Anna Hall, and Camille Protano transcribed more than 100 interview tapes.

More than 30 speeches drafted by Paul Murphy and Robert T. Fagan provided valuable background. My stellar administrative assistant, Kathleen Babbin, managed the flow of manuscript documents and related matters with aplomb. Patti Axelby and Mary Anne McCormack were adept at directing logistics and research support. Finally, my thanks to dozens who aided us on topics ultimately not included, especially to Philip A. Dur, Dr. Herman Weltens, Dr. Patrick Garcia, and Philip Houben.

DANA G. MEAD

Index